A Constant Forester

A journey discovering and using the positive interaction between people and forests

Paul Ryan

Copyright & Fiction

The copyright of this work is held exclusively by the author Paul Ryan and may not be used in any way whatsoever without the author's prior written consent

Acknowledgements

I would like to thank Jacky Martin, Trevor Armstrong, Raynette Mitchell and Libby Bowen, all members of our small writers' group for their encouragement, support, and guidance in both writing and publishing A Constant Forester.

I would like to thank those beta readers who provided feedback and ensured the story of A Constant Forester was more readable: Steve Jackson, June and Des Harries, Michelle Wilson, Terry James, Ian Hutchings, and Whitney Bauer.

In addition, I would like to thank Busy Bee Editing *(www.busybeeediting.co.za)* for their proofreading and editing of A Constant Forester.

Paul Ryan

December 2021

Contents:

The First Steps

My legs were filthy with mud and numb with fatigue while the humid heat caused sweat to trickle into my eyes, down my face and soak my shirt, as I slowly placed one foot in front of the other up another steep incline. On all sides were the tall trunks of forest trees with their dense green crowns, while lower down, saplings and undergrowth provided a thick cover on the ground. There was a smell of rotting vegetation mixed with the spicy scent of tree barks, and the damp exposed soil had the odour of bad drains.

Being exhausted and not fully conscious of my actions and surroundings, I grabbed a sapling to help pull myself up the muddy slope, when the large, heart-shaped leaf of a Stinging Tree slapped me across the face. Reeling back, half crazed with the sudden pain,

I tried to wipe off the stings. Gradually, the pain eased and one of my Papuan New Guinea co-workers gave me a hand to get to the top of the slope. From there it was an easier walk along a ridge to the tent flies comprising our camp.

I arrived with my thighs aching after eight hours of walking up and down steep hillsides, climbing over fallen tree trunks, setting up plots, measuring and recording data on trees in the plots, and then moving on to the next plot some 200 metres along our straight survey line. What made it harder was that the line was designed to go across gullies and ridges to get the maximum variation in vegetation types.

As I slumped on my canvas bed sleeve that was supported by two poles above the ground, my thoughts were not of regret or recriminations. I was tired and it was tough going over rough country, but there were no thoughts of giving up. A large hot mug of tea and a tin of peaches helped restore some strength, before a cool dip in a nearby creek to clean off the mud and sweat helped to make life easier.

This was one of my first days doing inventory surveys in the moist, evergreen forests of Papua New Guinea (PNG). It was disappointing, however, after all the hard slogging, to be told by the Team Leader, Rex Grattidge, when we got back to the base camp, that my efforts were not good enough.

I had not put in plots all the way to the end of the two-mile lines. We had just run out of time and steam after about a mile and a half. Not too bad I had thought, but it was not good enough. From that point on, I resolved to do better and did so over the next weeks and months. At the same time, I began to feel more comfortable with my chosen career as a forester.

PNG had been home since I was four, arriving in Rabaul, on the island of New Britain, with my mother and baby sister, Gayle, in February 1948. Dad, the local manager of Burns Philp, a trading and shipping company, had arrived in Rabaul in 1932, at the age of 24, doubtless looking for an interesting life with the company in this vastly different world, which some writers had referred to as 'The Last Unknown'.

My mother had even longer and closer ties with PNG, or at least with what was known as Papua before the First World War. Her father had arrived in 1897 and brought my grandmother to Port Moresby after their marriage in 1901. And so, my mother and her siblings were born in Port Moresby; something of a frontier town at that point.

Rabaul in the late nineteen forties and early fifties, was a picturesque town, encased in lush, green vegetation and situated around a harbour that was part of a massive caldera formed by some ancient volcano. It was and still is a highly active volcanic area, with the town being ringed by volcanoes; some dormant, some active. An eruption could occur at any time, and everyone had an escape plan. Dad had already experienced the violent volcanic devastation in Rabaul on May 27, 1937, when the two volcanoes, Vulcan and Matupi erupted: one on each side of the harbour.

In some notes he made in 1933, he comments on the volcanic nature of the harbour in a sort of unknown prelude of dramatic future events. He is referring to the highest and most notable of the volcanos, 'the Mother'.

'... The Mother in her majesty, provided a suitable background for the town and also impressed upon one its volcanic origin. At her base those extinct craters told, full well, a tale of the past and led one to contemplate on the future of Rabaul and its district should this stately lady choose to send forth the fury that is believed by all to reside in her bosom'.

The lush green vegetation dominated even the built-up areas with main roads like Poinciana and Mango Avenues bordered by large shady trees. The dominant tribe in Rabaul were the Tolai people, tall with handsome features that were more Polynesian than Melanesian. Most of the men wore only lap-laps around their waists, while the women or meries wore long blouses on top of their lap-laps.

We bought a lot of our fruit and veggies at the local open-air market or bung, where the smells of drying fish mingled with that of other produce and betel nut juice, which stained the ground red in all directions as well as the teeth and gums of the chewers.

We had servants who cleaned the house, did the laundry, cared for the garden, and helped with the cooking, although Mum did most of that herself. Perhaps it was the adaptability of the young, but I seemed to just accept it all and fit in.

A photo of Rabaul, 1962, showing the towering presence of the dormant "Mother" volcano to the left of which is Namanula Hill where we lived. The still active Matupi volcano is in the top centre.

In the late forties there was still much evidence of the war. Japanese POWs could be seen doing manual labour and they also collected our garbage under the watchful eye of a local policeman, who had a rifle with a fixed bayonet. I was a bit scared of the prisoners, particularly the ones who wore the little round dark glasses, which, to my mind gave them a rather sinister appearance. Wreckage of war equipment was everywhere, from planes and boats to guns, and even live ammunition. Unexploded bombs had to be dealt with and we would sometimes evacuate our house and go down into the town while the bombs were detonated. It was an environment that had few luxuries, although no hardships to speak of.

About 1952, we moved to Moresby, and I enjoyed life there in a carefree sort of way. Much time was spent on the sands and in the shallow reef strewn waters of Ela Beach, with many a red and sometimes blistering sunburn to show for it. Then in 1954, at the age of nine, I headed down to Our Lady of The Sacred Heart (OLSH) Convent in Bowral, NSW to start boarding school. It was quite an adventure travelling down on a double-decker sea plane, a Qantas Sandringham. I felt quite special, almost an adult, as I boarded the plane in the early morning on Moresby Harbour and was too caught up with the impending flying experience to be concerned about leaving my parents and heading off to an unknown destination. I told my mother not to cry as she hugged me, prior to my boarding the launch, which would take us out to the plane. Of course, she didn't take my instructions to heart and was sobbing as the launch pulled away from the jetty. My own tears would come later after I arrived at the OLSH Convent.

The water slapped against the plane's aluminium hull as the four radial engines produced a crescendo of power that had us skimming ever faster across the harbour. There was a marvellous sensation of speed as I sat watching the spray fly out from the side, until at last we lifted clear and rose above the harbour, still smooth in the calm of the morning. Clearing the hills near Tatana Island, the plane then turned and headed south across the coast and so to Australia.

I had no fears about my travel, only a sense of excitement and adventure. This was air travel with a touch of class, undertaken at a somewhat leisurely pace as the big seaplane lumbered through the morning sky. We landed at Cairns and came ashore to be taken to a hotel in town for a solid Australian lunch. I was an unaccompanied minor, but nobody seemed to be too concerned about me, and I wandered around the town for a bit before we headed back to the plane. After a late afternoon tea by the river in Brisbane, we arrived at Rose Bay in Sydney at about ten that night, to be met by my Aunt Eileen. The loneliness was to come later, after I travelled with other boys on the train from Sydney Central Station to the boarding school that was to be my home for much of the next two years. There in that alien and friendless environment, I often cried myself to sleep in the open dormitory until I got accustomed to being there. It was also the start of my developing a sense of independence and self-confidence that served as part of a survival mechanism throughout my life.

From OLSH I went up the road to Chevalier College at Burradoo, where I boarded for the next six years. The school was situated on 50 ha of rolling, partly treed countryside with its own dairy herd and a sheep dog we would borrow on occasions to hunt rabbits for dinner. They were good and formative years, with no real hardship, good friends and plenty of sport. As I was about to leave Chevalier my parents asked what career I had in mind. Over the preceding couple of years, I had considered several options including flying, going to sea and medicine. Now, when I was asked my reply was, "Something outdoorsy." I liked the outdoor life.

I was thinking of agriculture, which seemed the obvious outdoor career, when my mother suggested forestry. I don't know why, and I never asked her, but possibly she had done some research. Not knowing anything about forestry, she took me along to see a senior officer in the New South Wales Forestry Commission in Sydney. He explained all about it and I thought it was something I would like. So, we applied for two cadetships with the Department of External Territories: one in agriculture and the other in forestry.

I missed out on the agricultural cadetship, and for some reason that possibly only a seventeen-year-old boy could explain, I forgot about the forestry cadetship. In order to get sufficient funds to put myself through an agricultural college, I was working as a clerk with the Commonwealth Bank at their Brookvale branch in Sydney.

It was there, on a bright, sunny January day in 1962, that the bank manager called me into his office. I wondered what this was all about as I had already arranged with the bank to transfer to Moresby the following month. Without much preamble the manager asked me, "Do you know anything about a forestry cadetship from External Territories?" My mind clicked back a few notches and I told him I had put in for such a cadetship. "Well, it looks like you have won just such a cadetship. So, what do you plan to do?" Very quickly, though in a bit of a daze, I said I would take the cadetship. I wasn't quite sure where it would all lead, but it was a preferable career to banking and maybe just as good as agriculture.

There wasn't much time to spare to get into a university, and in the end, the only and best offer was at the University of New England in Armidale, on the northern New South Wales tablelands. So, instead of catching a plane up to Moresby in early February, I was on a train up to Armidale. After three years there doing a science degree, I moved down to the Forestry School in Canberra, which was about to become amalgamated with the Australian National University. There I spent two wonderful years learning about trees and silviculture, how to build roads and how to manage forests, as well as enjoying some great games of rugby as a winger and a vibrant social life.

First Taste of Life in the Bush

As the twin-engine Cessna 310 banked over the solid mass of forest below and made its approach to Alotau Airstrip I was both excited and apprehensive about what lay ahead over the next few weeks. It was December 1964, and I was accompanying a forest technical officer, by the name of Chris Brown, to the Sagarai Valley, just in from Milne Bay, on the eastern tip of the island of New Guinea. The rights to cut the wood in the Sagarai Timber Rights Purchase (TRP) had been bought by the government from the local villagers. Virtually all the forests in PNG were owned by the village communities. Our job was to put in the back boundary for the TRP before logging could take place, which meant traipsing through the forest, for some 40 kilometres, over ridges and creeks, putting in boundary markers as we went.

This was part of my work experience as a cadet forest officer during the long Christmas vacations. It was an introduction to working in the hot, humid conditions of dense tropical forests. It was physically hard, though I didn't mind and seemed to take it in my stride, learning about the bush as well as the flora and fauna in it. And the local Papua and New Guineans with whom I worked were good teachers.

Chris was an Englishman, and both a good bloke and a knowledgeable forester. He was a lean and practical man with a good sense of humour and with much experience working in the bush. A year or two later he told me how he had walked for two days through the forest, suffering from peritonitis after suffering an attack of appendicitis many miles from the nearest settlement. He survived, but it must have been quite an ordeal.

We landed at Alotau, the district headquarters, with all our gear and supplies for several weeks stay, including a quantity of food and booze in large tin boxes that would have to be carried to our destination by porters. The booze consisted of bottles of rum. Beer was too bulky to carry, and we had no means of chilling it. On the other hand, the dark Rum Negrita went well with lemon juice from the local villages and some sugar; what we called planters punch.

At Alotau, we met up with my cousin, Wendy Murphy, who was married to the district commissioner Des Murphy. Unfortunately, Des was stabbed to death by a disgruntled local near Kikori in the Gulf Province a couple of years later. Our family have always been scattered geographically and we keep running into each other in odd or out-of-the-way places. Apart from the social aspects, it was important to let Des know what we were planning to do and why, while at the same time picking his brains for any useful local information. The government launch then took us across Milne Bay to a village and mission station on the south-western shore. There we camped for the night in the local rest house, known as a haus kiap[1] in Tok Pisin, the lingua franca for much of PNG.

These haus kiaps were constructed of local materials, in the same way as a reasonable villager's house. They were usually raised above the ground on posts, with bamboo and woven palm leaf walls and a thatched grass roof. There would be two or three rooms with open doors that faced a veranda of sorts. The floor was uneven and made of split black palm trunks, making sleeping without a mattress a little uncomfortable; but the houses were dry and cool and comfortable enough. They were built and maintained by the villagers for use by government officers. Over the next few years, I stayed in a few of these haus kiaps, and most were quite comfortable, allowing one to camp for the night without having to put up a tent.

The author in front of a haus kiap, our accommodation in the local village, after a hard day's work in the forest.

1   A "kiap" is the Tok Pisin word for patrol officer, the local administrative officer.

Before settling down for the evening, Chris organised with the village chief or luluai to have carriers available to accompany us the next day. He also asked the luluai to send a runner to inform the next village along our route to have villagers ready to take over as porters at their village boundary, which was the customary thing to do. Then we dined on local mud crabs and rice with raisins. The crabs were a real delicacy. But the delicacy part was lost on my stomach, when I found myself awake a couple of hours later with the distinct feeling that the crab and my stomach were not getting on and that an eviction notice had already been issued.

The next morning my stomach was still misbehaving, but we were up early to help organize our party of porters for the trek. These were mainly men, clad only in their wrap-around cloth lap-laps. But there were several women, some of whom wore the loose-fitting, floral 'Mother Hubbard' dress with puffed short sleeves that had been introduced by the missionaries in an effort to 'cover their nakedness'. Other women just wore a lap-lap and were bare-breasted. All were barefooted.

They arranged amongst themselves who would carry what from among our collection of metal patrol boxes with food, books or papers, plus rolls of tents and bedding, bags of bulk food such as rice and sugar, assorted lamps, cans of kerosene and our kit bags. Poles were cut from the nearby bush to thread through the handles of the patrol boxes so that two men could carry a box, which could weigh as much as 70 kg. The men invariably carried these, but also other items, while the women, some of them none too young, would balance loads on their heads or across their shoulders. There was one woman, who must have been at least 50, not very tall, and quite slight. She leaned back against a rock while a fellow porter arranged a load on her shoulders, including a five-gallon drum of kerosene. Then, when all was arranged, she literally staggered to a walk, then kept on going - for the next three hours.

When all was ready, we set off at a brisk pace along a dirt track into the forest away from Milne Bay in a westerly direction. At first, in the relative cool of the morning, and with a somewhat alert mind and interest in the surroundings, it was not much harder than a pleasant stroll. However, as we moved away from the bay into more hilly country, and the morning grew hotter, the stroll became more of a chore. It didn't take long for the sweat to start soaking my shirt, though we were often in the shade of the forest trees. The heat in the open kunai grassland patches we encountered was oven-like and the light reflected from the razor-sharp blades of the tall grass hurt the naked eye with its intensity. I carried a water bottle and was grateful I did, though the water was warm and tasted of plastic.

Every hour or so we would halt for a quick rest; sometimes by a stream, where I could refill the water bottle and take a refreshing drink of the clear flowing water. I commonly drank from streams in the PNG forests without much concern about contracting a water-borne disease; something I would hesitate to do today even in a developed country. My one proviso was that the stream be flowing and passing through sunlight and that there were no villages known to be upstream.

After our brief respite, before we had cooled down too much, we would be off again, climbing out of the gully and trudging onward. Within a few hours, the novelty of the trek had worn off and it wasn't so much fatigue, but rather boredom that took over. My legs were carrying me along as if I was in a vehicle without feeling overexerted or tired, and this enabled me to take in the passing scenery or meditate on what was going on in my life and with my current girlfriend. Chris had developed a method of reading a book as he walked, glancing up every now and again to make sure his feet were heading in the right direction and the path ahead was clear of obstacles. I tried it, but found I needed too much concentration on the walking to be interested in the book.

When we reached the boundary of the first village the word had obviously been passed along as the next group of porters were waiting to take over. We lined up those who had brought us on the first leg and paid them off. The rate was a shilling or a stick of tobacco an hour for both men and women. The thick, tarry and sweet-smelling tobacco, which was often the preferred choice of payment, came with a page of newspaper in which to roll it. A portion of the tobacco would be pulled off the stick and shredded into the paper to make a cigarette that could be up to 20 centimetres long. This was usually lit from a smouldering stick, then, unfinished cigarettes were put behind the ear until the need came for another puff.

About mid-afternoon we emerged onto the flat plain of the Sagarai River and were soon at the outskirts of Sagarai Plantation. As far as we could see were regularly spaced tall coconut palms in fields of short-cropped grass. From the coconuts, copra, the dried white flesh, was extracted. This was used to produce coconut oil and desiccated coconut. After more than a kilometre we sighted the homestead. There it was in the midst of this great expanse of coconut palms, down by a river. Typical of many such houses, it was raised on posts with an open plan for the lounge and dining areas and a veranda enclosing the bedrooms, which made the place as cool as possible. Due to the hospitality of its manager we were to use this as a base camp.

By this time, after some seven hours on the track, I was no longer just daydreaming as I walked along. The comfort zone had gone, and I was starting to feel decidedly weary; while my legs were losing their feeling and not always doing what my brain told them to do. It was so nice to stop and sit down, and even nicer to have a hot shower and a couple of beers provided by the plantation manager. It didn't take us long to recover, though, and by the next day I was prepared for further treks. These weren't long in coming for as soon as we had settled in and organised our supplies we headed off into the bush, to start reconnoitring the area and putting in the boundary.

From the plantation, our work took us south into the coastal forest typical of PNG. Above a dense undergrowth of bushes and tree saplings rose tall rainforest tree species often supported by prominent buttresses. From the tree canopies hung vines, some of which contained water that we occasionally drank by cutting sections and allowing the liquid to flow down into our mouths. From the ground waved the long thorn covered canes of the 'Wait a While' or Lawyer Vine (*Calamus muelleri*). Before one realised it, one could lose their hat or find their shirt and arm 'stitched' with the backward facing thorns.

The terrain consisted of numerous short, steep ridges between small fast-flowing streams and my shirt was sweat-sodden within minutes of starting our climb to the ridge top. We camped out as we progressed along a ridge that looked out over the Coral Sea to the south of the TRP. Then every few days we would tramp back to the comforts of the plantation base camp to replenish our supplies and have a hot shower. It was hard and hot work, particularly with the extra effort of carrying my kit bag while slogging through the bush and marking the boundary, although we had employed a couple of local villagers to carry the tent fly and food.

Although much of the forest or 'bush' in PNG is isolated from significant human settlements, one doesn't see a lot of wildlife. There are no large mammals as these didn't make it across the Wallace Trench; that deep canyon in the ocean, near Sulawesi, which remained filled with water during the last ice age and so isolated PNG and Australia from the rest of Asia. We would sometimes come across a cassowary or hear the 'drumming' of a male as it pulsated its chest giving a mating call. Small wallabies occasionally hopped out of sight as we approached and there was plenty of bird life in the trees. The most notable of these were the large hornbills, which would sit in the treetops and, at our approach, take off with a slow, heavy, distinctive beating of wings.

We'd usually find a decent spot to camp near a stream. Then we'd pitch our tent fly using poles cut from nearby trees, with the locals doing most of the cutting, as my skills in that direction were far below theirs. We used canvas tent flies as it was too hot for full tents, and we only needed shelter from the rain. Several smaller poles would then be cut to set up the canvas bed sleeves. These had two poles either side to make a sort of stretcher, which was then supported at each end by cross pieces set into the ground. They made very comfortable beds, about 50 centimetres above the ground, secure from most animals, but not from rats or mice, which sometimes ran up and down inside the sleeve disturbing an otherwise good rest. The first time I experienced these it was disconcerting to wake in the wee hours to hear this scrambling going on in the hollow part of the bed sleeve. Though they seemed harmless, I thumped the sleeve a few times to scare them away, then went back to sleep.

As was usually the case, after a hard day's slog through the bush and setting up the camp we would strip and have a wash in a nearby stream to get rid of the sweat and grime. Then, feeling nicely clean and cooler, we'd relax in the cool of the late afternoon before dinner. It was all quite civilized and on many other occasions like this, I remember feeling a great sense of contentment. A couple of rum punches also added to the sense of wellbeing, sitting in this isolated site, hundreds of miles from so called civilization. Sometimes we would set up our camp near a waterfall or beside a lake with not even a village close by.

I remember saying on one or two such occasions, as we relaxed in such splendid isolation that tourists would pay thousands of dollars to be where we were, though perhaps in more salubrious accommodation. But we were here as part of our work and being paid for it. In later years, I often felt fortunate in having a job as a forester that so often was enjoyable and rewarding while being paid to do it. I wondered sometimes at the paradox of gaining such enjoyment from my work. Perhaps some lingering hereditary strain caused me to think that work had to be hard labour and not be enjoyed.

But this splendid feeling of isolation didn't mean the local villagers were not aware of our presence. They obviously had an interest in what we were doing as it was their land and forest and this was brought home to me quite clearly on one occasion.

We had climbed to the top of a ridge, miles from any village and, seemingly, quite alone. Chris then decided to demonstrate that we were, in fact, being watched. In a small clearing he proceeded to draw lines on the ground with a stick in quite an elaborate fashion. This had gone on for about five minutes, when two older men pushed their way out from the surrounding dense bush. I was fascinated by the fact that, unbeknown to us, we were actually being watched. It could also have been a little frightening if the 'watchers' were not friendly. However, in this case the two gents were just curious to know what we were up to, though probably reporting back to keep the other villagers informed.

Obviously, we were not seen as threats to their land or forest. We probably would have continued to have been unknowingly observed, but Chris's drawings had been too much for them and they just had to get a closer look and ask a few questions, all in a very friendly manner. We explained what we were doing, and they were interested to hear that our work was a forerunner to logging activities and some associated development of infrastructure for their area. They then proceeded to walk with us for a while as we continued the boundary marking, even helping out by clearing some of the bush in our path using the bush knives (machetes) they both carried.

A few years later, while doing inventory work in the Watut and Bulolo Valleys, I faced a much more hostile situation and had some difficulty explaining to villagers the purpose of marking out plots and measuring trees. On that occasion, we had to contend with local landowners armed with bows and arrows who cut down our tents, even though they had agreed to the TRPs in the area. It took many hours of patient talking in the village to convince them we were not planning to steal their resources. In hindsight, I felt it would have been both courteous and good planning to have informed the villagers in advance as to what we were about to do. After all, it was their land and forests.

We spent several weeks roaming the ridges at the back of Sagarai. Then, by the end of January, the work was finished, and we returned to Port Moresby. From there I flew down to Australia to continue my forestry studies in Canberra at the Australian Forestry School. I had survived, learnt a lot about self-sufficiency and self-confidence, and was as fit as a Mallee bull. I had also gained a new respect for the Papua New Guineans in the bush and as human beings. I was also grateful to them for the help they gave me, as compared to them I was like a babe in the bush and lacked their survival skills.

A Forester in Papua New Guinea

After graduating in December 1966 from the Australian National University and the Australian Forestry School in Canberra, I returned home to Moresby. And it wasn't long before I was being dropped in the deep end of forestry work, being assigned to doing forestry inventory surveys. My initiation into this was in the Wau and Bulolo area, where although the hills were not high, the slopes were steep. I wasn't unfit, but it took a few weeks and the loss of some 12 kilos walking up and down numerous hills through the dense forest before I had adapted and improved my fitness for the job. Though, I was still not up to the standard of the locals on my team. At the same time, I was gaining a familiarity with and a certain attachment to the forests with their damp, earthy smells and the occasional sharp scents from some shrub or tree as well as the fascinating and varying complexity of the ecology.

The usual routine on these inventories was to first establish a base camp with some of the comforts of civilization. This included a couple of kerosene fridges to keep the beer and meat cold, and a hot shower constructed out of a 44-gallon drum with a shower rose fitted to the bottom that could be filled with hot water by bucket from a nearby drum on a fire. We were broken up into teams of four; a team leader and three forestry assistants or labourers. I was a team leader and was lucky to have three experienced men from earlier inventories who knew the ropes on my team. These Papua New Guinea men were the most skilled bushcraft men I came across in my career. Often, they would pad through the forest in bare feet, though there were times, particularly in rocky limestone country where even their heavily calloused feet suffered badly, while good boots would be cut to shreds in short order.

We used helicopters to put teams into the field and do reconnaissance. These were mainly the three-seater Bell 47 3B1s with the bubble cockpit, like those on MASH. Taking off in one of these, particularly on the first occasion, was quite an experience. There is literally nothing in front or under your feet except the clear Perspex as you lift from the ground and then rise rapidly into the air, tilting slightly forward and then proceeding to skim over buildings and trees as you climb. As there were usually no roads, the alternative would be to walk into the inventory sample sites and that was time consuming.

But there was a certain element of danger flying around in helicopters in the mountainous and forested terrain. This was brought home when, on one occasion, I spent a day doing low circuits over dense forests in the rugged hills of the highlands, looking for another chopper that had gone down in the bush near Goroka. It was eventually found with all on board dead, having suffered a sheared drive shaft as it climbed to gain altitude over some ridges.

Often, if a helicopter has some height and then finds itself in difficulties it can auto-rotate down to the ground. This is an exercise whereby the pilot switches off the engine and allows the main rotor to spin as the helicopter drops. Then having got sufficient revs on the rotor, he can actually have some control using the pitch of the blades. The helicopter then falls gently with twirling blades like a descending winged maple seed. In this case, there was no chance for such an exercise.

Two of the three helicopter pilots we flew with in PNG died in crashes within a couple of years, one of whom, an ex-RAF bomber pilot, had already survived two tail rotor failures. When that happens, there is nothing to counter the torque caused by the main rotor and the helicopter starts to spin uncontrollably until the power is cut. It requires extreme presence of mind to carry out the right procedure and survive, particularly if the aircraft is relatively close to the ground. Bill eventually ran out of fuel and luck, in hilly, isolated terrain.

A Bell 47 3B1 helicopter on the ground at Baiyer River during one of our forest inventories.

Once the chopper had deposited us at our inventory site, we would establish our camp and then first thing in the morning, after a breakfast of baked beans or navy biscuits (hard tack) and a cup of tea, the four-man team would locate the starting point for our inventory survey line and then proceed to head off on the line, across the terrain, putting in sample plots, measuring trees and recording the data. This went on until about mid-afternoon, without a lunch break, when we would call it quits for the day and walk back down the couple of miles of line to our tents.

Back at our camp, the first task was to light a fire and get the billy on the boil for a good strong and sweet cup of tea. This was usually accompanied by a tin of some fruit like peaches. Then, we'd go down to a nearby stream and have a wash. The speed with which this was accomplished was dictated by the number of mosquitoes. In some places there were none and at others they were there in the thousands. When they came in such swarms, dinner of a plate of rice and tinned meat would be eaten sitting on one's bed under the mosquito net, being careful not to have any part of one's body touching the net.

The Papua New Guinean members of my team would often strike up a conversation as we ate our dinner or drank our tea. I learned about their attitude and fears in the forest; what they thought about eventually becoming an independent country; and some of their past experiences in the bush. On one occasion I learned how some people confused 'independence' with 'underpants' and felt they would all be required to wear underpants after independence. Another man explained that if independence meant that there would no longer be European police officers, there was no way any police officer who was not a member of his tribe could tell him what to do. With no background in politics, the whole concept of electing parliamentarians was alien to many, such as those who could not understand why President Lyndon Johnson could not be on the ballot, because they really wanted to vote for him.

After three or four days at one site, the helicopter would ferry us back to base camp where there was some half decent food and cold beer, and our clothes could be washed. Then after a day of such delights I would be briefed on a new site and off we would go again, with such a routine lasting from between two to three months. At the end of that time, chartered aircraft would return us, with our equipment and survey books back home.

A lot of 1967 was spent under canvas in the forest wilderness. Later that year I was officer-in-charge for an inventory around Mount Giluwe in the Southern Highlands, the second highest mountain in PNG at 4,370 m. There, we set up our base camp at the Ialabu patrol post, having bush material huts built for us with the assistance of the local Kiap (Patrol Officer), as it was too cold for just tent flies. The forests around the base and up the slopes of Mt Giluwe were different to anything I had seen before. They were a more temperate climate series of ecosystems. The lower slopes had dense, homogeneous stands of Southern Beech

(*Nothofagus*), while further up there were conifers like *Papuacedrus, Phyllocladus,* and *Podocarpus.*

Things had gone well during our two-month stint in the area, but when it came time to leave, I was nearly responsible for a disaster. We had chartered a Caribou transport and one or two other smaller planes to carry out the fifty or so personnel and our gear, from the local dirt airstrip. After two months of roughing it, everyone was looking forward to getting back to a few more comforts and families as we dismantled our camp and packed up the gear in anticipation of flying out.

On the morning of our departure, we moved ourselves and all our equipment and effects to the airstrip in time for the expected arrival of the aircraft. The morning was bright and sunny, and at 1,500 metres altitude it was very pleasant to sit and watch the skies for the incoming planes. But the scheduled arrival time came and went with no sign of any planes. An hour or so later, when they still had not come, I used the kiap's radio to find out what was going on. It seemed the pilots didn't share our enthusiasm for leaving Ialabu and were busy with some other job but were coming. Eventually, the Caribou appeared off to the north, slowly circled, and dropped down to land. At the same time, the sun disappeared behind rain clouds that were slowly building. After the Caribou taxied to a halt and the rear door opened, we all pitched in to load up as quickly as possible, knowing that the plane would have to make two or three trips before all the gear and people were taken out, and it was already late in the morning.

At last, with the cargo lashed down and several of our party on board, the plane taxied to the end of the strip to take off. That was when they found the problem, and we all heard it, the bang as the two magnetos for each engine were tested and one failed. Just to prove it wasn't an error they retested it and it popped a second time. My heart sank. I knew they wouldn't take off, though it was technically possible. So back they taxied and shut down. The pilots, who at this point seemed equally anxious to be away, said that they had radioed to Madang for a spare and it was on its way. But what the hell did that actually mean. It just seemed an off-handed estimate from some remote engineer, whose main concern for the day might have been whether he was going to make it with his new girlfriend that night, but not whether we would actually make it home from some remote highland's airstrip.

So, we sat back down to wait, calculating just how late the new magneto could arrive and be fitted to enable us to make it out that day. Our hopes were raised several times as light planes flew in, but they were government charters bringing supplies into the post, not the plane with the

Caribou magneto. Finally, after some two to three hours, the magneto arrived, and so did the rain, which had been threatening for some time. It didn't take long for the mechanic to replace the mag. I watched as once more the Caribou lumbered to the end of the strip in what was now a steady downpour. But it took off and turned towards the north. There was still time for it to offload its cargo and return for another load – if the weather didn't worsen. However, that sense of hope disappeared when another light government charter plane landed and the pilot informed us that the Caribou captain had closed the strip to his class of aircraft, due to an overly muddy runway.

I looked at the stack of iron patrol boxes holding our gear and inventory data plus the men still remaining and wondered what we should do, particularly as our camp had been dismantled. Then I had a brilliant idea, perhaps brought on by a comment made by one of the government charter pilots. There were a couple more such flights scheduled that afternoon to and from Mount Hagen, a principal town in the Highlands. Why not put the rest of the personnel, including myself on these, plus whatever gear we could fit and fly out, leaving the rest of the patrol boxes to be picked up next day or whenever the Caribou could return, with the patrol officer supervising. It was a somewhat self-centred idea, but at that point we all just wanted out. I did not have any travel warrants with me or sufficient travel budget funds to pay for the seats or cargo, but I did have excess baggage warrants. I agreed with the pilots that they would allow me to pay using such warrants. So, the rest of us flew out of Ialabu to Mount Hagen as so much excess baggage.

Boy was it good to climb aboard that plane, buckle up and have the pilot jockey into position at the end of the strip before racing down the runway and lifting off over the scene of our two months stay and our eight hours of frustration. It wasn't till the next day, as we flew by another charter back to Moresby, that I realized I had left all the inventory survey books on the Ialabu Airstrip. This was the outcome of our two months effort in the bush and the expenditure of some $80,000. Although they were packed in iron boxes, and I felt they should be safe from the weather, these were very valuable documents and shouldn't have been left just sitting on the side of the airstrip. It was not the sort of irresponsible action expected from an up-and-coming forest officer. Needless to say, it was a very sheepish Paul Ryan who reported to his superiors back in Moresby, that the outcome of all our recent efforts was still sitting in the rain at Ialabu. I spent an anxious few days until they finally arrived, none the worse for wear.

The Hidden Valley

They emerged from the trees and dense undergrowth surrounding our camp site in the forest on the edge of the river, as my companion and I erected poles for our tent fly. No doubt they had been watching for some time following our arrival by helicopter on the nearby riverbed and had finally decided to reveal themselves, either because their courage had been boosted or their curiosity had been piqued or a combination of both.

There were only men, and as they gathered around, I observed they were very short, almost pygmies, not being much above five feet tall, and were dressed largely in clothes made from bush materials. This consisted of a smooth bark belt into which was tucked a bunch of leaves over the rear end and a bunch of grass over the front. The women, whom we saw later, were dressed in a similar fashion, being bare breasted. A few individuals had pieces of western clothing, such as a shirt or shorts. Nobody wore anything on their feet. The people of the Jimi Valley were really not far removed from the stone age, having acquired steel axes and knives only in the previous decade or so, and, as we found, were still without files to sharpen such implements, in many cases. They were friendly, and through sign language and some Tok Pisin indicated they were prepared to help us make camp.

This was in mid-1968 as myself and Bob McKeowen, a friend, draftsman and colleague from the Department of Forests found ourselves in the Jimi Valley by the river of the same name. It seemed, at that time, the thickly forested valley of the Jimi River had been forgotten; a small part of Papua New Guinea had been largely passed over in the development process and progression into the modern world. Located on the northern fringes of the Western Highlands, where considerable outside investment had been made since the early 1950s, the people of the Jimi Valley were stuck in an otherwise bygone era. There were no roads into or in the valley and no towns. The people lived in small villages on the higher ground, where there was less chance of suffering from malaria. It was only a matter of a few years since the people had first made contact with 'white men'. General administration as well as law and order were undertaken by a patrol officer, based at Tabibuga patrol post, situated on a ridge at the eastern end of the valley. This was served by light planes landing at an airstrip carved into the side of the ridge and only approachable in one direction. Taking off, one looked down the grass strip that sloped away towards an empty void towards which the plane hurtled as you prayed that nothing untoward would happen to spoil the take off.

The Department of Forests had decided that the forest resources in the Jimi Valley should be acquired for potential logging operations. The main species of interest was Klinkii Pine, a species that was considerably valued for use in plywood and construction. The rights to cut the timber had then been purchased from the local people, though they really had no idea of the value of their resource and very little concept of the value of the money with which they were being paid. Their main concern was that the money be in coin, not paper notes, as the latter tended to deteriorate quickly when kept in the village, there being no nearby banks. Some $80,000 in coins were, therefore, flown in by helicopter and light plane and paid out to the locals.

The Department of Forests decided, that, having bought the timber rights, they had better find out the extent and nature of the resource, a rather back-to-front way of making a purchase. I was to eventually manage the inventory of the forests there. However, we first had to decide how we would tackle the job, given the fact that we had to assess both the Klinkii Pine as well as other merchantable species in the forest, obtaining a sample that would give a reasonable estimate of the volume of both types of trees. That is how Bob and I ended up being deposited on a rocky bank of the Jimi River, having completed a circuit of the valley, gazing down on the variegated green of different forest tree species, with the tall Klinkii Pines protruding above the canopy with their feathery-like tops.

From discussions with the inhabitants of the valley and the local patrol officer, we learnt that, like many other tribes in PNG, they had had a rough time of it during past generations and even currently. Malaria had been rampant and was still a major problem, particularly in the lower lying areas of the valley. It had decimated the population to such an extent that their numbers had been significantly reduced, even possibly halved. At that time, despite the development that had occurred elsewhere in PNG, the Jimi Valley people had been remote from any medical assistance as well as from ready access to goods or markets for any saleable products. They had only limited communication with the rest of PNG and no communication with the rest of the world, which did not know of their existence. Apart from the few modern tools they may have acquired from some distant trade store, their existence, as subsistence farmers and food gatherers, was probably much as it had been for centuries or perhaps millennia. They had no outside income, except for the money they received for the TRP. However, as with the majority of Papua New Guineans, they had their most valuable asset, their land ... and their trees.

To the people of the Jimi Valley, their forests were their heritage and a resource from which they obtained a subsistence livelihood; not just from wood, but from a variety of non-wood forest products, such as grubs, forest fruits, bush meat, bark and rope. This was similar to the other forest-based communities in PNG, and even elsewhere in Asia, Africa and Latin America. But these villagers, like elsewhere in PNG, were seeking development in the form of roads to link them with markets, improved health and education facilities, and access to commercial products. By allowing logging to take place within their forests they had been assured that such development would occur, although, they had no idea of how logging would impact their forests or their traditional forest livelihoods, and what exactly the development benefits would be or how sustainable they would be.

I mentioned that the people were not far removed from the Stone Age. In fact, the area was well known for its stone axes, which were very popular amongst collectors and tourists. These were of two types. There was the shorter, better balanced utility axe with usually a hard stone head that was actually used for chopping. Then there was the more ornate and counterbalanced ceremonial axe, often made with a softer black slate head, which was used for compensation and as part of a bride price. It was these latter axes that often found their way onto the curio or artefact markets.

Villagers clustered around the helicopter prior to our flying into the Jimi Valley.

During our subsequent timber inventory of the valley that year, we acquired several of these latter types of axes. Our first Minister of

Forests, Siwi Karundo, a man from Chimbu, in the Highlands, happened to be visiting our base camp, and so we asked him what the value of these axes was. He thought for a moment, then said, in Tok Pisin, "if you had twelve such axes, plus about twenty mother of pearl shells, plus fifteen pigs, it would be enough to purchase a bride like that," and he pointed to the Playboy centre fold for Miss March someone had pinned to the wall.

Having only a couple of such axes and no pigs I knew I was right out of the bride market. Unfortunately, so were a lot of other young Papuan and New Guineans, with older richer men often cornering the bride market and having several wives or potential brides, the latter sometimes being pre-teenagers.

Our aim was to see what the forest was like from the ground and how it compared to the aerial photos we had brought with us. We had our tent, a few clothes and food for about a week, so, with some help from the locals, we set up the tent near the river for our first night out and did a quick reconnaissance in the nearby vicinity.

Not far from our campsite we came across what appeared to be a road. It was built through high forest, with trees up to 70 centimetres in diameter and 40 metres high having been felled to create a 20-meter-wide swath for a right-of-way. A basic road form had then been constructed, entirely by hand. You could have driven a Land Rover down it, at least to the nearest decent water course. They hadn't mastered the art of building road bridges so there were no bridges.

This was an incredible effort using just hand tools and must have taken some time to complete. There must also have been an important purpose for building the road. When we asked the local people about it, they explained that it was built by them so 'that the cargo could come' and it extended most of the way down the valley, a distance of about twenty kilometres.

This was another variation on the cargo cult that had been prevalent throughout PNG since the Second World War. Usually, it took the form of people building airstrips and putting dummy planes made of wood and grass on the strip, and sometimes, on the coast, the people would build wharves.

The villagers then expected that planes or boats would come and deposit the 'cargo'. This they would expect to be food and goods of all kinds as they had seen happen with the troops during the Second World War and with government officers in more recent times.

To many of the villagers, who had little knowledge of the outside world, the arrival of all sorts of goods at such airstrips and wharves would have appeared to be like gratuitous gifts from the gods. The cult could have been somewhat innocuous if it hadn't been sometimes accompanied by a cessation of crop cultivation in the belief that it was no longer necessary.

The author with Jimi Valley people on the road constructed by them to allow "the cargo" to come.

Back at our camp, the villagers just sat on their heels and watched with quiet curiosity, as we unpacked and set up our beds. They were interested in what we were doing in their neck of the woods, and we managed to explain this to them.

Dinner was started before dark so that we could see what we were doing, and we had a wonderful meal, while sitting on the stones of the riverbed, with some villagers continuing to squat and watch our activities.

Everything is relative, of course, and it certainly wasn't high-class cuisine. But for the bush it was great. First, we had a sherry or two out of the same mug from which we then had some packet soup and finally Milo. The latter came after downing tinned stew and rice. The villagers pounced on the empty tins with glee, examining them with great interest, and then carrying them off for heavens knows what purpose.

The next morning the villagers were back again and asked if we had any files to sharpen their knives and axes. After some vigorous sharpening had taken place, they then proceeded to delightedly chop down a few medium sized trees in the vicinity to test the axes' renewed cutting potential, regardless of where the trees fell.

They offered to sell us fruit and vegetables, but when we asked about prices, it became obvious that they had little knowledge of the value of the currency. So, we agreed on some reasonable prices and proceeded to get a good store of fresh food to supplement our tinned diet.

Our work involved walking over as much of the valley as possible to see how the forest was structured. Most of this was along existing tracks that the locals used to move from one village to the next through the dense forest. There were some good-sized, fast flowing streams to be crossed and the local villagers were very adept at building narrow cane suspension bridges across quite wide waterways. It was an interesting experience to negotiate one's way across this wildly swinging structure on a narrow footing of bamboo, while clinging to the rattan cables and trying to avoid being mesmerized by the rushing river, some 20 metres below.

Crossing a cane suspension bridge with part of our gear.

As with a lot of lowland and mid-montane forests in PNG, the Jimi Valley Forest was not virgin or climax forest, but rather advanced secondary forest. This was the result of centuries of shifting cultivation by the local forest dwellers, who had cut small patches of the forest down, to plant their food gardens, possibly on a rotation of from 50 to 80 years. However, some species, such as the Klinkii Pine and the denser or harder wood species were not felled and could be up to 300 or more years old. During the subsequent inventory, we saw graphic evidence of this destruction and regeneration of the forest in the trunk of a Klinkii Pine we had felled to test for defect and decay. The tree's branches would be pruned when other trees grew up beside it. However, when the surrounding trees were felled to facilitate the planting of food, epicormic shoots in the tree trunk would then develop into new branches, and this happened every time some local cultivator cleared the forest to plant crops. What we saw in the "biscuit" cut from the log several metres from the butt were branch stubs imbedded at different depths in the log. This provided a log or diary of the dynamics of the forest surrounding this particular tree. It showed that, on average, clearings, presumably for crop gardens, had been made about every 50 years on about four or five occasions. The locals told us the pine was allowed to stand because it was believed to harbour the ghosts (masalai) of departed relatives.

Because of the need to live on higher ground away from the worst malaria mosquito areas, most of the villages were situated on ridges where water was often only available some distance down the hillside. So, for us to wash, it was necessary to either walk down to a stream or rely on the small quantities of water that could be carried to the village. This was done in long tubes of bamboo. Other villages closer to civilization would have used buckets or old tins, but these just weren't available in the Jimi Valley. Washing could then be a hilarious affair, with one of us holding on to the bamboo tube trying not to pour out too much water while the bather soaped himself up and then rinsed. All the while, a crowd of about ten villagers would watch fascinated at these strange antics. What caused even more wonder was when, on one occasion, we got a decent shower of rain, and both of us got out the soap and proceeded to have a shower then and there in an open area of the village. Of course, we had to put on an act and play the fool for the crowd, probably giving them something to talk about for months.

On the second day of our forest exploration, we had walked for some distance along the cargo road, towards the eastern end, when we came across a small group of men working industriously at clearing bush from the edge of the road. It was about mid-morning, and both they and us were sweating profusely from our exertions in the humid heat. We stopped to chat as they were interested in us and in what we were doing, and we were interested in learning about them. In the course of the conversation, one of these fellows asked if we would like some pawpaw (papaya) that was growing on the side of the road. We said we would love some. So, he cut down a couple of fruit and cut these in quarters, taking out the seeds with his bush knife. To my amazement and dismay, he proceeded to rub the pieces of pawpaw along his arms, collecting the sweat on the fruit before proudly handing it to us to eat. I started to protest that I didn't like salt on my pawpaw, but it was too late, and, in any event, it would have been a lack of courtesy to refuse. Both of us ate the fruit, putting on a brave face and expressed our sincere gratitude, knowing the honour they had paid us.

The act of covering the fruit with sweat was a way of preserving and recycling the salt that was available. Salt was scarce in the area, there being no local source and no trade stores from which the locals could buy salt. Traditionally, I learnt, salt may have been traded with people from the coast, but this was not a common occurrence. So whatever salt was present, including that in the body, was preserved. As a child in PNG, I remember watching villagers buying goods in the local trade store with salt being a major purchase. They would put their fingers into the salt, licking them with relish before they left the store. The workers from the highlands on our forest plantations would also save their salt rations till they had a bundle weighing several kilograms to take home as a valuable prize.

Our carriers resting on the track between villages.
Fresh leaves for the rear end each day.

Our reconnaissance of the valley's forests meant moving camp every couple of days and here we used the local villagers as paid porters. On one or two occasions we camped in villages, but accommodation in the form of haus kiaps was rare with almost no outside visitors to the area. On moving into or near a village to stay the night, we would be the centre of immense curiosity from all and sundry. Sometimes the old women would come up cooing and stroke our arms and legs (we wore shorts), fascinated by the blonde hairs. After establishing our tent and as we consulted our maps and notes, about a dozen villagers, including many children would crowd around the entrance to the tent watching our every move and quietly chatting amongst themselves, obviously discussing what we might be doing. These people had had very little contact with 'Europeans' and we were objects of fascination.

I had developed a bad ulcer on one heel from what had been a couple of mosquito bites and it was being aggravated by my continuing to walk with my bush boots on. However, I had been trained as a medical assistant during a three-week course at Port Moresby General Hospital. We had learnt to diagnose the major diseases, prescribe medicines, give injections, dress wounds and stitch up cuts, together with the usual St John's Ambulance First Aid. It was felt that such training would be useful as we often found ourselves in isolated situations with large groups who might need immediate treatment before we could get them to a hospital. The term 'medical assistant' was sometimes changed to 'medical assassin' by some wags who considered we had a license to kill, being allowed to administer such drugs as morphine and adrenaline. I put my training to use on several occasions, particularly for malaria and bad cuts that occurred with our inventory crews. However, it wasn't always easy when it came to treating myself.

For one of my colleagues, I would have prescribed and given a course of procaine penicillin by injection. However, I just couldn't get up the nerve to inject myself with the rather large bore needles that we carried, although I had seen one of my forestry colleagues do it. The alternative was to find a village medical aid who might be able to help, though I might have had my doubts as to his ability, or I could try and get Bob to do the honours, although he had never injected anything.

In the end, I managed to avoid both alternatives by using a technique I had discovered earlier. After dinner at night, I would bathe the wound in water as hot as I could stand. Now in these circumstances, particularly given the shortage of water, the best source was the remaining tea in the billy. By doing this for a few days and keeping a clean, well-padded dressing on the ulcer when I walked, it slowly healed itself. Many years after, I discovered that the tannin in the tea may have been beneficial in the cure.

We spent about a week in the valley before climbing back up the ridge to Tabibuga patrol post, from where we boarded a light plane and flew out to Mount Hagen. Later in the year we were back, but this time with an inventory team to find out how much timber existed in the valley. Our base camp was established in the adjoining Baiyer River Valley and a helicopter was used to fly in inventory parties. I made occasional trips back to the 'valley of the road to nowhere' to check on the accuracy of the work being done and to get a better idea as to the nature of the forest.

The villages were clean but being on higher ground to avoid mosquitoes meant they often lacked water supplies.

Having gone through the laborious and costly exercise of measuring and valuing the timber in the Jimi Valley, after the rights to cut it had been purchased from the local people, the forest was still largely intact, except for shifting cultivation activities, many years later. There was no feasible access across the range of mountains that enclosed the valley; but the people there still have their forest, unlike many other villagers in PNG who have seen their forests badly degraded by incompetent and careless logging of the few trees valued for export, in return for short term financial gains and limited infrastructural development.

Marriage and Madang

Early in 1969 I found myself in Europe, wandering from city to city by train and soaking up an entirely different type of culture and some extraordinary scenery. After a couple of years of work with the PNG Department of Forests and some months working during Christmas vacations while at uni and the Forestry School, I had accumulated some four and a half months leave; so, I decided to take three and a half of those months and see what Europe was like, calling in to New Zealand and America on the way.

I was now in a state of nervous excitement and anticipation as the tour bus I was on drove through the streets of Copenhagen, back to the Rathausplatz. Should I ask them for a drink or dinner. I was thinking of the two attractive blonde Canadian women I had approached in the Grundtvigs Church on our tour of the city. They had answered my somewhat inane question as to whether they were air stewardesses in a friendly manner. No, they said; they weren't air stewardesses, though they did work with Air Canada.

It would be easy to forego the angst of rejection and just get off the bus and not try to talk to them again. But I decided to wait after I got off, as they seemed rather nice. They were among the last to alight and were engaged in a conversation as I approached them, feeling both hopeful and a bit scared.

Then, they saw me and the taller of the two smiled and said something like, "Hello again."

I dove straight in and asked, "Would you like to come for a drink?" This was directed at the taller one with longer, straight blonde hair. The other I had noticed was wearing an engagement ring and so I felt she was of less interest.

"That sounds like fun," replied the taller one, who then introduced herself as Marion. Her friend's name was Lyn.

The three of us found a nearby bar and had a couple of drinks at a table on the sidewalk. That was followed by dinner during which I sensed that we were enjoying each other's company - so much so, that we met up again a couple of times over the next two days, before they flew out. I agreed with Marion to meet in London if I made it there before they left for Vancouver in about a week's time. That meeting didn't happen as I ended up touring fjords along the coast of Norway. However, once I was back in PNG after my three and a half months leave, feeling I had gained some knowledge of other parts of the world, I decided to drop Marion a line. This was a woman who I liked and would like to get to know even better, but we had not really spent much time together and I wasn't sure what her reaction would be. Marion replied in a friendly manner that left the door open for further correspondence. So, we started writing to each other, somewhat tentative at first as if we were both feeling our way through a medium that could create misunderstandings.

I had taken on the leadership of an inventory survey of the Tonolei Harbour area, at the southern end of the island of Bougainville in July for about two months. This was a mixed experience. Although, I had already been on several inventories over the previous three years and had led two of them, I seemed to struggle at times to get it right and there were occasions when I lacked the self-confidence and strength of character that a leader should have possessed.

We had established our base camp at what had been the site for a defunct logging and sawmilling operation, using a few fibro huts that were still standing for our office and senior officers' quarters. I instructed the technical staff and labourers to set up their tents on a nearby ridge. No sooner had my boss, Eric Hammermaster come on the scene to inspect operations than he upbraided me for putting those tents in such a difficult situation. Somewhat shamefaced, I ordered the crews to put up their tent flies on the flat ground surrounding our office and accommodation.

Then, a field crew managed to wreck our almost new runabout boat a day's walk around the other side of the peninsular that formed the southern side of the harbour. That happened just as the Director of Forests, Don McIntosh, turned up for a visit. I had the feeling that he and others may have felt I wasn't in good enough control of operations, although nothing was said. We also had a problem with several field crews developing nasty cases of foot rot. After about a month of spending long days in swampy conditions on some of the inventory lines their feet were red raw and painful. In time, we overcame this problem by ensuring those with affected feet kept them dry and aired while in camp and that their boots were also dried out. As time progressed it became a very congenial camp.

Marion and I had kept up an intermittent correspondence while I was in the wilds of Bougainville, and that became a bit more consistent once I got back to civilization in Moresby in late September. Towards the end of October, she decided fly to PNG and see me. As Marion's trip out came closer, so did our long-distance relationship, with letters arriving every few days. Meanwhile, I was getting myself into a bit of a quandary. I was so looking forward to seeing Marion, but I wasn't quite sure what I should be doing. I might have been 25 and had had several girlfriends over the preceding years, but I was somewhat naïve and sexually immature when it came to up close and personal relationships with women. I had never faced a situation like this before and it was all rather heady stuff. Here, I was with what looked to be developing into a really serious relationship with a beautiful, vivacious and self-assured woman. Where was this going? Where would she stay? What could we do together? How much time should I take off work? I would be the only person she knew, and the responsibility for it all was nerve wracking.

At base camp, Tonolei Harbour.

In the end, I muddled through, finding time from work to be with Marion, driving her around in my ancient, rather battered Peugeot 403 whose handbrake didn't work. I had developed quite a knack of using my heel and toe to go from brake to accelerator when starting on a hill. It also had a habit of sometimes just stopping, particularly after going through a large puddle. I usually managed to get it going again using a screwdriver and can of WD40 to open up and demoisturize the carburettor. However, on one occasion nearing Moresby on the road from Bomana, the engine stopped and refused to start. So, I figured the best solution was to thumb a lift back to town and return with my friend's VW. Marion was not impressed at having to wait by the dusty roadside for half an hour, minding our car.

Despite vehicle mishaps and my own inexperience, we became engaged towards the end of her stay. We flew down to Sydney together and bought an engagement ring before I saw Marion off on her Qantas flight back to Vancouver. I, then headed back up to Moresby to my forestry working life after what seemed like a fairy tale. It was only five months to our wedding date in July, but feeling somewhat desolate, those months seemed like forever, as my plane landed back at Jackson's Airport on another sunny day.

With work including an inventory survey around the Gogol River near Madang on the north coast, the time passed rapidly. I had two buck's or bachelor's parties; the first with the crew from the Gogol inventory survey at the Smuggler's Inn Motel in Madang. That was fairly tame, particularly compared to the party put on by my colleagues in Moresby in the back yard of a senior forest officer's house. By the early morning some of us were naked and covered in treacle and one had some nasty cuts from rolling on a broken bottle. Having driven home, I awoke later that morning to find the treacle-covered clothes I had dropped on my bedroom floor covered in ants.

The wedding was a small, though formal affair. Then, after a honeymoon in the interior of British Columbia, we flew back to Port Moresby. I had managed to be allocated a new house in the suburb of Gordon and had moved in a week or so before flying to Vancouver. Now we settled down to married life, though I felt some insecurity, feeling that such a drastic move for Marion would need a lot of support from me to help her adjust to such a different environment without her family and friends. The marriage may have been on the rocks one morning, when Marion said, "So, darling, what could I get you for breakfast?"

"How about tinned spaghetti on toast," I blithely replied, thinking of one of my favourite dishes.

Marion stared with a rather quizzical expression on her face. "I beg your pardon, what did you say?" It was taking time for her to adjust to strange Aussie eating habits.

In 1971, we moved to the beautiful town of Madang on the north coast, where I was now district forest officer. The Department chartered a plane to move us, a Short Skyvan. So, we loaded all our household goods and clothes, together with our new black Labrador pup, Beethoven, and a newly acquired rescue kitten, we had named Tuppence. Although Beethoven was tranquilized and, on a leash, the pilot was not happy about having a large black dog, stretched out in his plane.

My concerns about how well Marion would fit in and feel comfortable in PNG proved to be unfounded as she adapted wonderfully. She got herself a job with the office of the Harbourmaster in Madang and became adept at fending off enquiries for him when he was across the way at the Madang Club, until she could get his attention through the barman. We made a number of friends among the expats in the town, of which there was a varied assortment. There was a seamy side to life in the form of key parties, where couples would come to dinner and put their car keys in a bowl. Then, after dinner and liqueurs, the men would draw out a key and go home with the woman linked to that key. We made it clear that this was not our scene.

Our two-bedroom single-storey bungalow was beside the harbour near the airport, together with a few other government houses. I had a canoe made by a local villager, which we pulled up on to the shore opposite the house. We used this to paddle around the harbour and to nearby islands for picnics and swimming. However, we had to make sure our haus boi held on to Beethoven. If not, he would race across the intervening grass, dive in, and come swimming out to us in mid-stream. We were then faced with trying to get a rather large dog on board without capsizing.

I got on with my forestry work, which often meant time being spent out at Gogol, to the southeast of Madang, establishing tree plantations. A new pulp mill was to be established by a Japanese joint venture company, JANT, using mixed tropical hardwoods. I was introduced to the concept of cost/benefit analysis and spent time undertaking feasibility studies relating to the venture, in collaboration with the Japanese, with whom Marion and I became quite friendly. They were planning on cutting trees in the nearby Gogol River Forest to make wood chips, although, I hoped that they were saving the better species for other more profitable uses.

These forests were owned by the local people and the government had already purchased the rights to cut trees, but only down to a diameter of 50 centimetres. We needed to reach an understanding on an extension of their Timber Rights Purchase Agreement to include smaller trees that could be harvested for pulpwood. To that end, a kiap (patrol officer) and I spent a day flying from one village to another in a Jet Ranger helicopter, holding discussions with the forest owners in the remoter sections of the valley.

After our last visit for the day, at a village on the eastern side of the valley, we all piled into the chopper for the trip back to Madang where a few well-earned beers and dinner awaited us. As we sat in our seats, strapped in and waiting for lift off, there was the same sensation as getting into your car, turning the key, and finding all you get is a dead click. No power from the battery. So, what to do? We had no means of communicating with anyone, as the helicopter's radio relied on the battery and, of course, there were no phones or radios in the village or within 30 kilometres. The pilot had cancelled his Search and Rescue (SAR)[2] Watch with Air Traffic Control in Madang when he landed, so it was unlikely that people would be too worried if we didn't return, although if we had still failed to return the next day, they might have sent a plane to check and see if we were okay.

This, however, could mean that we might be stranded for two or more days. I wasn't prepared to just spend the night in the village in the hope that someone outside would take action. I felt I needed to do something constructive. So, I decided to walk for help – through the forest, and at night. It wasn't too far, possibly 25 kilometres to the nearest road and a further 30 kilometres to Madang. The villagers told me that there was, indeed, a path to the Gogol River, about six or seven hours away, or as they also expressed in Tok Pisin, "*Im i lon wei liklik.*" (Not too far). Once there, I reasoned, I could find my way across the river and up to the Madang Road, where I could try to get a lift into town in the morning. I borrowed a pair of walking boots from a local village policeman, as my shoes were not up to the sort of walking anticipated. Then, with a guide from the village, I set off just before sunset at about six p.m.

We didn't have a torch and there was no moon to speak of. Even if there had been, the dense forest canopy would still keep our path totally dark. So, before darkness fully set in, my guide cut two dried bamboo culms to make torches, which we lit when the light had gone. They enabled us to see in our immediate vicinity as we tramped along the muddy track, climbing over the occasional log, and wading through small streams. But, apart from massive tree trunks and tangled undergrowth next to the path, the surrounding forest was a black void.

A couple of hours into our journey, it started to rain. The track became a great deal muddier and the going more slippery and decidedly less comfortable as the heavy rain soaked my clothes. Fortunately, it was quite flat and, despite my concerns that the rain would douse the torches, they continued to burn. So, we could still see where we were going, although, at this point I was starting to wonder whether I had made the right decision, while at the same time hoping that the guide did, in fact, know the way. Shortly thereafter, we stopped at a village where we managed to scrounge a kerosene pressure lamp. This improved our ability to see, particularly when the rain stopped shortly afterwards.

---

2   All aircraft, on take-off in PNG were assigned a time at which they must report their position on an hourly basis. If nothing is heard from the aircraft a search and rescue procedure is activated.

Our stranded helicopter.

Finally, at around midnight we arrived at a village on the banks of the Gogol. A boatman was roused, protesting, from his slumbers, and we agreed on a price for him to take me across in his dugout canoe. This wasn't an easy thing in the dark and on this wide river that was somewhat swollen with recent rains and flowing quite swiftly. I didn't consider there was any alternative, although in hindsight it might have been more sensible to wait until daylight. So, after returning the borrowed boots, I slid down the wet and muddy bank and gingerly seated myself in the canoe. I tried to ignore the dangers as our boatman set out from the bank and rowed us across the fast-flowing current.

The light from the pressure lamp, held by my guide, showed only a few metres out from the bank, a swirling mass of brown water. The obvious direction was across the current, though that was sweeping us downstream at a hefty rate. I am not sure if there actually was a set landing place, but we could never have found it in the dark and with that current. So, we pushed on in our somewhat unstable craft, with the odd wave slopping water over the side, until, eventually, we made it across to the opposite bank, without capsizing or being savaged by a crocodile, which were quite prevalent in the area. I thanked and paid my guide. He would now have an even more difficult trip rowing back to his village, which was upstream from where we landed.

I made my way, barefoot and cautiously, up the bank and through some scrub. By now, the clouds had broken-up and a starry sky was giving me enough light by which to see. Reaching the dirt road to Madang, I found my bearings and discovered I was next to a vocational training centre. That was a bit of luck as now I wouldn't have to sit out the rest of the night on the

37

edge of the road or walking towards Madang. I decided I had a reasonable excuse to wake the local principal and his wife and banged on their front door. Needless to say, they got quite a shock seeing me on their doorstep, barefoot, wet through and covered in mud at one in the morning; but they kindly allowed me in and permitted me to silt up their shower with all the mud I had accumulated, before borrowing some clean clothes and settling down to sleep for what was left of the night, feeling somewhat pleased that I had made it.

The next morning, they drove me into Madang after breakfast. It was Saturday, and they were off to town for some shopping. Marion was just heading out as I drove up to our house. She wasn't worried as she had been in touch with Air Traffic Control who had said they were not overly concerned, thinking we may have stayed over for a party at the village. I immediately got onto ATC and told them of the plight of the helicopter and its occupants. The person I spoke to told me that, although they weren't concerned, they had diverted a DC 3 to check the area that morning. When they saw that all appeared to be okay with the chopper, no further action was taken.

The helicopter company, when I contacted them, wanted me to walk back in with a battery, but I refused. So, instead, they sent in a helicopter, diverted from the Highlands and everyone came out the next day. The day after, the rains came again to such an extent that the sand bank on which the chopper had been resting was flooded.

Early in 1971, Madang received word that the Duke of Edinburgh would be coming for a visit. He would fly in and then board the Royal Yacht Britannia for his onward journey. The town was abuzz with rumours and anticipation. Invitations were sent out by the District Commissioner, Desmond Clifton-Bassett, for various functions over the three days of the duke's stay. Marion and I, together with the Forestry Technical Officer, Dokka Reid and his wife, were invited for a garden party at The Residence of the DC. Others were invited to barbeques or dinner on board the Britannia. We were specifically instructed, particularly the expat ladies, not to dress up, so that the local New Guinea people would not be outdone. But that didn't stop the two main stores in town, Burns Philp and Carpenters, from quickly being sold out of dress material, long gloves, stockings and other items of formal or semi-formal dress.

There was also a certain degree of one-upmanship among certain residents with comments being heard like, "Oh, you're going to the reception, are you? We've been invited on board."

Marion, Dokka, his wife and I didn't bother with dressing up too much and arrived at the residency in good time. As other guests milled about around the front of the house awaiting the arrival of the duke, we moved down the lawn to the bar and proceeded to get ourselves a drink. There was a commotion as the duke arrived with people crowding around the driveway. We stayed where we were and continued drinking while watching what was happening. Then, the crowd opened and the duke himself, came sauntering down towards us. He greeted us warmly and asked what we did. We then had a short conversation, with the duke cracking some joke about forestry, and he turned back to the throng at the front door. Well, that was something to write home about, and we wondered why he had made a point of coming down to talk to a non-conforming bunch like us.

About mid-1971, I got word from the head of the Botanic Gardens in Lae, that a Russian survey vessel, on its way to the Antarctic, was to call in with a group of botanists to celebrate the anniversary of the Russian botanist, Nicholas Miklouho-Maclay's arrival on the Madang coast in 1871. I was to meet the Russian botanists and squire them around, including field trips to the bush.

In the process of organising things, people got to know about this planned alien visitation. Then one morning, I had a visit from the local ASIO (Australian Security Intelligence Organisation) officer, who had an office across from mine, where he seemed to spend most of the time reading the paper. "What's all this I hear about a Russian vessel due to call into Madang?" So much for our highly esteemed security service. I filled him in, presumably so he could report his 'intelligence coup' to his bosses in Canberra.

Some people were aghast that I would be going on board the ship, perhaps thinking I might get kidnapped and brainwashed. This was the height of the cold war and not long after Khrushchev banged his shoe on the podium at the UN. The district commissioner stated that the ship could dock to unload vehicles and equipment and allow scientists to come ashore, although it could not stay tied up and had to anchor in the harbour. I duly boarded the ship after it had docked and introduced myself to the respective scientists, who were all very friendly and seemed apolitical. We agreed on an agenda for their visit and then, having sounded out Marion, I asked them to come home and have a drink at our place, which they did. Ironically, Marion's favourite drink was a Black Russian (Tia Maria and Vodka, with no ice).

After we had shown the Russians some local hospitality, they invited Marion and me back on board for more drinks and dinner. By now the ship was anchored in the harbour, so we made our way out by launch and up the gangway. On board, we were treated first to straight vodka, which had to be tossed back in one shot. The first of these hit me behind the eyes, then the second went down without any pain. We were fed a rather tasty Borscht soup for dinner, followed by brandy and a tour of some of the ship's facilities. Descending down the steep gangway to the launch required some careful positioning of feet, but we both made it and, having somewhat ungracefully clambered up onto the dock, drove back home, feeling what nice people these Russians were.

One of the favourite watering holes in Madang was the Madang Hotel, on the point at the entrance to the harbour. It was there one evening that our esteemed Minister of Forests got into an altercation with one of the local police officers. I received a phone call the next morning asking if I could please come down to the courthouse where the minister was to come before a magistrate on a charge of affray or some such thing.\ I was to interpret as the minister's English wasn't too good.

I knew the minister having met him on several previous occasions, and I sat down next to him in the courtroom and tried to explain what was going to happen. He couldn't understand why he was being charged as he felt he was only defending himself after he had got rather drunk and been told to leave and was then manhandled out. The trial proceeded with the policeman involved giving evidence as to what had happened, together with a couple of other witnesses. All along, I was interpreting for the minister and at times he had to be restrained from leaping up and yelling at the witnesses and was told to sit down by the magistrate or he would be charged with contempt of court. The minister, having no idea about how the court operated could not understand why he couldn't object, and I had difficulty in explaining this and what 'contempt of court' meant. I felt rather sorry for him in this alien environment as he sat there mumbling to himself in Tok Pisin.

Then the magistrate asked the prosecuting counsel whether the police officer concerned was sober enough to make a judgement about the charge. "Oh, yes, Your Worship," the counsel replied. "He was quite sober."

"But how do you know?" persisted the magistrate.

"Because, Your Worship, he was playing darts."

"Darts? What is this darts?" asked the puzzled Papua New Guinean magistrate.

The counsel then proceeded to explain what was involved with playing darts, complete with appropriate actions. It went something like this, which, I proceeded to translate to the minister in Tok Pisin.

"You put this board with all these pig bristles on it up on the wall. There are lines with numbers fixed on the pig bristles. Then one man stands back from the board with pig bristles and numbers and he throws these little spears at the board. Then another man does the same and the man who hits the highest numbers wins the game."

The magistrate was mystified, and the minister was arguing quite loudly that this was a silly game and what did it have to do with anything.

In the end, the magistrate accepted that the policeman involved must have been sober enough to play such a game and proceeded to allow his testament. And that testament wasn't good for the minister as it seemed he created quite a ruckus. However, after several hours of testament and late in the afternoon, the defence council raised a point of order or procedure about certain options not being explained by the magistrate to the defendant So, the court was adjourned until the next day.

The next morning, another magistrate, flown in from Wewak, up the coast, concluded that it was a mistrial and said that the minister was free to go. No further charges were pursued. The minister was completely bamboozled by the whole procedure as he was only trying to defend his dignity as any red-blooded highlander would do. If this had been at his home, spears and arrows could have been involved. Here nobody was hurt and yet there was this day long court case accusing him of harming someone, then it all amounted to nothing.

PNG had adopted a form of self-government in the 1960s and independence was in the wind. Government positions were being 'localized' with Papua New Guineans replacing expats in jobs, starting at the top and the bottom. Knowing that sooner or later I would have to look for another job and because I was feeling somewhat isolated from forestry work decisions in Madang, I thought it best to make a move. So, in May of 1972, I resigned from the Department of Forests. I had earlier acquired Canadian Landed Immigrant status, and, so, Marion and I flew over to live in Vancouver. I saved the government some money by not following the usual practice and using plywood to make our packing crates. Instead, I went to the local sawmill, whose owner I knew, and bought numerous wide boards of New Guinea Rosewood and Walnut. I reasoned that I could use the timber in Vancouver to have furniture made, which is what we did. I also made a cage each for Beethoven and Tuppy for their long trip across the Pacific.

Another Side of Forestry - Consulting

It had been decided before we left PNG that, in Vancouver, Marion and I would join with Marion's Mother, Dorothy Grimston, and set up a galley selling PNG and other Oceanic art and artifacts in Gastown, a new trendy area of downtown Vancouver. To this end, I had purchased a considerable quantity of artifacts from in and around Madang before leaving, much of it originating in the Sepik River area. This was shipped over to Vancouver, so that shortly after our arrival we had some 21 tons of artefacts in wooden crates dumped on the front lawn of our new house.

Running our own business was a tiring, though somewhat satisfying, endeavour as we had a good collection of interesting and hard-to-obtain pieces from PNG. I had boned up on the ethnology and meanings associated with the various figures, masks and other carvings and enjoyed satisfying the enquiries from numerous, curious customers. In fact, our business gained a good reputation for its artifacts, and we shipped numerous items to customers in the US and other parts of Canada.

After a very slow 1973/74 winter season, I felt I had had enough of the gallery business. Although our gallery had been moderately successful, obtaining new and interesting supplies from PNG was difficult, and I wasn't interested in other sorts of art for sale. It was time to get back into forestry. However, I didn't much fancy tramping through the ice and snow of British Columbia's winters to manage forests. So, I contacted a couple of forestry consulting firms, with Forestal International being the more promising. Coming from a public service background, I wasn't used to bargaining for a salary. So, when Bill Webb, who was Vice President, asked what I might expect, I considered my last salary down in PNG, added a bit and said, "about $13,000 a year."

Bill said, "I feel we can do better than that." And when they rang to offer me a job, I started at around $22,000.

Forestal was the forestry division of Sandwell and Company, a major pulp and paper engineering firm, which had built a considerable number of pulp and paper mills, both in Canada and around the world. I joined them in March 1974 and found I was with a good group of foresters and forest engineers who were quite easy going and welcoming. Morning and afternoon coffee and tea breaks in the drafting office were a time for a type of social bonding with all manner of topics discussed, including work issues and tales of happenings on jobs, which were largely overseas.

My first assignment was with a team that was determining how forestry and forest industry operations could be more efficiently carried out in Turkey. This meant spending four months there helping to redefine management and silvicultural regimes for their forests. Little did I know that the assignment would drop me into the middle of a war.

Although Marion was amenable to my taking the job with Forestal, the four months of separation was difficult for both of us. David, our first son, had arrived the previous July, and Marion was not happy about being left with a young child, although she felt she could manage. Marion and her mother were continuing with the gallery, which was another burden for her, although before the year was up, we would sell the business. The night before I left, in July, I sat on David's bed and gazed at him with an overwhelming ache while stroking his head, feeling the bond between us and not wanting to leave him.

The Turkey experience was a daunting task and my first experience of 'pushing the envelope' in consulting. though, I was also excited to be venturing into many unknowns, both culturally and forest-wise. Although I had studied the silviculture applicable to the pine and spruce forests in Turkey, that was all academic, and my experience had all been in tropical or eucalypt forests and plantations, but I was in good company. Brian Jones, a short, stocky, taciturn Brit was also on the team, as well as a couple of forest engineers and the team leader, Bob Church. As we would be dealing with many Turkish forestry personnel who didn't speak English, we all attended classes to learn at least some basic Turkish before we left. This at least gave us a basis on which to build once we were immersed in the country and its culture.

Flying over the almost treeless Anatolian Plateau, then passing over minarets as we came into land at Ankara, I was very much aware that this was a different sort of country. Stepping off the plane onto a tarmac with machine gun-toting soldiers was not the usual airport welcome and gave me a sense of unease; and one sensed a certain tenseness in the air across the capital. Turkey and Greece were at odds over Cyprus. Relations between the Greek junta that had seized power in 1967, and Archbishop Makarios, the President of Cyprus, were at breaking point, and Turkey was concerned for the Turkish Cypriots.

It all came to a head after we had arrived and were already undertaking field trips. On 15 July, Greek army officers in Cyprus instigated a coup

44

that overthrew President Makarios. Then four days later, Turkey invaded Cyprus. It was a Saturday, and Brian and I were overnighting in the sleepy town of Canakkale on the Dardanelles. On the opposite shore stood the imposing Kilitbihar Castle, built in the fifteenth century. It lay just north-east of the battleground, on the Gallipoli (Gelibolu) Peninsula, on which thousands of ANZACs and Turkish soldiers gave their lives in 1915.

We had paid a quick visit to the castle the previous day before taking the ferry across to Canakkale, having spent the previous two days in the company of a rather hawkish Turkish forester checking out forests around Edirne, not far from the Greek border. He had boasted that the Turkish army could cross the border and be in Athens in a matter of days; and that night, as I tried to sleep in Edirne, scores of army vehicles, including tanks on trucks, moved through the town, heading for the border. It was obvious that something was definitely going to happen, and, sure enough, it did.

We heard the news of the Turkish invasion at breakfast in our small hotel. Of course, the news on the TV was all in Turkish, requiring our Turkish counterpart to interpret it. I was feeling nervous. Here we were in a foreign country that had just gone to war with its neighbour. Would the Greeks retaliate by bombing Turkey? What should we do? With the invasion and Turkey now being on a war footing it was unlikely that we as two foreigners, would be able to continue wandering around the countryside for our field work or if, indeed, it would be safe to do so until the situation became clearer.

Down on the shore of the Dardanelles it was quite eerie. Normally, there would have been several vessels either heading towards the Sea of Marmara or out to the Aegean Sea. That morning there was nothing, not even a rowing boat in sight. We decided that, as it was the weekend, we would spend the time on the beach awaiting advice from our project manager. If there was no word we would then head back to Ankara.

The next day, word came through to head back to Ankara with all speed, though keeping a low profile. It turned out that the Canadian Embassy had also been trying to contact us as they were organizing an evacuation flight out if needed and wanted to know where we all were. There was some strife from the project manager for not letting him know where we were or for not coming back earlier. One lesson I learnt was to have a transistor radio so I could pick up the BBC or other news and get an outside view on any such crisis.

Back in Ankara, we noted that the Ministry of War was only a block away from our hotel; perhaps far enough if Greek planes decided to bomb selected targets in the capital. I managed to get word to Marion through the company that I was safe and in Ankara. Our normal communication was by written mail, and letters could take a week to get to or from Canada.

Once the situation in Turkey became more stable, we continued with our field work; although, there continued to be much hype about the war, with the press fuelling national sentiment against the Greeks. There was also some antagonism against foreigners and particularly the British, who had moved a squadron of Phantom jet fighters to the Greek side of Cypress to protect their interests. Sometimes this hype would boil over during discussions with Turkish foresters, which led to the occasional tense situation.

We were using Ankara, as our base. The city is situated almost in the dead centre of the country on the dry, mostly treeless, Anatolian Plateau. It was not always like this. The story goes that Tamerlane (Timor the Lame), the ruthless Mogul conqueror, hid his army in an oak forest prior to his defeating the Turks near Angora (Ankara) in the fourteenth century. Today, the once verdant oak forests have been reduced to patches of low oak scrub (maki), the result of forest destruction for agricultural and grazing lands, as well as overcutting for fuel and construction wood. In places large stumps of ancient oak trees could still be seen, reminders of what once was a more forested landscape.

Our many and wide-ranging field trips revealed that there were dense forests on the escarpments to the Plateau. These ranged from dense spruce and fir stands with almost solid rhododendron undergrowth two metres high in the northeast, to less dense pine forests in the drier regions to the west and south. In between, along the Black Sea Coast and towards the western escarpment, were more open beech forests.

Our field trips took us across the northern half of the country by road, from Kars and Artvin in the east, near the Armenian and Georgian border, to Izmir on the Aegean Sea and Edirne on the Greek border, in the west. We usually stayed in hotels or forest guest houses and experienced a range of Turkish cuisine, often from wayside eateries with dubious hygiene regimes. There was many a convivial night spent with our Turkish forester counterparts eating and drinking. As the fiery raki took hold and dulled the inhibitions we might be found out on the floor performing Turkish dances.

But an indelible memory of my time in Turkey is the toilets. These were usually the squat variety, which I am not fond of. In our Ankara office, the toilets had a habit of flushing without warning, which could lead to an embarrassing situation with wet trousers if one was caught with one's pants down. Apart from a concession to foreigners in our Ankara office, there was no toilet paper, just a jug of water to cleanse oneself, with the left hand, of course. In the field, many of the toilets either didn't flush or weren't flushed and stank so badly you could find your way to them on a dark and moonless night. I refused to use them if we had bush or forest nearby, as an alternative. I must have commented or complained enough because on the eve of my departure from Turkey my counterparts presented me with a bronze miniature Turkish toilet.

As we travelled around Turkey looking at forest operations, we also came across the residue of some 6,000 years of history. The towns and the countryside were littered with numerous ruins dating from the Mycenean Greek and Roman periods, through to relatively modern examples from the Ottoman Empire such as Top Kapi Palace and the Aya Sofya in Istanbul.

The legendary city of Troy, just south of the Dardanelles, had been reduced to a series of stone walls outlining various structures, and the ruins were many kilometres inland. The seafront and port of Troy had been silted up by sediments caused by overcutting of forests in the hinterland.

We passed through the town of Yassıhüyük, some 80 kilometres south-west of Ankara, the site of Gordium and the Gordian Knot. This was an elaborate and involved knot, with no visible ends tying the yoke of the chariot of Gordius, the founder of the city, with a pole. It was believed that whoever could untie the knot would go on to conquer Asia. In 333BC, Alexander the Great called into Gordium, tried to untie the knot and being unsuccessful, he pulled out his sword and cut it through.

Two of my Turkish forestry counterparts and myself.

47

I was certainly being extended beyond my forestry comfort zone. Not only was I supposed to be some sort of expert, but also an expert on northern hemisphere temperate forestry. It was a wonderful learning experience, and I took copious notes as we talked with Turkish foresters and tramped through numerous forests. I had picked up the concept somewhere that writing things down helped the memory more than just reading or listening, and of course one then had a record for later reference. It was the start of compulsive note-taking over many years of assignments in numerous countries.

After some time working in the country, I was forced to consider what my role was as a consultant. One or two of our Turkish counterparts from the General Directorate of Forestry (Orman Genel *Mudurlugu*) were questioning why the Turkish Government had employed a team of foreign consultants, who were not familiar with Turkey or its forests, to restructure their industrial forestry operations when they felt adequate expertise for doing that existed in the country. It was a legitimate question, and being the sensitive being that I am, I also wondered why we were being paid so much money to teach the Turkish foresters what to do about their forests and how they should be managed. Talking the situation over with my Canadian colleagues, I concluded that we were in fact fulfilling a useful role. We shouldn't pretend we know everything about forestry in Turkey. What we could provide was expertise in taking the information we acquired from our Turkish counterparts and our own observations and using our own expertise from elsewhere to produce a workable plan and recommendations, including the technical and financial feasibility of investing in various forestry or forest industry options.

For all this tripping around the Turkish landscape we used old Willeys Jeep estate wagons, with Turkish drivers of about the same vintage, both being provided by the Orman Genel Mudurlugu. Having been in the country a few weeks, Brian Jones and I, together with a Turkish forester, set out to do some reconnaissance of forests towards the west of the country. It was July, the height of summer on the Anatolian Plateau, and the temperature hovered around or above forty degrees Celsius. It was like opening an oven door to step outside. The vehicle we were taking should have been in good condition, having been checked out after our first trip when, amongst other things, we felt the steering was a bit loose. As we were chatting and eyeing the rather desolate, almost treeless, landscape about 100 kilometres south-west from Ankara and halfway to the town of Afyon, we noticed steam erupting from under the bonnet.

Pulling over to the side in the parched countryside we waited till the engine had cooled down. We found that the radiator had almost boiled dry. On examining the cap, I found the gasket was gone.

"Oh," said the driver.

"You remember we had a problem with the gasket being damaged on the last trip?"

"Well, I just decided to throw it away." There was a sort of logic to this thinking.

After two rather incredulous gasps of, "You did what!" from Brian and I, we then had to figure out what we could do. Perhaps we could hitch a ride from a passing vehicle. But we needed transport for our field work. In any event, as we stood by the side of the road, I noticed that hitching a ride may not have been a plausible option as there was a distinct shortage of vehicles passing – in both directions. I also noted there wasn't a living soul or building to be seen. There wasn't even a tree, just a few goats nibbling on the scanty bushes and dried grass in the distance seen through the shimmering heat. One other thing I noted was that we had no spare water, only a reasonably full 2-litre bottle of drinking water, which wasn't much for a parched radiator.

Stopped at a farmhouse on the edge of the forest in Eastern Turkey with our trusty Jeep estate wagon.

The driver remembered that there was a service station a few kilometres ahead. Maybe, we could just make it, with a bit of care. So, after waiting for about an hour until the radiator had cooled sufficiently, we tipped in our precious bottle of water. The driver managed to start the engine, then he slowly climbed to the top of the next hill, where he put the gears in neutral, turned the engine off and coasted down to the bottom. He repeated the operation on the following hill. Luckily, there were only two or three hills before we were able to glide into a service station, where, somehow, a radiator cap with a gasket was found, plus a good supply of water.

Rain and Snakes on the Osa Peninsula

If you have a problem with snakes, don't go tramping around the Osa Peninsula in Costa Rica at any time, and if you don't like getting wet don't go there in the rainy season. Something in the vicinity of four metres of water pours out of the sky in an almost constant deluge over several months. Being ignorant about both these factors, I found myself on the Osa Peninsula for six weeks in the middle of the rains - not that I had a choice, as this was an assignment for my company, Forestal International.

It was May 1975, and I, together with a colleague from Forestal, John Phillips, found ourselves climbing out of a single-engine Cessna on an airstrip cut out of a solid mass of forest with no other sign of habitation around. We had bumped and dodged our way through and around a series of threatening cumulonimbus clouds as our Costa Rican pilot flew John, myself and our gear in the overloaded plane from the capital, San Jose. This venture into such a wet, green wilderness was all because some Japanese-American consortium wanted to know if there was enough potential to set up a wood chip mill on the peninsula.

The Osa Peninsula is a rather isolated area in the south-west of Costa Rica, adjacent to the Panamanian border. There were no towns, just an undulating, mottled green carpet of dense forest covering a rugged landscape. Scattered settlements were inhabited mainly by squatters, with whom the owners of the land had an ongoing feud that occasionally resulted in the burning of houses and the shooting of people on both sides. This was something else I didn't know about when I climbed out of our cramped seats in the chartered Cessna.

We were met at the airstrip by the local forest manager from the company who owned the forest. He, then, drove us in a rather dilapidated Land Rover to a bunkhouse, situated halfway up the side of a ridge, our accommodation for the next six weeks. After we had taken one load of luggage in from the back of the Land Rover, which was parked by the side of the house, we found, upon coming out to get more of our luggage a couple of minutes later, that the Land Rover was missing. A quick search of the area revealed that it had rolled back along the driveway, and over the edge of a steep embankment coming to rest, upright, on a grassy field below. On the way, my case had fallen out of the back and had been run over. Amazingly, the Land Rover was unscathed and, apart from my damaged suitcase, nothing was broken.

Our main activity was the tedious process of carrying out an inventory of the forest, which meant establishing sample plots all over the place and measuring trees. To help with this we had a small team of local technical people from the company. However, I felt very much at a disadvantage, at least initially, because the only Spanish I spoke had been learned from a phrase book I had picked up in Vancouver after I heard I was to come on this job as the forest workers didn't speak a word of English.

As I was supposed to be in charge and compiling the inventory data, it was a bit of a challenge. To the few words and phrases, I had learned, I quickly added enough Spanish to communicate with my co-workers, particularly such key items as the numbers, when to have lunch or set off for home, and some items of food. Luckily, they were a friendly and easy-going bunch who were quite patient with my language deficit.

It was rough going with a lot of walking and climbing steep ridges to establish sample plots and survey the forests and topography with a view to a possible logging operation. On a couple of occasions, we camped out overnight in a friendly settlement. The work was made harder by the almost constant rain. After a few days I had no spare dry clothes to put on. So, each morning I would dress for breakfast in my only dry shirt and trousers and then reluctantly change these for wet clothes before heading out to the field. Back at the bunkhouse in the late afternoon I would change back into my dry outfit.

It was a miserable experience, and nobody had bothered to inform me it was the wet season before I left Vancouver. I did devise a sort of poncho from a piece of plastic sheeting to keep me somewhat dry and warm when we stopped to measure trees or have lunch. The rain turned any open ground into sticky, glutinous mud that made walking and climbing more difficult and sucked the sole off my new pair of sturdy bush boots. As we spent hours tramping through the rain showers and scrambling up steep, densely forested slopes, my thoughts turned to Marion and my son, David, snug and dry back in Vancouver. I was also keen to get back and finish the conversion of our garage into a den, of which I was particularly proud. Eventually, after about three weeks, the rain eased and occasional dry periods occurred, even sunshine. We had the relative luxury of some clean and dry clothes, laundered by the woman who cooked for us.

And then there were the snakes. I had not come across so many in so short a time, even during the many years I was working in the forests of Papua New Guinea. And here, on the Osa there were a couple of particularly poisonous species. The one we came across most often was the very dangerous

Terciopelo[3] or Fer-de-Lance, a venomous pit viper that could reach a length of two metres. The other main type was the Coral snake. These are small, vibrantly coloured, highly venomous snakes. Its neurotoxic venom is the second-most deadly of any snake.

Walking up to a tree and about to measure its diameter, I was saved more than once at the last moment by a shout from one of my co-workers as I was about to step on a Terciopelo, coiled up in between the buttresses. After I had jumped backward to safety, my co-workers would lay into the snake with sticks. Sometimes we would see two or three of these snakes in a day. I decided to start carrying antivenom, which I had acquired from a pharmacy in San Jose, although I would have been reluctant to use it except as a last resort.

About a week into our wandering around the Osa I learnt that there was a serious problem with wild pigs. My co-workers related how the pigs hunted in packs, forcing people up into trees. This assignment was turning nasty, and I wasn't feeling comfortable, and yet we had a job to do. We were also more aware of vengeful, gun-toting squatters; especially after we heard that a botanist was shot in the same area while he had been out botanizing. Apparently, he was killed in revenge for an earlier shooting by authorities of one or more of these poor, though illegal squatters.

Between snakes, squatters, and pigs, I was becoming concerned for my own safety and decided to take up the forestry foreman's offer of a gun to carry with me. It was a 357 revolver and carrying it did give me a greater feeling of being safe. As things turned out, I didn't need to use the gun and I am not sure how effective I would have been against a narrow moving target like a snake. We avoided the squatters. If we found there was a squatter settlement nearby, we would carefully make our way behind a ridge and go out-of-sight through the forest until we had bypassed the settlement.

We managed to finish the assignment without coming to any harm and headed back to San Jose. In fact, the worst thing that happened to me was coming down with a severe stomach complaint on my return to San Jose. On the Osa Peninsula, our meals were rather basic and unappetizing, consisting of rice and beans, occasionally with some egg thrown in, sometimes with some tapir meat. So, as we toiled up yet another ridge, John and I would dream aloud about the meals that we would have back in civilization. As it turned out, I was lucky to keep down a glass of boiled milk and some scotch. I was still dry retching as I got on the Pan Am 707 to fly out to Los Angeles and home to Vancouver.

---

3   *Bothrops asper.*

A Year in Burma

As I crossed the sun-baked tarmac at Bangkok International Airport to board the Union of Burma Airlines Fokker jet, I wondered how easy it would be to work and live in a country with a president who had just banned the playing of rock music. To me, and I think to a lot of other people who may at least have been vaguely familiar with the country, Burma, in 1977, was something of an enigma. I had read what I could on the country before leaving home in Vancouver, but there wasn't much recent objective material that had not been published with a decided bias by the Burmese government.

Much of this was the flowery self-aggrandizement that was typical of centrally controlled regimes. The little I did know about the country portrayed a repressed people controlled by an almost demonic regime under the presidency of General Ne Win. The regime had established a brand of tunnel-visioned socialism that recognised only its own self-serving ends. The result had totally impoverished the country, while maintaining its isolation from the rest of the world.

Sandwell/Forestal had won a contract to provide a team of forestry specialists to assist the Burmese Government to improve their forest management and industries. It was an eighteen-month assignment and I had been selected as part of the team of four foresters from Forestal. It was an exciting, though somewhat daunting prospect. On such long postings it was usual for spouses and children to go along. However, I would be going without my family as it was not sensible to take our two young sons, particularly three-month-old Michael, to a country with dubious health facilities and other major drawbacks. I was not happy about this, though I did arrange to come back for home leave every few months, at my own expense.

The flight to Rangoon was only about an hour, most of it over seemingly unending green jungle. The petite female flight attendant, dressed in the traditional Burmese way, and her male counterpart, who wore dark trousers and a white shirt, served us small, stale sandwiches and sweet tea in plastic cups. The plane was only half full and the passengers were mainly Asians, with a sprinkling of Europeans. I noticed that the flight attendants seemed somewhat self-conscious when serving the Europeans, perhaps, I thought, because they recognised that such fare was well below the standards of other more prosperous airlines.

As the plane flew low over scattered houses and agricultural fields on the outskirts of Rangoon and touched down on the cracked concrete runway I wondered, with some trepidation, what was in store for me over the coming year. The history of the country was fascinating, but during the previous twenty or so years it had been almost totally cut off from the rest of the world. Few visitors or tourists came, and those that did were only issued a seven-day visa and were restricted in their movements.

The Burmese Way to Socialism, brought in by the autocratic General Ne Win, had not only deprived the people, particularly the farmers, of income, it had totally wrecked the economy. In addition, several insurgent groups, with whom the army fought ongoing skirmishes, controlled about 40 percent of the country. Some of these ethnic groups, such as the Karens and Kachins, had been promised autonomy after a period of time, following independence from the British in 1948, but this had subsequently repeatedly been denied to them.

Rangoon was such a contrast to vibrant and crowded Bangkok. Here, the prosperity of the British colonial period was evident in the wide boulevards and many fine public buildings and residences; some with quite imposing architecture. However, a combination of the tropical climate and a lack of maintenance had reduced these once fine buildings to grey, often windowless, nondescript hulks. A bit of paint and some good old soap and water with 'elbow grease' would have greatly improved their sad visages. Similarly, adding a few panes of glass for windows would have improved the effect. It really was sad to see what must have been such a beautiful city having declined into such disrepair.

The trees were still there, though, lining the streets and boulevards of Rangoon; the rain trees spreading their massive branches to form archways, and the rosewoods with their perfumed white blooms. They had seen the British colonizers who had planted them, followed by the Japanese invaders, who had followed as latter day less benevolent colonizers. Then there were the Burmese themselves, who had been there all along, though they were still not in a position, as a nation, to control their own destiny in a democratic process. This was a nation in waiting. The pagodas and Buddhist temples were also still there, clothed in gold as they had been for centuries. Dominating these was the imposing golden spire of the Shwedagon Pagoda on Sing Uttara Hill, near the city's heart, representing the quiet and karmic faith of a patient people.

By comparison with the car-choked and polluted streets of Bangkok, the traffic in Rangoon was sparse and the few vehicles present were mostly 30 to 40 years old. A typical example of these was the rather dilapidated

1937 Hillman in which I went to view some prospective houses one afternoon. The small, always overloaded buses seemed to have a permanent tilt, caused by the large numbers of people who clung precariously to one side from the windows and hung out of the doors. On one occasion, we came across the distressing scene of a bus, which had just tipped over as it went around a corner, crushing several of those hanging on under its side.

Together with the three other Canadians in our team, I spent the first two weeks in the Strand Hotel. At this point, the building was only a relic of what once must have been a small, but rather magnificent hotel. Parts of the old grandeur were still there in the colonnaded dining room with its high vaulted ceilings, the beautiful, polished wood floors and stairs, and the rosewood furniture in our rooms. But the sparkle had gone as had any semblance of efficient service.

The food in the dining room was depressingly mediocre. The bathroom had no hot water, and the overhead fan in my room had only one speed – supersonic. The scurrying cockroaches in the rooms and rats that seemed to have free rein of the hallways and balconies pointed to the lack of pride and care inherent in a decadent government enterprise. There were no tangible incentives to do a good job, only the desire to maintain one's personal pride, and even that was difficult under the prevailing conditions.

Our personal belongings that had arrived by ship were cleared by rather officious customs inspectors, who thoroughly searched through the boxes looking for offending items. These included subversive reading materials. Perhaps because they were not literate in English and just to make sure, they sent off three books I had brought: a Caterpillar tractor handbook, a book on forest inventory, and a novel. All were returned uncensored.

I eventually moved into a small house, down a quiet lane, in the suburbs of Rangoon. At least it was quiet most of the time, except when a series of nearby loudspeakers erupted in a horrible cacophony of sound before dawn, to raise the faithful to prepare food for the Buddhist monks. On the other hand, I inadvertently reaped a benefit from the same self-serving government leadership with my power supply being rarely interrupted, as it often was elsewhere in the city. This was because a neighbour on the same lane was a senior minister in the government.

My landlord was an army colonel by the name of U. Lan Wei. This almost bald, bespectacled, taller than average Burmese was a medical doctor and the officer in charge of the army's paramedical unit. He was a rather atypical military type and a kind and helpful landlord, a devout Buddhist as well as a very intelligent man, who spoke six languages.

He proposed that his batman, who was living in a small adjacent house be allowed to stay on, at no expense to me, as a general factotum or mali. That was fine with me as I needed a trustworthy soul to look after the place during my absences in the field and to do some cleaning and gardening. At one point, I also thought of employing an Indian cook, but Lan Wei didn't feel that was necessary.

In any event, he felt such a person may not have been trustworthy, because, as he said, "There are so many rogues and bounders around amongst such fellows."

I enjoyed Lan Wei's company on several occasions. He would drop round on the pretext of being a landlord, and usually bring over a bottle of his homemade wine. Both, the red, made from damson plums, and the white made from cashew fruit were very drinkable; and between that and some of my scarce supply of good scotch, we would sit and have some revealing, in-depth discussions that included politics and religion. Through Lan Wei I gained more insight into Burmese culture and their way of thinking.

On one occasion, he illustrated the almost fatalistic acceptance of one's karma or situation. His sister, who was also a medical doctor was suffering from a severely bleeding peptic ulcer. She begged Lan Wei to give her a transfusion to save her life. But he refused, saying that this was her karma, and she should accept that she was going to die. She continued to plead with him until, finally, he agreed and set up a direct transfusion from himself. "And, you know, she lived," he declared in an almost disbelieving voice.

The prevailing climate of government mistrust and repression was a constant cause of uneasiness to me with the only sources of solace and comfort being my Canadian team members and their families and a few other expats I met through the British, Australian and American Embassies. To help meet people and to partake in the local scene I joined the Rangoon Dramatic Society and gained a part in a production of *The Little Hut*, a romantic comedy with only three parts – two men and one woman – all shipwrecked on a small tropical island.

I also became a member of the Rangoon Golf Club, where my colleagues and I would occasionally venture onto the fairways, which had a habit of swallowing balls during the wet season. The ground was so muddy and soft that a good, lofted drive would land and bury itself, perhaps never to be seen again unless you walked right over the top of it. To my mind there was something of the colonial days in being a member of the golf club and the Rangoon Yacht Club, based on Inya Lake in Rangoon. The lake was more than a kilometre in diameter, and occasionally we took out small sailing boats that may have dated from the Colonial era.

The repressive situation was worse for the Burmese, including several counterparts and friends that I made while in the country. There was an overriding sense of fear of 'Big Brother', represented by the internal security people and the army.

Burmese friends and counterparts would rarely visit me at my home, because it was probably watched, and they ran the risk of being reported to internal security. This could mean their being interrogated about their visit with, perhaps, a level of suspicion thrown over them. On the other hand, Lan Wei said that he preferred to visit and chat with me, as a landlord, rather than with his army colleagues, because he just couldn't trust them.

In many aspects of our life, the kindness, friendliness, and hospitality of the Burmese was overwhelming. As we got to know several of them, their personal plights under the oppressive regime imposed by President Ne Win became more obvious. Everyday food and consumer goods that we took for granted in Canada or Australia, like cereals, butter, tea, or coffee were not available, and if they were, it was through the only slightly concealed black market where prices were exorbitant.

In a letter to Marion, I noted an example of this. '*The wife of the Assistant to the Director General of Forests has been very kind, but little comments have come out such as the fact that their children can't wait to just have a look at Jackie Phillip's (*the daughter of one of my Canadian colleagues) *toys. They only have one toy – a tricycle that is far too small for any of the three of them. Toys are just too expensive. Her husband likes to play tennis but can't afford to buy tennis balls.*'

After an initial couple of weeks of meetings and settling in, we started our field work in early February. I have often felt fortunate that, as a forester, my work took me into the bush and rural areas of a country. It is there that one sees and experiences more of the true feeling of a country; and so, it was with Burma, although there was a down side; As some 40 percent of the country was under the control of insurgents at war with the government, we had to be careful, and our Burmese minders were not about to allow us to get into harm's way. The previous occupant of my house in Rangoon, a German, had been kidnapped by the Kachins and held for ransom, which the Burmese Government refused to pay. Eventually, he was freed after someone paid something. So, for most of our travels outside Rangoon we were accompanied by a platoon of rather motley looking solders, or sometimes a squad of armed police.

Our first field trip was to forests in the Pegu Yomas, the low range of hills north of Rangoon that act like a spine to the country. As in many of the forests in Burma there were numerous teak trees, and I got my first look at these specimens of luxury timber *au natural*. Teak was so commonplace in Burma that it was often used for house construction, as well as boatbuilding. They even used it to cover electrical wiring on house walls. Well, at least the white ants wouldn't eat it. As my landlord, Lan Wei, explained, when he decided to build his house, teak was more easily available than other woods, and so that was what he used for framing the house.

With United Nations and Canadian colleagues in Pegu Yoma forest.

Riding through the thickly forested, hilly landscape or walking along dusty forest tracks, I observed how the forest was growing, and reflected on how forests, or nature in general, has a mind of its own. As forest managers, we can try to understand how the 'mind' of a particular forest will react to certain circumstances and practices; but, not infrequently, that 'forest mind' will react quite contrarily. My job was to evaluate the techniques being used to manage the forests on a sustainable basis, particularly the teak, and to recommend how to ensure that sustainability. But I was faced with forests that definitely had minds of their own.

The British had introduced what was called The Brandis Method[4], whereby only trees over a certain size or diameter were permitted to be cut. The theory was that by doing this, younger trees and saplings would be allowed to grow and replace those trees that had been removed. It was determined that a cutting cycle of 35 years was sufficient time for a new batch of suitably sized trees to be ready for harvest.

Teak trees don't mind the company of other species or bamboo. However, they demand light to grow and not too much competition from rapidly growing bamboo and other non-teak trees which occurs after opening the forest by felling trees. This can foil the growth of young teak trees and seedlings. Initially, the British foresters had reportedly treated the forest successfully to encourage young teak tree growth. The high cost of such silvicultural treatments meant they were abandoned or only partially undertaken. The result was, as a couple of young Burmese counterparts, U Than Shwe and U Pe Thein pointed out, there were an insufficient number of young teak trees waiting to grow into merchantable sized trees. If the status quo continued, the species would quite quickly be wiped out; not a good thing for a country dependent on this valuable wood for export, nor for the continuation of the species.

On a logging road in the Pegu Yomas, Burma.

The teak sustainability issue was exacerbated by the state-owned Timber Corporation cutting more than its allocated annual allowable cut. It

---

4   Dr. Dietrich Brandis, who was the first Inspector General of Forests for India, which included Burma, from 1864, introduced a system of scientific sustained yield management for Teak to Burma in 1858.

was doing this in only 60 percent of the forests, while the other 40 percent was being exploited by insurgents, particularly in Karen State, adjacent to the Thai border. All this made it difficult to come up with a workable sustainable management plan for teak. After about a year of field visits, collecting data and considering sustainable forest management options, that aspect of our report was not acceptable to the government. They didn't like us telling them that as they had no control over large areas of insurgent controlled forests and that their current silvicultural management was deficient; and, as a result, the annual allowable cut of teak would need to be reduced. We were threatened with being expelled from the country unless we amended our report and so, a compromise was reached that had little bearing on sustaining teak in the country.

The Burmese used elephants to pull out the teak logs after having ring-barked the trees a year or so earlier to lighten their weight. It was interesting to watch the partnership and understanding that existed between the mahout and the elephant, with the former usually being paired with a given elephant from training during the elephants' working life of several decades. With only two or three trees being cut and logged per hectare, using elephants had a relatively low impact on the forest, although it was a slow and tedious process. The logs were often piled into water courses to await the onset of the rains. The increased water flow would then float the logs downstream, where they would hopefully arrive and then be rafted to sawmills.

The trip through the Pegu Yomas was an introduction to Burma's rural roads as well as to rural life. Off the main road along the Irrawaddy River, from Rangoon through Prome, the roads were unsealed. By the end of a day's travel, we would be covered in fine, red dust, including on our hair and eyebrows. Stopping for the night in small towns like Toungoo, the local foresters plied us with Mandalay Rum and beer and served up embarrassingly large quantities of Burmese food, which was generally quite tasty. The nights were spent in forest rest houses, sleeping on bare boards or straw mattresses that were hard and lumpy.

Late one afternoon in mid-February, Bill Webb, our leader, John Rithaler, our logging expert, and I, plus four Burmese forestry counterparts boarded a ferry heading to Bassein (Pathein), a town on the Irrawaddy River some 140 kilometres to the west of Rangoon. Burma has three large river systems, the Sittang, the Salween and the Irrawaddy. The longest is the Irrawaddy, now called the Arrawaddy. This flows from the mountains and gorges of Kachin State in the north, through thickly forested land north of Mandalay. It passes through the 'Dry Zone' in the centre of the country, by the ancient city of Pagan, where the landscape is hot, flat and red, with only scattered trees and scrub, until at last it reaches its delta nearly 2,000 kilometres to the south.

With elephant logging no teak trees were inaccessible.

Our boat journey would take us through the Irrawaddy Delta, a huge area of low-lying land extending from Rangoon west to Bassein. Perennially lush and green, like most deltas, it was rich with alluvial soils that are wonderful for agriculture; but there was still much forest present, including the dense stands of mangroves that bordered the myriad waterways. The problem was that the wood from the mangroves was a major source of charcoal, particularly for Rangoon and Bassein. As a result, these valuable forests that also served as breeding grounds for fish and crustaceans had been disappearing.

At Rangoon's busy docks, with the help of a porter, we made our way through the crowds. The atmosphere was one of busy chaos. Passengers included families with bundles of belongings, individual businessmen or government officers. Mixed with the passengers, were numerous hawkers, noisily advertising their trays of cheap fried food, cigarettes, or fruit. The late afternoon sun glittered from wavelets on the brown, slow-moving river on which several small to medium-sized cargo ships were tied up at the long series of wharves on the city side.

On the far side, to the south, was Insein, an industrial and residential area, with generally poor quality houses. Plying between both sides were a series of taxi boats. These small, open, wooden craft embarked or disembarked their passengers at numerous small landing stages or just onto the muddy riverbank. The single oarsman would then methodically push and pull his stern oar to propel the ferry slowly across the river to the opposite side, with the water often lapping perilously close to the gunwales of the crowded boat.

We all had first class accommodation, which entitled us to a cabin. Those humble souls that preferred or were forced to travel steerage or second-class did not have cabins. They just had to arrive early to get enough deck space for their belongings and themselves. Bill and I were together in a cabin, although we weren't the only ones sharing the cabin. As we opened the door there was a frantic scurrying and six large cockroaches scampered under the beds. There was also a four-inch diameter spider who appeared the next morning – much to his everlasting regret. By cruise line standards, the accommodation could be termed 'sparsely appointed cabin for two on the upper deck'. We had a wash basin with periodic running cold water, while the lighting was 'subdued' as of the four or five light fixtures, only one had a bulb.

After leaving Rangoon, we moved at a good pace along the waterways that included a series of canals connecting stretches of river delta. As the sun edged towards the horizon, small boys could be seen guiding home the family's buffalos and farmers were finishing the last of their rice seedling planting for the day, calf-deep in the dark muddy water of the paddy fields. In the occasional villages, the smoke from cooking fires drifted lazily in the still air, with the women squatting on their heels preparing the evening meal. Interspersed along the waterfront were stands of mangroves with their dense green foliage and, as the tide was low, I could see knee roots rising above the brown water and the spiky pneumatophores[5] projecting, like a bed of nails, from the mud. Occasionally, patches of dryland forest would appear on the higher ground.

On the river or at its edge, there seemed to be constant activity. There were fishermen or commuters in small boats, little boys jumping in for a swim and every now and again a small or medium sized wooden craft would chug past carrying charcoal from the mangroves or some other local produce. There was a tranquillity about the passing scene that seemed absent from the more hurried pace of Rangoon. Life seemed more peaceful in these villages, where livelihoods were often based more on subsistence crops than on earning a meagre wage.

The trip took 18 hours and sleep was hampered by the screaming of the ship's whistle, which would announce our arrival, our imminent departure, and our departure from three stops on the way, as well as warning other boats, large and small, of our presence. The darkness, which only allowed a vague outline of the passing scenery, was pierced on a regular basis by a beam of light from a spotlight on the bow of our ferry that swung from one side to the other to help the helmsman steer along the water course. Both the man in charge of the light and the person steering had probably made the journey countless times and knew what to look for.

At least that was the reassuring thought I allowed myself. Occasionally, the beam would pick out a solitary small craft making its

---

5   Pneumatophores are the spike-like protuberances that appear above the mud and allow certain species of mangrove roots to breathe.

slow way. Otherwise, the light only showed the dark delta waters and fleeting images of trees or structures on either bank.

Early morning saw us heading upstream on the Irrawaddy itself. The river was some 200 metres wide and a dirty grey-brown colour, with villages and agricultural fields on either side. As we came closer to Bassein, more buildings crowded the high banks. Bassein, the regional administrative headquarters, appeared to be a bustling township, as we manoeuvred to our jetty at eight in the morning. There was an untidy collection of boats, some wooden, some steel-hulled, tied up to the shore. Smaller wooden craft moved at varying speeds, but all seemingly with a purpose, up and down or across the river, carrying people and produce.

After making our way onto the floating dock we were hailed by a couple of local forestry officers, who took our bags and showed us the way to a nearby Forestry Department jeep. It was a short drive to the forestry compound, where, after a quick wash in a rather run-down wooden guest house on stilts, we sat down to an unappetizing breakfast of cold greasy eggs and soggy toast. After some introductory discussions in the office of the regional forest officer, we boarded a Forestry Department work boat, with the lovely name of "Magnolia", and headed further up the river.

The forest here was different to that seen in the Pegu Yomas, with very little teak. There were a lot of other useful hardwoods, which were being taken out by skidders[6], buffalos and elephants. In a scenario I came to expect throughout Burma, only one of five skidders were working, there being a lack of spare parts to fix the broken-down machines. The buffalos were used in pairs and on flat country, only having about 20 percent of an elephant's capabilities to do the job. The logs were loaded onto trucks for a journey along poorly planned, constructed and maintained roads to a dump at the Irrawaddy River. There, after two months, they would be rafted using Giant Bamboo (*Dendrocalamus gigantea)* or Tinwa Bamboo (*Cephalostachyum pergracile*) culms for buoyancy.

Watching the rafting process, I was told that it took about 20 men to make a 100-ton raft in a day; no mean feat, although rather laborious. A group of the men would then build huts and live on the raft to protect and steer it as it drifted or was towed to a sawmill site.

Unfortunately, a lot of the area had suffered from a cyclone a year or two earlier and there was a real mess of fallen trees and branches on the ground. Walking in this forest was extremely time consuming, with a lot

---

6   Skidders are tractor-like vehicles, usually articulated, that are used to pull logs out from the forest.

of climbing over fallen tree trunks and cutting through tangles of branches. It was here that we had an encounter with a tiger. Making our way down a creek we rounded a corner and there, just ahead, was a magnificent, stripped specimen. It was feeding on a freshly killed deer and on spying us, took off into the surrounding dense forest though not without a frustrated roar. We were equally taken aback, but quickly made our way past the kill and headed off along the creek, continually keeping our eyes peeled in case the tiger desired some dessert.

After a few days roaming waterways and visiting logging activities, in a fairly relaxed manner, we embarked on a ferry for the return trip to Rangoon. Compared with our former ferry, the first-class accommodation on this occasion was rather abbreviated.

The ferry was a long twin-deck vessel, open on the sides all around except for a cabin-type structure with windows on the upper deck in the bow, and below this was the small, enclosed wheelhouse. The upper deck cabin was our first-class accommodation, and we made our way there through steerage class. This was the open deck on two levels, where individuals and families were organising their space amongst their bundles, boxes, and cases, and I am not sure where the toilet was, if indeed there was one.

Our slightly more respectable accommodation consisted of a communal room for sitting, eating, and sleeping. It wasn't terribly big, being about six metres long and narrowing from about five metres where one entered to a couple of metres at the bow. There were sliding wooden shutters on the sides, and in one corner, at the wider end, there was a toilet of sorts with no water, but lots of smells. Along the walls were arranged four narrow thinly padded benches, and these could also serve as bunks. There were no sheets or pillows.

Of the ten first class passengers, four of us got the padded benches, the rest got the unpadded floor. When an eleventh passenger arrived on route, the only space left was under the table. What first class offered was relative privacy from the hoi polloi and better shelter if it rained. To make life interesting we ran aground in the middle of the night, though after some time and much shouting by the captain and crew, the vessel was refloated.

Not being able to sleep very well, I got up and wandered outside onto the steerage class deck. I was careful not to tread on any sleeping bodies as I made my way to the rail, and then spent some time gazing out at the dark passing scene as a wonderful cool breeze took the heat from my body. The steady thump of the ship's engine, the slight swish of the wake, the breeze, and the darkness combined to provide a very tranquil state of mind.

66

Although the means of transportation in Burma during the late seventies lacked even the basic necessities and was far from comfortable, the Burmese people with whom I travelled and associated with were usually first class. I wondered how they managed to not only exist, but maintain such equanimity under the difficult social, economic, and political conditions imposed by the country's ruling class.

On occasions, my Burmese colleagues and friends were quite outspoken about their feelings concerning these conditions. But there was no overt action, and I sometimes marvelled at their restraint in not revolting against the regime. Reason suggested it might well have been a useless gesture, as history was later to prove, when an uprising in 1988 was ferociously suppressed and again when Aung San Suu Kyi won the election in 1990 and democracy appeared within their grasp but was subsequently smothered by the military dictatorship. However, I also felt the karmic acceptance of their fate, as engendered by their Buddhist faith, played a big part in helping to accept and cope with living.

After a couple of weeks in Rangoon we headed north in early March, by which time the doldrums were starting, with higher temperatures and increased humidity. This situation would increase to sauna-like conditions through April until the monsoon broke in May. It was a time when sleep was difficult; the sheets on my bed would be soaked with sweat shortly after I lay down despite a fan in my room and with the combination of a lack of sleep and the steamy weather, tempers were short.

Heading to Mandalay, we flew, courtesy of Union of Burma Airways. At Rangoon's Mingaladon Airport we edged our way through a mass of swarming passengers and baggage to check in. Then we waited. Our Fokker Friendship had something wrong with one of the wheels, which required the attention of some ten mechanics and 'advisors' for about an hour. With a lack of spare parts in the country I didn't wish to speculate too much as to what was going on. We were finally asked to board, and we stuffed ourselves into the rather worn seats. The interior of the plane hadn't seen a cleaner for some time, and I fervently hoped that the more vital parts, like engines and avionics, received more care.

Having some preconceived images of Mandalay, mainly gained from Kipling's poem, '*On the Road to Mandalay*' going through my head, I was disappointed by the town. Kipling used a lot of poetic licence in his poem as "*the old Moulmein Pagoda*" isn't in Mandalay and isn't by the sea. There were some impressive pagodas, like the Mahamuni Pagoda, but otherwise the town seemed to consist of unkempt wooden houses in narrow streets on the banks of a slow-flowing, muddy Irrawaddy River.

We didn't stay long, though, as we were booked on the night train to Katha, further north along the Irrawaddy. Luckily, we managed to get 'upper' class sleepers, which weren't much, though better than the wooden benches in 'ordinary' class. Originally, the team had planned to travel to the town of Bhamo, further up the Irrawaddy and take the ferry downstream to Katha, checking out the forest as we went. However, a week earlier that ferry was ambushed by Kachin rebels and several lives were lost in the ensuing gunfight, a reminder of the insurgent menace in some parts of the country.

On reaching Katha we found our Burmese counterparts were somewhat on edge about the insurgents who were known to be in the area. The army escort provided to us was of a different calibre than the more bedraggled troops who usually accompanied us further south. These men looked and behaved like troops who were used to battle conditions. Their vigilance and concern made us, in turn, more wary, and I certainly took the threat seriously, though I'm not sure how real the danger actually was. Our escort would not allow us to travel into certain areas and every time we stopped to inspect some aspect of a forest, the soldiers would head out into the trees, guns at the ready, to form an armed perimeter. Though I wasn't too concerned, I was glad to move out of the forest and on to the rest house. In the end, nothing untoward happened, though we did have a bit of excitement one night as we camped out in a forest rest house, recently constructed of wood and bamboo.

The soldiers were billeted with us and as I lay there trying to get to sleep, I heard a truck noisily approaching along some road nearby. It seemed to be making heavy weather of it as there was a lot of changing of gears and revving of the engine. Then, suddenly, there was a shouted challenge. There was no change in the engine noise from the truck and then, a further challenge was issued. But on came the truck with the uneven revs continuing from the engine, when, suddenly, two gunshots were heard. The truck stopped. Our guards moved like lightening, flattening themselves in defensive positions on the floor of the rest house with weapons at the ready. I debated whether I was safer on the bed or under it, on the thin split bamboo floor, as I listened to yells and shouts from the direction of the truck. I decided to join the soldiers on the floor.

All was quiet for a few moments until the truck started up again and an 'all clear' was shouted. We learnt the next morning that the driver of the truck, which was carrying bamboo, was rather inebriated on local liquor, and with the noise of his engine, hadn't heard the challenge and didn't react till a shot went through the windscreen of his cab.

From the steamy and insecure atmosphere of Katha we headed up the catchment of the Chindwin River in our new Range Rover, to the cooler and calmer atmosphere of the Chin Hills. This was an area where regular foreigners hadn't been since independence in 1948 and it was, in many ways, a treat to get into these less frequented back blocks of the country. However, the roads were all unpaved and torturous, not having seen a grader or any other noticeable form of maintenance for years. They were particularly bad on the lower, river valley areas, with its dry Teak and Dipterocarp forests.

Half a day was spent driving up the river valleys often flanked by rice paddy fields that were being ploughed and readied for the coming monsoon season. Buffalos slowly pulled the crude wooden ploughs that were being guided by barefoot farmers through the dark mud, while white cattle egrets busily investigated the insect or worm possibilities. There were also patches of dense forest, with many species, like Teak, leafless at what was the end of the dry season, and there was very little undergrowth, giving a dry and desolate appearance. The occasional group of monkeys playing near the roadside did liven things up somewhat.

After lunch at a forest rest house, we started to climb into the hills, with the road constantly winding round spurs and ridges as we gained altitude. The rice paddies in the valley bottoms were left behind and we drove through a dry wooded and largely leafless landscape. There were occasional fields for dry cropping that clung to the sides of steep slopes, many showing the effect clean cultivation has on such slopes with the scars of soil erosion cutting into the landscape and laying bare the soil structure below. Finally, after several hours of this dusty climb, we reached a sort of plateau, and shortly thereafter our destination for the day, the small administrative headquarters town of Falam.

The Chin Hills Division was one of the more backward areas of Burma and had seen very little development, with farming being the primary occupation together with some work in the pine forests that were scattered throughout. This included the tapping of pines for resin to make turpentine and other products; what is sometimes referred to in the trade as naval stores, presumably from the time such products were in high demand for wooden sailing ships[7]. There was an independent mentality among the Chin Hills people that was refreshing in a country that seemed cowed by the long and oppressive arm of the state security services. The Chin people considered that they were a long way from the seat of government in Rangoon, a situation they preferred, and like some errant schoolboy

---

7   In modern usage, naval stores apply to all products derived from pine sap, that is used to manufacture soap, paint, varnish, shoe polish, lubricants, linoleum, and roofing materials.

out of the reach of the headmaster, they got up to their own version of insubordinate activities.

It was refreshing and somewhat amusing to discover some of this independent spirit during our first night in Falam. The local administration and foresters had arranged the usual dinner for us. However, this one was to be followed by a dance. The Burmese would not usually go to such lengths among themselves. But foreign visitors were a rarity in this corner of the country, off the regular tourist/business track. So perhaps it was just our hosts' way of making a bunch of Canadians and one Australian feel at home while at the same time thumbing their noses at the government in Rangoon.

Although rock music had been banned by President U Ne Win, it was wonderful to see these local officials, completely undeterred by this ban or perhaps in spite of it, call on some enthusiastic local musicians. They were a serious and slightly nervous group that turned up in the dining room of the forest rest house, complete with some well-worn electric guitars and a drum set, and wearing jeans instead of the usual wrap-around longyi. It may have been the first time they played to outsiders. However, it didn't take them long to liven up the night with renditions of Buddy Holly, Elvis, and several other rock stars.

As I found elsewhere in Burma, the younger generation, i.e., anyone below forty, loved western music, but perhaps because of the country's isolation the music was ten to fifteen years old, though far from being passé.

A small group of local schoolteachers and nurses had been pressed into service as partners for us foreigners. They were a bit shy and needed encouragement on our part. So, we gallantly asked them to dance, and we all ended up having a great time. This was helped along by liberal quantities of rice wine and a rather competitive drinking system. A clay pot, about 40 centimetres high was filled with the wine. A piece of banana leaf was placed about two centimetres below the surface of the wine with a bamboo straw through it. The idea was that if one took a drink from this communal pot you had to drink down to the leaf each time in one shot, about the equivalent of a cup. The pot was then topped up for the next drinker. Getting into the spirit of things, I had about four draughts of this dicey, but drinkable brew in between trying to teach a couple of slender local ladies my version of rock and roll.

The next morning was not one I awoke to with 'Ode to Joy' bursting from my lips. In fact, I seem to remember being on all fours over the hole-in-the-floor toilet once or twice during the night. Needless to say, I felt decidedly seedy as we set off for more bumping along dirt roads to another destination in an even more backward area. Sometimes these social activities end up being a sort of endurance test above and beyond the usual terms of reference for the job on hand, though in the end, it was all part of a great experience.

We were heading into Naga territory where a local tribe of the Naga people lived. The term Naga refers to a conglomeration of several tribes inhabiting the north eastern part of India and north western Burma. Historically, the Naga had a fearsome reputation for taking strangers heads off their shoulders. Though we weren't expecting to lose our heads, I was still feeling I would like a replacement when we arrived in the early afternoon. After a formal greeting we were shown to some very basic traditional wooden huts with not much more furniture than single iron beds with thin mattresses, our accommodation for the night.

However, far from being allowed a rest from our efforts of the previous night and our road trip, our hosts smilingly and ever so graciously presented us with several bottles of the locally made wine just to make us feel at home. They then told us there was a party in our honour later in the afternoon. This was all getting to be a bit much and so unlike the rest of Burma, where we were lucky to get a bottle of Mandalay rum from our local hosts.

As on other similar occasions, when I have been expected to go beyond my job description or terms of reference by consuming copious quantities of alcohol of a somewhat dubious nature, I groaned silently and probably aloud. After taking a few sips of our hosts' offerings, I decided this was a particularly poor batch, tasting something like a mixture of diesel fuel and methylated spirits. I would have preferred, even in my delicate state, to have gone for a hike of several kilometres to see some forest, though I doubt our hosts would have accepted the preference.

So, off I headed with my colleagues to fulfil our social obligations. The function was being held in a dusty arena, around which were gathered several locals seated on wooden benches. We, the visitors, were seated in the centre of all this. It was as if we were the main attraction and entertainment. A couple of welcoming speeches were made, to which our leader, Bill Webb, replied. Then we got down to the drinking and eating – and dancing.

As part of the hospitality, we were proudly served more rice wine from an earthenware container by a gentleman who took his wine steward duties seriously. It was the same dubious vintage they had so graciously provided earlier. These people either had no concept of what a reasonable rice wine should taste like, or our tastes differed markedly. Then again, perhaps this was the best they could do given the materials to hand in this outpost of a rundown country. Either way, it didn't help my constitution given that my stomach and head were still feeling the effects of the previous night's drinking.

I wasn't sure what to do, but I wasn't going to drink too much of the concoction on offer. So, I took the opportunity, between the odd sips, to tip portions of it onto the dusty ground on which our chairs had been placed. It was getting dark, so people were less likely to notice, and I did it quite surreptitiously between my legs. However, because of the rate it kept disappearing from my mug, this had the undesired effect of leading our hosts to believe I really liked their liquor.

As a result, our conscientious wine steward kept filling my cup while others urged me to drink up. I was then asked if I would care to chug-a-lug the entire contents, but I resisted the offer, as it could have had disastrous effects on me and the tone of the whole party.

This time the dancing was traditional tribal. Folk songs and dances are essential ingredients of the Naga culture. In the spirit of local camaraderie and with the help of their local spirits, as well as a little coercion from our hosts, I and a couple of my colleagues, decided, to get up and join in. The choreography consisted of interminable stomping around in a circle to the beat of drums simulating either a vanquished enemy being subdued, or a herd of deer being rounded up. I couldn't decide which.

There were times when we were supposed to waddle around in a squat, simulating what I can't remember. This became rather tiring after a few minutes and my thigh muscles screamed to be allowed to resume a more natural pose. However, when I attempted to get up, an old crone behind me, would push me back down again. By the time we headed for our beds I feel both hosts and guests had enjoyed each other's company, and one couldn't fault the enthusiastic hospitality of the hosts.

That was the end of our being feted in the Chin Hills. After another couple of relatively cool days of work and nights spent in rest houses amongst the pines, we descended back to the heat of the plains and the Irrawaddy River. One night was spent at a forest rest house near Pakokku on the edge of a dry and dusty Dipterocarp Forest and scrub, before being ferried across the Irrawaddy to its east bank, in what was now the driest part of the country, with only scattered low trees and shrubs growing from the baked red earth.

Our route back to Rangoon then took us through the fascinating and ancient city of Pagan, which dates from about 850AD, and was the home of the Burmese kings for some 400 years. During this time the citizens of Pagan and the surrounding area managed to construct about 400,000 pagodas.

In Buddhism such construction of pagodas is regarded as a meritorious act and despite past sins helps to ensure a higher status in the next life after reincarnation, which is all very nice if one has the money to pay for constructing the pagodas. It seems as though achieving Nirvana is so much easier for the rich, like so much else in this life.

Pagan was sacked during military action in 1299, when many of the pagodas and other buildings were severely damaged. Nevertheless, there are still 200,000 pagodas standing throughout the area, with most of these now in various states of ruination, but many still have features that are worth seeing. It is a site much visited by Burmese Buddhist pilgrims and foreign tourists.

There was much to see among the decaying ruins on the dry red earth plain, covered mainly by patches of thorny and acacia scrub. These decayed ancient buildings provided an insight into the man-made magnificence that once existed.

Thinking of Pagan still brings an image of an enormous red sun setting over a red, dusty, and largely treeless landscape that is broken by the crumbling images of scores of pagodas; a physical reminder of a more glorious past for Burma, when, perhaps, life had more order and meaning.

We dined well at a tourist hotel in Pagan, then spent the night at a guest house on the slopes of the extinct volcano, Mount Popa, after roaming the hot and parched countryside inspecting eucalypt plantations. From there we made our way back to Rangoon by way of Meiktila, where we saw more planted eucalypts and played nine holes of golf. As I noted in a letter home, it was good to be back at my house where I could eat a few things I had been dreaming of, sleep in a flea free and more comfortable bed, and catch up on news from the outside world via my Grundig radio plus recently arrived letters. I had also found it a bit of a strain spending three weeks with the Burmese and their way of doing things. They were tremendously generous, hospitable, and friendly people, but we didn't fully understand or appreciate each other's habits.

As is usual with such field trips, there was a mixture of visiting offices in the towns that formed divisional headquarters as well as getting a feel for forestry field operations. A compulsory courtesy visit to the administrative head of the division was part of the itinerary, which, although seemingly a waste of time, was a political necessity, and it often helped to smooth out logistics. The forest offices, where we'd stop to pick up data, and, perhaps a cup of tea, were, more often than not, a set of run down and dirty rooms in rather worn out older buildings. The windows often had a greyish translucent coating of dirt, indicating they had not been washed for months, while it had been years since the internal or external walls had had a coat of paint, resulting in a dirty, peeling white crust on the concrete.

We would sit on rickety chairs in the divisional forest officer's office, which would have stacks of files tied up with pink ribbon on his desk, on shelves, in and on top of the cabinets and even on the floor. Those on his desk were for immediate action, whatever that might mean. It was quite depressing when I considered that the Burmese Forestry Department dated back to the mid-1800s and, after all that time, there didn't seem to be much of a sense of pride in their infrastructure; although such pride is hard to come by when money for maintenance and repairs is almost non-existent.

The lack of money hampered everything from infrastructure maintenance to forest silvicultural activities, and the forest officers weren't paid much either. The lower echelon earned up to about US$50 a month for the first fourteen years of their service. It was amazing that they turned up for work at all; but they did, and they had a sense of pride in their profession, despite the many financial, security and political handicaps.

Several foresters with whom I worked were extremely diligent and innovative and we shared some enlightening experiences in the field as well as several very informative conversations. It was a shame to see such enthusiasm unsupported.

Usually there was no running water in any of the guest houses at which we stayed. The bathrooms were makeshift affairs with a couple of 200 litre drums containing water and a dipper that was used to wash off the layers of dust and grime. It may have been a bit rudimentary, but it was effective and refreshing, before settling down to a tot or two of rum on the veranda with our Burmese counterparts.

There was usually a pit toilet out the back, which required a torch at night, not just to find the path and the door, but also to guard against the odd viper or cobra, which were not uncommon. The thin, hard, horsehair mattresses on the wooden bed frames were usually covered by a clean sheet, however, the mosquito net often had a few holes in it, which, of course, the mossies always found.

In July, I went home to Vancouver to spend some much-needed time with my family. Being summer, it was wonderful to be outdoors with them, and David, at four, was at an age when we could do a few things together. It was heartbreaking to leave them when I headed back to Burma, six weeks later.

On my return, in September, the team agreed that I should investigate, on the ground, the feasibility of doing an inventory of bamboo stands in Arakan State. The area was classified as 'black', meaning it was under insurgent control. I found myself in this invidious position because the Burmese Timber Corporation and Forest Department were really keen to build a pulp mill in north-west Burma, using the particular species of bamboo that grew there, *Melocanna bambusoides.*

Several months earlier I, together with a couple of my colleagues and Burmese counterparts, had spent a day flying low over this entire section of the Arakan coastal region in a Twin Otter aircraft, doing an aerial survey. At that point we figured we would be moving too fast in the plane to be targets for the insurgents on the ground.

It was amazing to see these large contiguous areas of pure bamboo. Unlike most bamboos, which grow in clumps containing several stems or culms, the *Melocanna* grows as single stems to a height of nearly twenty metres. So, the effect from 500 feet was like looking down on great fields of grass, stretching as far as one could see. Of course, with bamboo being a member of the grass family, *Gramineae*, there was some substance for the analogy. There must have been tens of thousands of hectares of the stuff. But the species has a quirky sort of problem; when it flowers, which it does about once every fifty years and then en masse, the whole lot dies. You then have tens of thousands of hectares of dead bamboo. Consequently, investing in a pulp mill that relies on *Melocanna* as a source for making pulp can be a risky business.

But, apart from the uncertainties of a bamboo supply for anyone contemplating construction of a pulp mill in this part of Burma, we also knew that the presence of insurgents in the area would make any operations difficult, including undertaking an inventory of the resource.

Earlier, in April, several of our Canadian team plus Burmese counterparts used a large launch to travel up the Kaladau and Lemro Rivers in the northern part of the Arakan region, viewing the forest as we went. These were reasonably sized streams and we managed to get quite a distance inland. However, we were well aware that insurgents were active in the forests on either side of the rivers and the presence of a dozen well-armed soldiers on board to ensure our safety was a constant reminder of the potential danger.

It was a relaxed way of viewing the forests of trees and bamboo as we motored up and down the streams, but the fact that we were in 'enemy territory' meant we couldn't fully relax. There were times when the soldiers ordered us below decks when we went through parts of the country where insurgents had been seen recently. This was to ensure the insurgents were not alerted to the presence of foreigners whom they might wish to kidnap for cash. Although we knew of the danger, we still chafed at being ordered below and felt that it was probably unnecessary as the insurgents most likely had word from local people about our presence anyway.

On occasion, we were allowed ashore, and we walked into nearby forests along muddy tracks, accompanied by forest officers and our military escort. Otherwise, we spent most of our time on the launch.

Our meals were basic Burmese fare and two meals a day consisted mainly of a sort of chicken curry, made from fowls that were kept under woven covers at the stern. They got a few scraps of rice from the cook and gradually disappeared as the trip progressed, while the chicken in the curries became leaner and tougher by the day.

It was interesting to watch the cook in action using his pestle and mortar to grind spices and then use a small charcoal stove to cook several dishes on limited open-air space at the stern. The meals were far from luxurious. In fact, they lacked vegetables, as they did on many of our trips through Burma. As a result, after a year, I developed a folic acid deficiency, which caused me to lose some 15 kilograms in weight.

Despite the known presence of armed and belligerent insurgents, and after much discussion with our Burmese colleagues, it was decided I should do a ground reconnaissance of the areas more to the south, in the vicinity of the Dalet and the Ma-e Rivers, to check on the feasibility of actually carrying out an inventory of the bamboo.

The problem was that in contrast to the area around the Kaladau and Lemro Rivers, which had insurgents present, but not necessarily in full control, the insurgents virtually controlled the area where I was now destined to go. I certainly had misgivings about travelling in the area, but as the Burmese were very keen on establishing a pulp mill, we decided to see what the War Office thought about it. My reasoning was that if it was that bad, they would not let me go and I was hoping they would say, "No".

Surprisingly, the War Office allowed my trip to go ahead, which resulted in a confrontation with the divisional military commander in Akyab. In reply to his asking why I was insanely insisting on going into the area in question, I said we were interested in determining the feasibility of doing an inventory of the bamboo forests, which the government hoped would support a pulp mill.

After some thought, he agreed that I could go, but told me not to be too hopeful about fulfilling my mission. It would be up to the commanders on site to decide if, and how far, we could progress into the hinterland.

To make sure I had reasonable protection he ordered that our launch be accompanied by a naval gunboat. This imposing grey vessel was moored at the docks when I arrived there that afternoon, and it dwarfed the launch being provided by the Forest Department, which would otherwise have been our only means of transport.

Lying in the grey, brown choppy water, the gunboat was about thirty metres long with a Bofors heavy calibre gun on the bow and a solid looking heavy machine gun at the stern. I also found that a platoon of armed soldiers had been assigned to protect me. I wondered what their actual orders were, but nevertheless felt as if I had some sort of vice regal status and was about to go off and inspect the nether regions of the empire, not just a few stems of bamboo.

The gunboat commander, dressed in his all-white uniform, was a very pleasant man with no apparent airs of importance. He greeted me cordially and suggested I might like to travel in the roomier comfort of a cabin on the gunboat, instead of a padded bench on the launch that I would otherwise have had. I didn't hesitate to accept.

About mid-afternoon we left Akyab, which is situated on flat land formed by the estuaries of two large rivers and has really nothing to recommend it. Our two vessels headed across the wide river mouth and out into the Bay of Bengal as we sailed down the coast to the southeast. The seas were choppy, but not enough to cause more than a slight pitch on the gunboat, though the smaller launch was making more heavy weather of it. After sailing for several hours, we swung into Hunter Bay and there we anchored for the night, close to the shore. I dined with the commander and two of his officers on Hkauk Swe, a spicy chicken, coconut and noodle stew, fried fish and steamed rice, before retiring to my cabin for an early night.

The next morning saw us slowly making our way up the Ma-E River. At first, there were mangroves lining the banks with their complex root systems and masses of green foliage, the lower sections of which bobbed up and down in our wake. As the salinity dropped and the ground became higher, the mangroves disappeared, and I could see low scrub and fields associated with the occasional village. Then the trees closed in, right down to the river edge in places. The river narrowed and, at times was not much wider than our boat. The thought passed my mind that such conditions were ideal for an ambush, should the insurgents know of our presence and feel so inclined.

A couple of hours from the river mouth we came in sight of the local army command post. It consisted of a collection of wooden and bush material houses on a ridge, in clearings cut from the forest, overlooking a bend in the river. It seemed a pleasant, if remote, spot. There was no sign of any other human activity, with any farms being left behind us, downstream. After we had moored to the bank and a wooden gangplank was put in place, I went ashore and met the young local officer-in-charge, a lieutenant, who had been expecting me. He told me the area further upstream was a free fire zone, meaning that the army could shoot at anything that moved and, obviously, the insurgents could reciprocate. Despite this, he was prepared to let me go to the limit with an escort. I wondered why, despite my wishing to enter designated insurgent territory the military kept passing the buck to the next lowest on the chain of command. Maybe the military was also interested in the pulp mill or maybe the insurgent threat wasn't as bad as reported. In any event, the danger level seemed to be increasing as I moved closer to my goal of inspecting the bamboo forests. This didn't bode well for doing an inventory, let along establishing and supplying a pulp mill in the area.

The lieutenant gave me the use of a small boat with an outboard motor, threw in half a dozen soldiers and said we could see how far up the river it was feasible to get before his men decided it was too risky. I looked up the river. It was wider here than where we had passed downstream, about thirty metres wide, and seemed slow moving and peaceful with thick forest growing on either side. However, the idea of travelling up it, into insurgent territory, made me nervous. On the other hand, I reasoned that the soldiers were not going to get into a shooting match for my sake and that they should be familiar with the area and what was going on. Besides it was all arranged, and I was interested in actually getting into some bamboo forest, which wasn't present in the immediate vicinity of the base, so I decided to take a chance and accepted the offer.

We set off upstream, while I kept my eyes wide open for both insurgents and bamboo, wondering if some sharpshooter was constantly watching from the dense jungle ahead on either side of the river. We didn't get far, though - no more than about a kilometre upstream when the soldiers decided it was too dangerous to proceed further. I had certainly felt exposed out in midstream and the sergeant in charge of our little unit did, in fact, suggest we made ready targets for alert insurgent snipers. I wasn't going to argue but asked that we go ashore then and there to have a look at the forest and bamboo. After all, I hadn't come all this way just for the boat ride.

Unfortunately, from a bamboo perspective, the best that we could do was to walk up a nearby hill to some scattered stands, where I made some notes, before heading back. The soldiers probably thought I was a bit nuts, but I did want to try and at least see as much as I could to be able to make some judgements on the inventory design, if somebody was crazy enough to proceed with it. However, assessing the insurgent problem in relation to accessing the resource was also important, and I certainly had some information on that.

After thanking the commander and his men for their efforts, I reboarded the gunboat and we headed back down the Ma-e and proceeded south for several hours along the coast to the Dalet River. After meandering through divided waterways, where, at times there was thick forest, and, at other times farmland, we arrived at the military outpost. This was a different situation to that on the Ma-e. The camp was within a heavily fortified wooden stockade, surrounded by deep ditches. It was a somewhat depressing place. Recent rains had turned the surrounding ground on this bend in the river into a mass of mud and all the trees within 300 metres had been felled to provide a clear range of fire. They were obviously prepared for trouble. The local commander told me that the camp had been completely overrun about 18 months earlier, with much loss of life among the soldiers. This was not encouraging news.

I was told the insurgents almost certainly knew we had arrived. In fact, it seems we had been travelling through insurgent territory as we made our slow way up the river. My overactive imagination produced visions of them planning some sort of raid and advancing on the boat and the camp, intent on cutting off our retreat to the coast, though I was probably overestimating my worth.

On this occasion, I was prohibited from moving any further upstream to view the forest. I was getting a little concerned and readily accepted the situation. The gunboat captain was also worried as it was getting late in the afternoon and, given the local security threat from the insurgents, he wasn't keen on spending the night there or trying to make his way back downstream in the dark.

In any event, I couldn't really see the point in going any further, because, unless the insurgent situation changed dramatically in our favour, carrying out an inventory of the bamboo would be nigh impossible, even with a massive army presence. So, the gunboat was turned around and we retraced our route back down the Dalet River to the coast, with sailors manning the guns fore and aft.

As I leaned on the steel side of the ship, gazing out at the passing scenery in the late afternoon light, I half expected there to be some sort of ambush as I felt the insurgents would not want to miss an opportunity to have a shot at the Burmese military. But we reached the river mouth without incident as a massive round orange sun slid into the Bay of Bengal. Another night was spent anchored not far from the shore and the next morning we headed back up the coast to Akyab, from where I managed to catch an afternoon flight back to Rangoon on a Union of Burma Airlines Fokker jet. It was a relief to be back among my colleagues in a less threatening environment than the previous three days.

The result of all of this mucking about in boats on the Arakan Coast was that we told the Burmese authorities back in Rangoon that, given the nasty security situation in the area, it would be too difficult to do an inventory. However, the Burmese did not give up lightly as someone high up was keen on that pulp mill being built. At one point, in our discussions, they actually proposed providing a company or two of soldiers to guard us while we did the inventory, but that would not have been practical. We pointed out that even if the inventory was successfully undertaken and showed adequate stocks for a pulp mill, massive protection would then have to be given to any bamboo harvesting operations and the mill itself. Consequently, we also recommended against any pulp mill being built until the insurgent situation greatly improved, which didn't make us very popular.

I told my colleagues in Rangoon, quite frankly, that I didn't consider the risk of kidnapping or death while undertaking an inventory of the bamboo was something that we should be expected to do as part of our job, particularly when the chances of achieving a worthwhile outcome were somewhat remote. The Burmese Government was disappointed, though eventually, I heard several years later, that a pulp mill was established further south of these troubled areas. I am uncertain as to how it is fairing, but I wouldn't have put any money on its chances of being successful.

People and Trees

After a rough sleep on the Ariana Afghan Airlines flight, I awoke to a brilliant blue sky and the high and barren mountains of Afghanistan. The view from the plane was beautiful in a stark sort of way, with the western side of the mountains still in shadow while the eastern side reflected the rising sun. Despite the beauty of the scenery, it was rugged country, and I would not want to get lost down there.

I had been back in Vancouver for six months or so after cutting short my Burma stay in December 1977, to be with Marion and the boys, when Don Laishley, a Vice President in Forestal, called me into his office. The World Bank were looking for a forester to put together a fuelwood plantation and poplar management component for a rural development project in Afghanistan. Now, by this point I had become somewhat used to being asked to go to different countries on assignment. But Afghanistan was something else, and only three months earlier a violent *coup d'état* had deposed President Daoud and a Russian-backed government under a chap called Taraki, and nobody was quite sure what the next move by the Russians or the Americans would be.

I told Don that I was no expert on fuelwood, except on how to chop it, or on poplar management, but had enough forestry knowledge and common sense to make a reasonable attempt, and I could learn as I went. I am not sure that should have been the criteria for me getting the job, but off I was sent. It wasn't the first or the last time I had to learn and improvise on the job, but I must have done enough of it correctly because over the succeeding years I kept being asked by the Bank to do more work. This Afghanistan assignment was a new facet of my forestry career that would introduce an important and interesting role in my future life as a forester. It was the start of my work on wood as a fuel and also an introduction to an institution that would play a major role in my career over the next three decades.

And that is how I found myself in a room at the Grand Hotel Krasnapolsky in Amsterdam trying, unsuccessfully, to find a number for Ariana Afghan Airlines in the Amsterdam phone book. I checked my ticket that had been issued by the travel agent back in Vancouver and, sure enough, that was the airline on which I was expected to fly from Amsterdam to Kabul. So, I tried KLM and asked if they were the agents for this, hitherto, unknown airline. There was a pause for a few moments but back came this nice lady to say they were and, although there was no record of my booking, which was hardly surprising as Ariana's computer system had been having problems for some time. That was a euphemism if ever I heard one. Nevertheless, I had a seat if I wanted it. Sure, I did. I was contracted to do a job, and this was the only way in. I wondered what I was actually in for.

The plot got curiouser when I checked in at an almost deserted Schiphol Airport the next evening. There was some discussion as to whether I needed a visa for Afghanistan or not. Nobody seemed sure and, obviously, the question must not have arisen very often. I told the pleasant Dutch female KLM check-in agent that I had been told one would be issued at Kabul Airport. She and her supervisor finally agreed to check me in, probably because it was the Afghan Government airline taking me in and not KLM, and that same airline would have to take me out if I was not legit. When I asked about boarding passes, the check-in agent said these would be issued at the gate.

So, I wandered down to the gate, where another three passengers were idling away the time. There was no sign of any agent from Ariana and so we all waited. Finally, at about the time we should have been boarding, if there had been a plane to board, a slightly balding gentleman in a sports jacket, carrying some documents, came through the door and started arranging things behind the agent's desk. He then announced, in a loud voice, that the plane was somewhat delayed, but would arrive shortly. I sauntered up and, having got his attention, asked if I could get a seat assigned.

"That won't be necessary," he replied, smiling at me. "We aren't too full."

Sure enough, it seemed as though there was a dearth of people wanting to fly to Afghanistan as no one else had joined our small waiting group.

Eventually, the plane, a shortened version of the Boeing 707, referred to as a 720, turned up. We boarded, to be greeted by a friendly and smiling all male crew. I selected a seat from the hundred and eighty or so available and buckled up. Next port of call was Paris Orly Airport, where we let off a couple of passengers and replaced them with two or three new ones. It appeared the plane did a circuit of several European cities before heading back to Kabul.

Our last stop, at around midnight, was Rome. The passengers stayed on board while they loaded vast quantities of freight. I struck up a conversation with a couple of the cabin attendants, who asked if I would like a drink. I was a bit surprised, knowing the strict Moslem code under which the country operated. There wasn't much choice, and I wasn't really interested, but the attendants were all into G and Ts (gin and tonics). Seems it was their favourite tipple, Moslems or not.

So, there we were standing on the broad steps that led up to the rear doors of the plane, under a balmy, starry night chatting away for some time. The crew, in their white shirts, black ties and black trousers, were tossing back G and Ts and regaling me with tales of Ariana. They were quite proud of their airline and its association with Pan Am, who, apparently had a large shareholding and did training as well as maintenance. I wouldn't have been surprised if the plane wasn't second-hand from Pan Am. While I was engaged in this conversation, I was informed I would have to change my seat and move further forward. There was too much cargo for the holds, so they had decided to stow the passengers' luggage and a few other items on the seats to the rear of the plane; just placed there, unsecured. I was not surprised, just another unconventional approach to air travel on the part of Ariana.

On arriving at Kabul, I was met by a local World Bank officer with a vehicle. The atmosphere was still unsettled following the recent coupe and I detected a degree of tension, even oppression, in the air, with a noticeable Russian military presence. The few civilian aircraft at the airport were outnumbered by military cargo planes and fighters; all Russian. The streets, through which we drove to the Kabul Intercontinental, our home for the first week, were dirty and the buildings drab in contrast to the brilliant blue sky that served as a backdrop to the city and its surrounding, largely bare, dun coloured hills. The hotel, perched on a hill overlooking the city, was almost empty and manned by the surliest bunch of staff I have encountered in a hotel, particularly one of such lineage. The receptionist gave me the impression I was interrupting some other more important personal activity, while later in the hotel restaurant the waiters would eventually condescend to acknowledge our presence handing out somewhat grubby menus.

Russian military personnel were everywhere in Kabul. There was a sense of expectation that further violent events were in the offing with the fate of the country in the hands of the Russians, or the Americans. As things turned out, a little over a year later, Taraki was murdered, and another government installed with a pro-American head by the name of Kamal. Shortly after, the Russians, not liking this state of affairs on their back doorstep, invaded Afghanistan, got rid of Mr Kamal and appointed their own man as president.

Village scene with houses made from mud the same colour as the countryside, which had virtually no trees and very little other vegetation.

I joined the other members of the World Bank team under the leadership of a New Zealand livestock man - Vince Ashworth. We connected with our Afghan counterparts. Mine was a young forester who always wore his dark brown suit to the field and never looked like he had planted a tree. My insistence on trudging through poplar plantations during field visits was not really to his liking; perhaps he considered it beneath his professional status or that he might get his shoes dirty.

The team headed south for a week of travelling around the back roads of Ghazni and Wardak Provinces. The countryside was absolutely barren and looked as if it hadn't rained in a thousand years. This grey-brown, mountainous landscape was occasionally broken by small patches of green, representing small oases, often at the base of hills, where streams from mountain springs irrigated village fields and, perhaps, a stand or two of poplars. On occasion we would come across a small valley with the floor a mass of green irrigated Lucerne, which only served to accentuate the stark aridity and bare nature of the surrounding country.

The villages blended in with the countryside, as the houses and their surrounding high walls were all made of the same dun coloured mud. The thick mud walls provided wonderful insulation against the great temperature variations, from 30 degrees below in winter to 40 degrees plus in summer. I spent one night inside such a mud house but found the lack of air circulation too stifling and so, in the wee hours of the morning, I moved my sleeping bag out onto the mud path in the front of the house and had a restless sleep underneath a brilliant star-studded night sky. Other nights in the field were spent like the locals, sleeping on the flat roof of the house where we were staying.

The mud building where I slept outside on the ground.

The rocky, desert-like, mountainous landscape had a sort of grandeur and beauty about it. This was particularly so in the late afternoon and early mornings, when the light was softer, and the shadows cast by the mountains contrasted with the sunlit mountain sides. It is a harsh environment for both man and most beasts, and must, to some extent account for the rugged nature of the tribal people who inhabit this land; the faces of older men often as weather beaten as the landscape in which they eke out a living.

I came to respect and admired the farmers we met to discuss their situation and how the project might improve their lot, including the extreme scarcity of firewood. For all their difficulties in both their farming and daily living, they were invariably gracious and friendly.

My colleagues, an Ethiopian economist and a German agronomist, and I were sometimes invited into farmers' houses, in line with the very courteous Islamic concepts of hospitality. Like all the houses in the area they were made entirely of mud. Inside the somewhat cramped quarters the air smelled of stale sweat and acrid smoke from a smouldering fire.

As we sat or squatted on a rug-covered mud floor, the farmer would serve us with tea (chai) and flat bread (Nan). Sometimes we even got a little chicken soup. It may not seem like much, but it was probably the best meal the farmer could provide, perhaps even depriving himself and his family of some of the food with which they were depending on that day, and it was all done with great courtesy and kindness.

Wood fuels (charcoal and firewood), as in many other developing countries, comprised the major source of energy consumed, particularly for households; but it was extremely scarce. There just wasn't enough woody biomass in the form of trees or even bushes. Reasonable fuelwood had a higher price than lumber. However, most rural families used just brushwood, twigs and leaves and then, in many cases, only had one fire a day, and thus only one hot meal may have been cooked a day. But, even this one fire was fully utilized as I observed in several houses.

Local ingenuity put the fireplace or conical shaped oven lower than the regular floor, and then with the flue going through the thick baked mud floor it helped to heat the house in winter. Part of the flue also went under one or more sleeping benches to heat these. The system is referred to as Tabakhan. The Romans used a similar 'hypocaust' system.

Collecting biomass for fuel had stripped the mountains bare of most of the small bushes and shrubs, including camel thorn. Often the plants were pulled out by the roots negating any chance of regenerating. The result was a lack of browsing for sheep, goats, and camels, but even more devastating was the almost total lack of water absorptive capacity. Consequently, a minor storm could cause flash floods and destroy lives and property with devastating efficiency as happened during our visit.

My World Bank agronomist colleague talking with Afghan farmers in the field

We drove around the hills and valleys of eastern Afghanistan in a Russian jeep. It wasn't comfortable and it wasn't dust proof, but the driver knew his stuff. However, we discovered he had a problem that was worrying him. Unbeknown to us, there was a government regulation limiting the number of kilometres any vehicle was allowed to travel in a given time period, there being fuel restrictions. Being the sort of conscientious workers that we were, we had forced our driver to drive beyond the limit, although, at the time we were ignorant of any such limits. His dilemma came to light when we caught him reversing all over an open space by the road while we had been off visiting a farmer. He thought that if he went backwards, so would the odometer - thus reducing the kilometres shown. I don't know how long it took for him to realise that he was still actually adding kilometres not subtracting them.

There was certainly a darker and disagreeable side to Afghanistan, which pervaded our whole stay in the country. Apart from the political and security tensions, there was the pervasive poverty, in both the rural and urban areas; but in the towns, this was exacerbated by the filth and lack of hygiene. One of my most vivid memories is of men swatting and defecating, in the open, on the stony edge of a polluted stream in the centre of Ghazni town. We had stopped at an Afghan version of a café to buy the local speciality. This was a sort of cold vermicelli topped with ice cream, which had been made and kept cold by snow brought from the Hindu Kush mountains, many kilometres to the north. It was not a pleasant experience sitting there eating our rather dubious sweet treat, while only forty metres away men were casually relieving themselves and the odour of sun-dried faeces permeated the air. I later saw similar practices in India, but this was the first time I had seen such casual disregard for hygiene or public wellbeing. Sure, they had to go, but was the ground so hard or shovels and picks so scarce that they couldn't dig a few pit latrines.

By the time I came to leave Afghanistan I was glad to board the Ariana flight back to Europe, particularly as I had to smuggle out the films I had taken, plus a roll from the World Bank Resident Rep. taken during the recent coupe, showing, amongst other things, Russian planes bombing Kabul. They didn't find the films, which were in my suitcase, though I did have to take off my shoes for the security search on the way through to the departure lounge. This was an uncommonly rare experience at airports in those days.

Arriving at the relatively new Washington Dulles Airport, I had no trouble getting a cab to take me to my hotel, the Georgetown Dutch Inn, in the upper middle-class leafy suburb of Foggy Bottom, only 10 minutes' walk from the World Bank offices and another five to the White House. It was late summer and much of the drive along the Dulles Toll Road through Northern Virginia toward the Potomac River and Washington D.C. was through treed countryside. Crossing over the Chain Bridge from Virginia to Washington D.C., I could just see the tall spire of the Washington

Monument. Here I was in the capital of the USA, and I felt a little awed. It was my first visit to a city that I would get to know very well over the next 40 years.

Our Russian Jeep and the driver who drove backwards

I spent a couple of weeks at the World Bank, putting together my report for the Afghan project, and visiting some of the famous sites in my scarce free time. Having seen the conditions in the field, I was in a quandary as to what to do about growing fuelwood in such an arid and harsh environment. This was a new situation for me and had me worried, particularly as this was my first assignment with the World Bank. One just couldn't recommend certain species with any assurance that they would grow in an unirrigated situation, and there weren't any local plantings of species apart from poplars, from which to choose. I decided on a stepped approach, beginning with trials of species I felt had a chance. Then after a couple of years, when one at least knew which would survive, a more ambitious planting programme could begin, while the trials continued; to determine the best species. This seemed like a sensible approach.

It was a somewhat awesome experience working with such a prestigious organization as the World Bank. I was anxious to do a good job and a bit anxious that I might not measure up to what I felt were quite high standards. As it turned out, I must have done a good enough job because before leaving Washington I was asked could I join a forestry appraisal mission for a project in Greece. It was to be the last project funded by the Bank in Greece, which had graduated to other sources of lending.

So, later in 1978, I flew to Greece for three weeks of whirlwind travel around the forests of the country, from the Peloponnesus to Thrace. Unlike most visitors to that country who came to visit ancient historic cultural sites, we spent our time in out of the way forests. However, we did enjoy the local culture as far as food and wine were concerned, sometimes being feted by the local foresters, with bottles of retsina wine[8] in shady, mountainous, forest surroundings that also smelled of pine resin. There were also some memorable seafood dinners at open-air restaurants down by the harbour at Piraeus. I eventually got to see the Acropolis just before flying out to Washington D.C.

These trips weren't too long and the rest of the time I spent in Vancouver with extra time being allowed off to spend with the family in lieu of weekends and holidays I had worked, while I was on assignment. Late in 1978, I was asked to assist with another World Bank project - this time in the Philippines. It was for three months based at Cebu in the Central Visayas Region. I flew out in January 1979, travelling now on a Canadian passport that I had obtained with some difficulty because of my absences from the country, prior to my application.

I thought it would be a good idea to become a Canadian citizen if I could still keep my Australian citizenship as I was working abroad for a Canadian company, sometimes in difficult situations, and I wanted to participate more fully in Canadian life. I had been informed by Australian Embassy officers while I was in Burma that I would not lose my Australian citizenship. 'Once an Australian, always an Australian,' I was told. However, as it turned out, I found when I went to renew my Australian passport that I had forfeited my Australian citizenship. It took me ten years and some law changes in Canberra before I was reinstated as an Australian.

The assignment in the Central Visayas region of the Philippines was my first real experience in community-based forestry, or what some of my colleagues back at Forestal referred to as 'Mickey Mouse forestry', not the real thing as far as they were concerned. However, as I was to discover over the succeeding years, this type of forestry involving the community would become a major means of managing otherwise unmanageable forests, particularly where such forests were already under threat from impoverished communities within or on the fringes off the forest. At the same time, such regulated management could have significant livelihood benefits for these same communities.

---

8   Retsina wine is a traditional white or rose Greek wine flavoured with pine resin. The origin is said to have come from when amphora was sealed with pine resin to prevent wines from spoiling.

As my flight from Manila turned to land at Cebu Airport on Mactan Island, I looked from the glittering blue waters of Cebu Strait where Magellan had sailed on his expedition's circumnavigation in 1521 before dying on Mactan Island, to the steep cultivated ridges inland from the city. On the island of Cebu and some surrounding islands the removal of trees to provide farmland as well as wood for fuel and other purposes had laid hillsides bare to the effects of torrential rains. The result was that most of the topsoil had been eroded, and in some cases a certain amount of the subsoil. This meant that soil fertility was badly compromised, and farmers were having a difficult time growing crops with adequate yields.

Together with a small group of scientists from the University of Los Banos, the objective was to recommend a sustainable solution to the problem. A key element to the solution was to introduce an agroforestry element whereby nitrogen fixing trees or shrubs would be planted in rows across the slope between agricultural crops such as maize. The principal nitrogen-fixing tree used was *Leucaena glauca*, known locally as Ipil, Ipil. The species had already proved very successful in reforesting numerous degraded areas in the country.

This approach came under a banner named 'Social Forestry'. It was being put forward by development agencies like the World Bank as a means of establishing trees on private or communal farmlands, to provide wood for fuel and building materials as well as fodder and fruit. In the case of agroforestry, the trees would also provide fertility to interplanted crops and promote soil and moisture conservation on slopes. It was a new approach for me and other foresters, and we were all learning and making mistakes. As traditional foresters we had been trained that it was our job to manage the forests and the local people were regarded as unnecessary if not a hindrance and a threat to good forest management, and in some cases, they were that.

Now, we were meant to accept that local communities were also stakeholders in the management of forests and certainly in the management of woodlots and trees planted on their farmland. This meant that there needed to be communication and understanding established with members of the communities. In hindsight, my approach and that of some of my colleagues was a rather patronizing and top-down one, which only demonstrated our ignorance, particularly from a sociological aspect. I found myself sitting on a log in a village on a hot and steamy afternoon explaining to a group of half-interested villagers that they had a firewood supply problem or an erosion and soil fertility problem in their farms, and then explaining how they could plant certain trees or bushes to overcome their problem. The villagers seemed to be somewhat agreeing with what I was saying, although I wasn't sure that this would result in positive action on their part to solve what I perceived to be their problem.

During those early years of my community-based forestry I didn't appreciate that the villagers to whom I was speaking may have had a series of problems, most unrelated to there being a dearth of trees, and some of those problems were more important in their eyes than the lack of trees or wood. It also took me a while to realise that many villagers may have had considerable historical knowledge regarding the sustainable management of their nearby forests or woodlands, and that as farmers, they were adept at planting and growing crops, including trees. I wasn't a very good sociologist, and it took several similar projects over a few years before I realised the need for an expert sociologist's input in designing such community related forestry projects.

In the Central Visayas I muddled along with my Los Banos colleagues and came up with what we thought would be a workable and fundable project. I enjoyed myself while we did this. My base at the Hotel Monticello in Cebu City was comfortable and the staff very attentive; even providing a cake for my birthday and flowers for Valentine's Day. Every few weeks, I would fly up to Manila to discuss our progress with my World Bank masters, while staying at the grand old, luxurious Manila Hotel. I like to think that the project that eventuated with World Bank funding due to my efforts and those of my Philippine colleagues did improve the agricultural yields of farmers on Cebu and greatly lessened the erosion problem, although I have no idea how it all finally ended up.

Following on from my Philippines assignment, in 1979 I got my first job with the Food and Agricultural Organization of the UN; more specifically with their Investment Centre, which prepared projects for World Bank funding. We went to Indonesia, where we spent several weeks before returning to Rome, preparing a forestry project for World Bank funding. In January 1981 I was back in Indonesia. This time I was on an assignment from Shell International, who had a Non-Traditional Business Division that, among other things, considered pursuing forestry ventures. In conjunction with a potential partner, an Indonesian forest industry company called Porodesa, Shell was looking at forestry related investment possibilities in Irian Jaya, the western half of the island of New Guinea.

It had been an interesting week since flying over from Jakarta and then down to the small town of Fak, Fak on the southwestern coast. From there I spent some days in the forest, further down the coast. Coming back to Fak-Fak meant a night trip by small boat. Our only navigational aid was an outline of the nearby coastline by starlight, as we ploughed through a choppy swell in the dark. From Fak-Fak, a small, twin-engine, Briton Norman Islander flew me to an isolated airstrip, further east, on the edge of the Gulf of Ambon. Surrounded on all sides by the dense green tropical jungle that characterized much of coastal Irian Jaya, the strip was remarkably well maintained, probably being left over from the Second World War. The smoking cigarette dangling from the mouth of the pilot as we came into land emphasized a general nonchalance about the Indonesian approach to life and work, I had noticed on several occasions.

On landing, we taxied to an old Quonset hut at the end of the strip that must have been another remnant from the Second World War, to find a DC 3 that could have been of the same vintage. A European in old shorts and a T-shirt emerged from the hut and glanced in our direction, though without a great deal of interest, as if the arrival of planes in this remote corner of civilization was commonplace.

For me, the appearance of a 'white man' in this green wilderness of western New Guinea was a totally unexpected sight. He was a suntanned, stocky character, with short graying hair and he looked as if he had seen some rough situations. He didn't seem surprised to see me, but, then I had the impression that not much in this world would surprise him. He was friendly enough as he introduced himself as Captain Jack. His accent betrayed him as an American, and he confirmed this and explained he was there as a check pilot on DC3s for Bourak Airlines, an Indonesian domestic airline, aligned with Porodesa. He then took me into the hut and showed me one of several small rooms, where I could bed down for the night.

Captain Jack was pleased as punch with himself because, before leaving Balikpapan, on the east coast of the island of Kalimantan (Borneo), he had managed to obtain two cases of spirits for a song from a newly opened supermarket, which hadn't got its pricing sorted out.

"Some idiots must have put the wholesale instead of a retail price on, so I helped myself to a couple of cases before they wised up."

This windfall gave him about a bottle of hard liquor a night for the month he was due to spend at that isolated airstrip, while flying in support of a Marathon Oil drilling operation in the interior. The fact that he was flying each day, usually in the morning, after so liberally dousing himself with alcohol, didn't seem to bother him. But then we were in the Wild West (or East) of Indonesia, where regulations and law enforcement were scarce on the ground and in the air.

That night Jack regaled me with stories of his many years' experience as a pilot while we filled ourselves with one of the bottles of spirits; Scotch whiskey as I recall. He used to fly for Air America, which I had never heard of. Captain Jack then explained that Air America was the CIA airline, and he had done two straight tours of duty with them in Vietnam, during the height of the American involvement there in the late sixties. He specialized in flying DC3s. I asked who or what he was carrying on all these flights.

"Oh," he volunteered somewhat cryptically. "Various personnel and equipment; although sometimes our cargo was just human ears."

He confirmed my suspicions that this grisly cargo had been cut off Viet Cong troops shot by the South Vietnamese or Americans and were required to confirm the body counts.

He finally had enough of Vietnam and the killing, mentally, emotionally, and physically, but wanted to stay on in Asia; so, he moved to Indonesia, where he joined Zamrud Airlines. I thought I knew all the regional airlines, but I had never heard of Zamrud, and with a name like that it would be hard to forget.

"Yea, well, it was set up and owned by a bunch of senior army officers, who had more money than management sense and they were too greedy," Captain Jack informed me.

The airline flew mainly DC3s, of which it managed to crash and lose three. It was supposedly the largest airline in Southeast Asia in the late sixties/early seventies, until they ran out of cash, which the colonels had managed to squander. It ended operations in 1982. But this wasn't the captain's first work in Indonesia or Irian Jaya.

He had been in what was to become Irian Jaya prior to the 1963 annexation of, what had been Dutch New Guinea, to Indonesia. As the captain was rather short on details about who he was working for on this occasion I wondered if he wasn't part of the shadowy arm of the CIA once again or associated with something or someone equally clandestine, linked to the Indonesian government.

The annexation had required a plebiscite by so-called representatives of the Dutch New Guinea communities. These simple, unsophisticated village leaders from the bush had been feted by the Indonesian government to convince them of the 'good life' that would await their people if they voted to join Indonesia. According to Captain Jack, one of the final acts of persuasion had been the delivery of scores of Johnson outboard motors to remote villages, even though many were miles from the nearest water body. As Captain Jack tells it, he was the only non-Indonesian allowed in Dutch New Guinea at that time, and he described how he landed on numerous bush airstrips and unloaded these outboard motors, (known to this day as 'voting motors') to eager villagers.

I left him the next day, aboard a Porodesa company launch, to do some more forestry reconnaissance work in the hinterland. There, I spent nearly a week on the boat and in the bush, gaining an impression of the local forest resource. It was clear that the 'voting motors', and other promises prior to annexation, had done little to endear the Javanese intruders to the local inhabitants, who, I observed, had been treated shamefully by the Javanese, in a superior patronizing way.

Our launch for exploring forests in southern Irian Jaya.

On my arrival back at the bush airstrip, Captain Jack was into his second case of spirits, and it appeared that I would be helping him out for another night as the charter flight, which Porodesa had arranged for me, couldn't make it. It had been arranged that I would fly out with the venerable captain the next day to Manokwari, in the North West, from where I could get a domestic flight to Biak and so head back to Jakarta.

After sharing another bottle that night (vodka I think it was this time), Captain Jack was in the cockpit, with his Indonesian pilot by six next morning, looking hale if not too hearty. I threw my gear in the back of the DC3 and climbed aboard. Much of the cabin space was taken up by empty 44-gallon fuel drums that were being taken back to the Marathon Oil field site. I threaded my way forward up the sloping floor in the unlined fuselage, between the drums that had been lashed down. There was a double seat just before the forward bulkhead and I was settling myself down when the captain asked if I wanted to come into the cockpit for the takeoff. Sure. Why not? So, I squeezed into the rather small space available, just aft of the two pilots as we taxied out to the runway. I looked for a jump seat on which to sit, but Captain Jack just turned around and yelled over the engine roar with an ignitable, spirit-sodden breath. "There isn't a jump seat. Just stand there and hold on,' which I did.

He pushed the throttle levers forward and the engines responded with a thunderous roar that felt as though it would shake every rivet loose in the plane as, with increasing speed, we headed towards the trees at the end of the runway. Clearing them with a few feet to spare, we rose into the clear morning sky above the dense jungle mass I had been exploring during the previous few days.

Then the Captain, after telling some distant air traffic controller that they were airborne, pulled off his earphones and stated quite laconically, "I could really do with a fag, but we've got all those fucking drums in the back."

I felt for the man but was thankful he was at least cautious to some degree and mindful of the risk posed by the combination of fumes from the drums and naked flames.

A couple of minutes later, though, I had changed my mind as Captain Jack, who had obviously been giving the matter some thought, suggested. "Let's open these front windows. Take her up to six thousand feet (we were at three). That way the air will be expelled from the rear of the plane, together with any fumes. Then we close the windows, come back down to our current altitude to decrease the suction on the drums and light up."

I looked at the Indonesian pilot, who was in the captains left hand seat and he was either as baffled by Captain Jack's scientific logic as I was or agreed with the captain's logic, and needed a smoke as badly as the captain, or was too scared or polite to say anything to this veteran on his right. In any event, he made no comment.

I asked the captain if he was sure he knew what he was talking about, but he assured me he did. So, thinking that anyone who survived four years with Air America in Vietnam carting human ears around had to have some survival instincts, I said no more; but I held my breath and took a sort of fatalistic approach to the whole thing as we proceeded to climb, after getting permission from the air traffic controller. No reason was given for our change in altitude, and no one asked. After all, the sky over Irian Jaya wasn't anything like the east coast of the US or Australia as far as having numerous other planes in the area goes. The windows were opened as we went. Creaking noises came from the empty drums as the air pressure decreased, but the captain explained what it was and seemed to take it all in his stride, as if he had actually done it before. After several minutes at our new altitude, the captain decided we had flushed enough fumes out and descended. He then proceeded to light up. I waited for the flash and explosion, but I guess Captain Jack really did know his stuff.

The rest of the hour and a half long trip was uneventful, and I moved back to the main cabin and settled down in my seat, alternating between reading or watching the mountainous green landscape pass below. At Manokwari, I shook hands and thanked Captain Jack as we taxied to the front of the small terminal. Then, with the engines still running, I threw off my bags and jumped down on to the tarmac. Walking towards the terminal, I turned and watched Captain Jack wave from the cockpit as the trusty old DC3 engines increased their revs and, with its nose in the air, the plane moved back to the runway. I haven't seen him since, but I still have the T-shirt he sold me as a memento for $5. It is now in a somewhat ragged state, but the message on the front, in green and red is still clear:

FLY

ZAMRUD

Indo. Nasi goreng

AIRLINES

And on the back, showing above and below a traditional Indonesian three-wheeler taxi with wings, and Captain Jack holding the wheel with one hand and a foaming glass of beer out the window with the other, the message says:

THE BEMO[9]

IN THE SKY

---

9   Bemos are three-wheeled motor scooters used as taxis.

Into Africa

I awoke from a cramped and uneasy sleep, stretching to get the circulation going in my limbs and removed my eye shades. Light was filtering through the windows. Others in the cabin were stirring and, down the aisle, two of the cabin crew were starting the breakfast service for those who were awake and interested. I didn't really need food at this point as it was only a few hours since we had been served a late dinner, but not being sure when the next meal would be, and out of habit, I pulled out my tray from the armrest and indulged myself.

Before the trays had been cleared away, we had begun our descent towards the solid layer of white cloud below. I watched as we entered the cloud; skirting the top and cutting through the occasional protruding pieces, before being completely enveloped in the white mist. Shortly thereafter I caught glimpses of scrub and hills, cultivated fields and isolated small houses as we emerged beneath what was now a grey mass. So, this was Kenya.

It didn't look wild and threatening from 5,000 feet, but from the state of the few roads and the houses I could see, it definitely looked under-developed. There were no busy motorways or even any paved roads visible. There was no verdant green, well managed farms as seen in North America, Europe or Australia. Instead, the landscape consisted of light brown grassland, scattered trees, and patches of cultivation.

The plane continued to descend and turned, banking as it did so, to reveal the suburban outskirts of the city. Here, at least there were some paved roads. But there were still a lot of dirt tracks running between increasingly dense collections of squat mud-daubed buildings that were about the same colour as the dirt on the roads. We passed over a major thoroughfare, a widish paved road with a stream of vehicles moving slowly along, even at this early hour. Then we were over the verge of the airport and flaring out to land. As we taxied towards the terminal, I noted that the dry grass was uncut and the airport buildings unkempt as if nobody really cared.

This was my first African experience. It was 1981, and I was heading for Lesotho to undertake an assignment identifying a soil conservation and forestry project for the Food and Agricultural Organization of the United

Nations (FAO). The travel agent in Vancouver wanted to know if Lesotho was a city or a country and, in fact, I wasn't too sure about where it was in relation to South Africa and other southern African countries. I didn't know what to expect from Africa, having read accounts of some of the early European explorers, such as Burton and Speke, the highly organized kingdoms on which they and the slave traders intruded, and then, of more recent conflicts and disasters.

The journey took me through Johannesburg, where apartheid was very much in evidence. My passport had a South African visa attached as a separate page, so after my trip, there would be no evidence to other countries that I had been in South Africa. I didn't know what to expect as I approached the immigration officer at Joburg Airport. But after one or two questions regarding my visit, he stamped my visa page and I emerged out onto the concourse to a chorus of voices urging me to take their taxi. I spied a man with a sign board and my name from the hotel at which I was staying. I signalled to him, and he took my case and ushered me to a minibus parked nearby, much to the consternation of the taxi touts.

The next morning, there was a real chill to the air as I walked across the tarmac to our HS748 turbo prop aircraft, my connection to the small city of Maseru, the capital of Lesotho. At Maseru, customs and immigration procedures were rather low key and perfunctory, before a taxi took me to the Hilton Hotel, my base for the next couple of weeks.

Lesotho is a tiny landlocked country, surrounded by South Africa and dominated by the rugged peaks of the Drakensberg Range that climb to 3,000 metres. Maseru was not what I expected of an African city. It wasn't much more than a rather large town and acted as a sort of 'sin city' for the South Africans, with gambling and porno movies in abundance, mainly at the two main hotels, the Hilton and the Holiday Inn. It was quite a different experience walking into the lobby of the Holiday Inn, a chain that advertised 'No Surprises', to find slot machines all over the place and large posters advertising such dubious movie treats as 'Debbie Does Dallas' and 'Caligula'. It was almost surreal to have such entertainments in a small African country, whose people would almost certainly have no funds for gambling and have scant knowledge of porn movies.

A lack of wood for fuel and massive erosion caused by denudation of the hillsides were the problems for which we were endeavouring to find solutions for funding by the African Development Bank. Based in Maseru, my colleagues on the mission and I travelled extensively throughout the country. There was a distinct lack of trees across the landscape with much of the less mountainous countryside being dominated by grasslands. We spent time talking with villagers alongside their distinctive round huts made of wattle and daub, with no windows and conical grass roofs through which the smoke from their cooking fires filtered; there being no chimneys. These rondavels were probably much the same as those the people had used for hundreds of years.

The villagers, who were dressed in what seemed to be largely hand-me-down western clothes, were welcoming and happily explained their situation with regard to the lack of wood for fuel. They were proud of the small woodlots they had planted with the help of foreign aid, to help with their firewood supply and to also provide poles for building. Later, back in at FAO headquarters in Rome, in a cubby hole of an office, my Swedish colleague, Per Ohlson, and I, worked out a plan for funding the growing of more woodlots in the country. Unlike Afghanistan, there was ample evidence of what species of trees would do best as both the climate and soil were reasonably favourable for growing the trees.

My next trip to Africa was to Zimbabwe in 1983, arriving on a British Airways 747 and being ushered into a small, cramped immigration and customs shed adjacent to the small airport terminal. Zimbabwe, in those days wasn't hard to take, and provided further insights into the African culture and environment. The country had just emerged from several years of civil war, following the Unilateral Declaration of Independence by the, then Prime Minister, Ian Smith, and the racial overtones from that earlier era and permeating up from South Africa were very much in evidence. This was borne out by attitudes to the other person on this World Bank supervision mission who was an African American woman, representing the Bank, and in charge of the supervision, Diane White.

We stayed at the best hotel in Harare, Meikles, when I was not in the field; and the staff there weren't sure what the relationship was between this black woman and myself. This was particularly evident in the dining room when we went for dinner. Perhaps many waiters and white guests were wondering about our relationship, although it was purely professional. I thought it was rather fun to goad the white Zimbabweans and South African guests at a time when the abhorrent policy of apartheid was in full swing in South Africa. It was more difficult at the Forestry Commission, which seemed to be one of the last bastions of white supremacy and where I had to be more circumspect. There, the managing director and his senior officers almost totally ignored the mission leader in favour of talking to me, which I found rather distasteful. Diane was aware of the bigoted attitude, of course, although it didn't seem to get her down.

These first two African countries were quite a positive experience. The people were generally friendly, and services operated reasonably efficiently then; although the situation later changed in Zimbabwe under the despotic rule of Mugabe, and I experienced some of this as I continued to do forestry work there until 1998. By contrast, the situation was not as comfortable when I flew into Nigeria in June 1984. I had had word of the country's reputation for corruption, and it was with this in mind that I somewhat nervously boarded the British Caledonian DC10 for the flight down from Gatwick Airport, London.

I felt even more ill at ease on my arrival in Lagos, not knowing what to expect, but wishing I could be somewhere else or just stay on the plane with its familiar atmosphere and reliable crew. It was a feeling I experienced many times on arriving at some African country's rundown airport. The feeling of security associated with a familiar culture that one takes for granted is about to be left on board the plane, if it wasn't left behind when we boarded. All that pampering and luxury of upper-class travel is also left at the aircraft door, together with scattered blankets, discarded eye shades, socks and other detritus used by the disembarking passengers. But there was a job to do and, so, I had to carry on and deal with things as they came.

Nigeria isn't the largest country in Africa. That distinction is reserved for Sudan. But Nigeria is the most populous and probably has had the largest cases of corruption, graft, or just plain theft of public monies on the continent, with billion-dollar figures often being mentioned. This has a lot to do with the fact that there is a lot of wealth generated from oil. It should be a rich and prosperous country, with its oil exports, while having the potential to be self-sufficient in food production. Misuse of their natural resources and poor governance have instead meant that the country has gone from being an exporter to an importer of wood, with much of their previously rich forest resources heavily degraded or destroyed.

My first confrontation after arriving was with the immigration officer. As in many African countries, this, officious official would sit at a raised desk. This enabled him to have a sense of superiority as you stood there, feeling suitably inferior while trying to see what was being done with your documents. I approached the Nigerian immigration officer, looking down at me.

'Ok, this is it,' I thought. What was I in for and how much would I have to pay? However, although he wasn't particularly friendly, nothing untoward happened. Nevertheless, I was quite relieved when I then discovered that a representative from the United Nations Development

Programme (UNDP) had been sent to meet me inside the customs area, and so I passed with no harassment through customs and was officially transported to the United Nations guest house. In fact, that trip didn't go too badly as my colleague, Jim Redhead, and I were escorted around by United Nations officers and had our arrangements made by the UN.

On my subsequent visits in 1991 and 1992, while working for the World Bank, I was not afforded such protection and found that all sorts of people were involved in trying to extract that extra bit of money, ranging from taxi drivers and hotel clerks to officials at the airports and the police. They were usually quite open about it. I also discovered that it was a dangerous business getting transport from the airport to one's hotel at night. In fact, if one wanted to get to the airport from downtown for late-night flights to Europe, it was advisable to travel before seven p.m. even though that meant waiting around for four to five hours until the departure of one's plane. Many drivers considered it too dangerous to drive after dark as there was a constant fear of hold-ups by armed gangs, though I never experienced any. When I first heard about this problem, I was interested to see what the drive from the airport was like, imagining it to be through open countryside or bush where bandits could safely operate. However, the route passes entirely through built up urban areas. So, obviously urban law and order is a problem even for such public main thoroughfares.

On the later trips, in 1991 and 1992, although the World Bank resident mission arranged for a travel agent or a bank car and driver to pick me up, those people didn't actually come into the airport to ease the way through immigration and customs, as the United Nations person had done. I also discovered that I still had to be careful with these pickups as more than one Bank staff member had been met and whisked off by con men who said they were there to meet the person. These thieves were quite clever and knew the look of the black briefcases with which Bank staff were issued in those days. On seeing someone carrying such a briefcase and knowing that the person was expecting to be picked up, they approached and said they had been sent by the Bank to pick up the person.

I know of one such staff member who was then driven off to a secluded spot and robbed of everything he had, and another who was saved from such a fate by a watchful police patrol. I would ask for identification if I didn't know the driver or, on the few occasions when I came back on local flights and nobody was there to meet me, I checked that the taxi driver had his taxi driver ID. All these shenanigans and constant threats to my property meant that I had to be vigilant, and they added a touch of spice and tension to the visits.

Leaving Nigeria was as much of a problem as arriving, perhaps even more so. The worst time I had was on my departure in 1991. I ended up paying six people money, starting with the official who issued the airport tax receipt. The usual approach was for them to ask, "Have you anything for me," while they had your ticket or briefcase or passport. This was done quite openly with other officers nearby, but then they were all probably playing the same game. On this occasion, most of the requests came from security people and there seemed to be an inordinate number of security checks. I knew that refusal to cooperate could result in my briefcase being upended and searched minutely, so I passed over US$5 or some Naira on each occasion.

Eventually, I did get fed up and refused to pay, saying, "I gave to your mate over there so go and get your share if you want," or some such statement. On my last flight out of Lagos in February 1992, there were announcements about not paying airport officials, though it still went on.

The graft and corruption also manifested itself in the decrepit state of the airport facilities and illustrated how such practices, combined with poor management, were wasting valuable resources, and degrading public investments. The airport had, apparently, been designed along the lines of Amsterdam's Schiphol Airport, the epitome of a modern, well-run airport at that time. I have been through it on several occasions and have always been impressed by the quiet efficiency with which operations occurred and passenger movements were facilitated. but Lagos airport was a stark contrast to Schiphol.

Many of the aids just did not work, mainly through a lack of maintenance. This applied to flight information boards, electronic security systems, and escalators. The bathrooms/ toilets were awash with water and many commodes didn't work. In fact, one particular bathroom resembled a Roman ruin with pieces of porcelain lying around like so many dismembered figures. The situation on the tarmac wasn't much better. On one occasion, I noticed our Lufthansa plane was taxiing particularly slowly and that there were few, if any lights, on the taxiways. I found out that these had either been stolen or had not been replaced when they blew. Then there were the planes that were held up at a remote and darkened corner of the airport as they were taxiing, and thieves would then open the cargo hatches and steal containers.

At times it appeared as though near-anarchy reigned in the country. The poor state of the airport was symptomatic of so much infrastructure in Nigeria, and, in fact, in many other African countries. Maintenance was just not done or only done to a limited extent. It had low priority, largely because there was just no money to be skimmed off the top in graft from maintenance as there was with new construction.

As in other African countries, there was very little money in local coffers for maintenance, with much of any designated tax revenue being siphoned off by unscrupulous politicians and bureaucrats. For the same reason, roads were usually badly maintained, foot paths a hazard on which to walk and there were frequent power outages. The latter could also be caused by people stealing the copper transmission wire.

It was clear where the priorities of politicians and bureaucrats lay - certainly not with the public. This attitude often started right at the top, with some of the leaders of Africa's poorer countries being disgustingly rich on a global basis. One leader who impressed me by not belonging to this notorious club was Julius Nyerere, the former and first President of Tanzania. His socialist economic approach may have led to the economic woes in his country. However, to the end, he appeared to lead a simple life without a great deal of material trappings, and he endeavoured to maintain the integrity of the government, even after he formally left the political arena, although his efforts were thwarted to some extent by the later crop of political leaders.

I had the honour to meet him unexpectedly in Western Tanzania. We had suffered a puncture and were pulled over on a dusty country road when this none-too-modern Peugeot 403 sedan pulled up and out climbed President Nyerere. He walked over and asked if we needed any help. We had a short, pleasant conversation about the forestry project, which I was involved in and then he climbed back into his car and drove off.

If flying into and out of Nigeria was eventful, flying inside the country was also an interesting and somewhat traumatic experience. On my 1984 trip, I travelled north to the city of Kano in a Nigerian Airways Boeing 737. It was a relatively orderly process, with the only disruption being a fight on the tarmac between an overbooked passenger and airline officials before we took off. This involved much throwing of arms in various directions and shouting by the passenger, while the airlines ground staff calmly tried to get the point across that there were no more seats.

From Kano, we drove back to Ibadan in the southwest of the country, some 800 kilometres. It didn't take long to discover that driving in Nigeria could be quite a hair-raising experience, with no adherence to speed limits, and the evidence of numerous accidents left by the roadside.

I decided to calibrate the road safety situation by counting the car wrecks on the side of the road. Over a 100 kilometre distance, there were 110 wrecks. It then struck me that there were an inordinate number of tanker trucks among the wrecks, often with evidence of fires.

Over the next 800 kilometres I counted 90 such tanker trucks. I was told that the tanker drivers were in the habit of selling the fuel on the way and then deliberately wrecking the truck to cover their misdeeds.

On a World Bank mission to Nigeria in September of 1991, I was looking at the supply status of wood fuels, particularly in the drier north of the country. Once again, I had occasion to travel to Kano by air. However, by this time a rather competitive internal airline system had evolved. Air Nigeria now had to contend with three or four private airline operators, who must have turned up at a fire sale for second-hand, twin-engine, BAC111s, which had long since left regular service in saner parts of the world.

Burnt out tanker trucks, a not uncommon site on the main roads in Nigeria

The World Bank staff in Lagos warned me that the whole business of getting on a flight was somewhat chaotic and that I needed to be careful and then they left me to my own devices. By then I had experienced several other examples of Nigerians' demanding approach to relieving me of my money, including persistent attempts by prostitutes to get into the room at the hotel where I was staying. First were the phone calls, saying the girl I had asked for was downstairs waiting to come up. When this ruse failed, an overpainted and underdressed pushy woman would knock on my door.

On opening the door, I was greeted by, "Hi honey. I'm here. Aren't you going to ask me in?"

There was no escape, even on my morning run. One proposed that if she could stay with me to the end of the street, I should sleep with her. I managed to outdistance her, an easy feat with her high heels.

I, therefore, was feeling decidedly uneasy and insecure and felt I had to be constantly on guard. Flying to Kano seemed like it would be a bit of a scramble when I discovered it wasn't possible to make bookings. The procedure was that one just turned up at the airport in time for scheduled flights and trusted to luck that you could get on a flight, although, as I discovered, there was more than luck to the game.

So, it was with some trepidation that I took a taxi to Lagos Airport, not knowing what to expect, but being ready for anything, as my taxi drew up at the terminal. It was like the American wild west in Africa, with the same disregard for law and order, and all sorts of locals out to 'make a buck'; only this time, the cowboys wore dirty tattered shorts and didn't use lassos to rope you in, only a confident insistence to give you a hand as they made a grab for your suitcase.

As I stepped onto the curb, tightly clutching my brief case, while trying to cover my pockets at the same time, I was met by a young tout and, not knowing a good tout from a bad one I trusted my instincts and let him take my suitcase. Well, he didn't look any worse than the others I saw hanging around.

"Where you going?" he asked.

When I replied, "To Kano." He directed me to the check-in counter for Okada Air, in a rather makeshift structure with a counter and set of scales for weighing baggage. As it turned out, he proved to be quite efficient and, for a few Naira, the equivalent of 50 US cents, he saw me through the business of buying a ticket and checking in my bag.

There were no security checks, and, having got my ticket, which served as a boarding pass, I walked into the departure lounge. This was one very large room with several wooden bench seats stuffed to overflowing with enough passengers to fill about six or eight planes. They were dressed in both colourful, traditional Nigerian garb and western clothes, all with several bits and pieces of baggage. It was hot with no movement of air from fans or air conditioners, and the odour of sweating humanity was all pervasive.

I had been sitting there for about 10 minutes, feeling a little alien in the sea of Africans, waiting for some announcement, and wondering what happened next, when another tout came up and asked if I was on the Okada Air flight to Kano. I said I was, to which he replied, "Come. You have to board your plane."

Feeling a bit confused and not sure if this was some ruse, but still feeling I knew what I was talking about as I had been around a lot of airports, I told him the flight had not been announced and that, anyway it was still some time before departure.

"No," he stated emphatically, "You have to come now," while at the same time trying to grab my brief case.

'Well,' I thought, 'maybe he knows something I don't,' remembering it was, after all, Nigeria and not London or Sydney.

So, while still being wary of some scam, I picked up my bag and kept up with him as we went out the door of the terminal and through an opening that had been cut in the fence (not a gate) onto the tarmac. There we joined a group of other people who were lining up at a plane that was just disembarking passengers.

It was then that the 'penny dropped' and I realised that having a ticket didn't necessarily mean I was on the plane. It seemed that everyone that checked in got one and it was first in, first on. I was very grateful to this young bloke and gave him a 'little something' accordingly.

I made it on board and settled down for the flight. There were no safety drills, not that anyone would have listened or obeyed the instructions anyway, but we did get a plastic cup of tea and a biscuit on the hour's flight to Kano. I didn't worry too much about comfort or safety or plane maintenance and just hoped the plane made it to Kano.

I was on my way, and it was part of the experience of working in a country like Nigeria. It's amazing how one rationalizes undertaking otherwise difficult and unsafe practices when there aren't any readily available alternatives and worrying about such things would put one in a perpetual state of anxiety.

In Kano, I checked into a small but relatively clean hotel. It was mid-afternoon and I had time to organize the hire of a car and driver for the next three or four days. It was then that I began to feel unwell, and after a half-eaten dinner, I was quite feverish with an increasing temperature. This was a classic case of malaria, which I had suffered from several times since my childhood days in PNG. Although the definitive diagnosis requires a blood test, there are some tell-tale symptoms, one of which is the speed with which the disease develops. Shaking with ague and feeling rather alone, I took a curative dose of Fansidar and Chloroquine and hoping that all would be well, I spent a few feverish hours shaking in my bed before the drugs had the desired effect.

By the next morning, the fever had gone, just in time for me to have some breakfast and head out on the job, though I was feeling rather debilitated and quite light-headed.

I spent about five days staying in Kano, using it as a base for travelling several hundred kilometres around northern Nigeria in a rental car, which was driven by an ex-army sergeant. This thick set, traditionally garbed individual drove at breakneck speed on the highways but slowed down on the many less frequented roads we took, as I checked out how energy in the form of firewood, gas and kerosene was supplied and used.

There was quite a paradox with regard to the supply of kerosene and petrol. Even though Nigeria was an oil exporting nation and an important member of the Organization of the Petroleum Exporting Countries (OPEC), there were severe shortages of both these fuels in the country.

In fact, Nigeria was importing some 350,000 tonnes per month of premium motor spirit, the petroleum industry's nomenclature for petrol. This was because the three refineries were producing well below capacity due to maintenance problems, and because the price of these fuels was officially fixed at only 4 US cents per litre. The result was that distributors would rather sell across the border in Niger and Cameroon where prices were more like 25 to 30 cents a litre.

Filling hire car with 'brown market' petrol in
northern Nigeria.

One could get 'brown market' petrol on side roads where suppliers had large above-ground tanks. However, we had problems with such petrol because of sand that had worked its way into the tanks. It was the time of the Harmattan, the desert wind that blows from November to March from the Sahara and fills the air with a constant pall of fine sand and dust. This not only contaminated fuel, but also made people rather irritable. My driver would periodically have to stop and clean out the thick layer of sludge in the bottom of the fuel filter in the Peugeot.

There was also a paradox with regard to tree cover in the northern half of the country. A lot of the woodlands, which were poorly managed government forests and regarded as a common resource for plunder, had been cut down for fuel and building materials, leaving only scattered trees and grassland.

On the other hand, the farms tended to retain a number of trees both for animal shade and because the trees produced commercial products like Shea Butter (*Vitellaria paradoxa)* or Desert Date (*Balanites aegyptiaca)*.

When I arrived at Kano Airport to board my flight back to Lagos, I found that the Okada Air flight was cancelled and, so, they put me on an Air Nigeria plane that was coming through from Rome. Air Nigeria hadn't really improved much since I last flew with them in 1984. In fact, so bad was their reputation that they were refused landing rights in Rome until they paid their fuel bills and then all fuel sales were on a cash basis only. As a result, the pilots carried thousands of US dollars in cash, which must have provided all sorts of temptations for fiddles.

They put me in first class. I don't know why; perhaps because I was a foreigner who looked like he was worth something. What little comfort I experienced on the hour and a half flight to Lagos was offset by the dismay I felt when I saw, that on arrival we were taxiing to the international terminal.

Of course, we would, being an international flight, but I had a strong feeling that no special arrangements had been made for local passengers, who had boarded at Kano, to pass through immigration and customs. This meant that I and several others would be like bait fish to the immigration and customs officer sharks.

My concerns were fully justified, but I wasn't going to let these bastards take advantage of me, just because of some Okada Air and Air Nigeria cock up. It was chaotic as several Air Nigeria passengers endeavoured to persuade officials that we had just got on in Kano. This was as we were being directed, with others on the same flight, who had travelled from Rome, to go through immigration clearance procedures.

There was also another international flight that had just arrived, and I took advantage of the turmoil, with so many passengers milling around to pass the various barriers, to convince officials to let me through without too much questioning.

I was back in Nigeria in February 1992 doing further work on an energy issues and options study for the Bank. It was necessary to visit Kano again, as that was where there were major problems with wood fuels and other forms of household energy. This time I thought I knew the game plan for getting on a domestic flight and had developed a somewhat cavalier attitude to the unavoidable wild west show at the airport. I should have been more on guard for the unexpected.

On arrival at the terminal a young, self-assured tout, dressed in grubby shorts and a shirt with no shoes, asked what flight I was on as I was getting out of the taxi. When I said, "To Kano," he grabbed my bag and, instead of going into the large shed they called a terminal, he walked around the side and, so, I thought I had better follow him. We ended up on the tarmac side of the building where he put my case down and explained that the last flight of the previous day had been cancelled so the flight I was after was not just overbooked, it was likely to be double booked. Nevertheless, for a price, he would see what he could do. I felt I might as well try, seeing I was now at the airport and needed to get to Kano.

Firewood and children in northern Nigeria.

While he wandered off to scrounge a seat, I hung around in the hot sun, wondering just what I was getting myself into and feeling out of place in what in any other airport probably would have been a restricted area. The tout returned after a bit to say there were two or three no-shows from the previous night, but he would need double the fare of 400 Naira (about US$35) to get the tickets; obviously paying off someone on the way I reasoned, or was he? I wondered to what extent I was being taken for a ride, particularly being a white foreigner, but it was still only about US$70 and a very reasonable price for an airfare over that distance, forgetting this was not reasonable air travel.

A little while later back comes this character with a ticket, but when I looked at it, I saw there was another person's name as the passenger; a Nigerian name, quite obviously not me. Somehow, he had managed to buy some other passenger's ticket and goodness knows where that other passenger was at that time. When I raised this problem, having already paid the 800 Naira, the tout told me it would cost me US$60 in cash for his services in getting the ticket and then negotiating with the airline to ensure I got a seat, although he assured me, I would be on the plane. I refused to pay him until I saw that, in fact, I could actually get on the flight, and, as I was to find out, this would be a close call.

There was an air of expectancy as a large group of people, me included, waited for the plane scheduled to take us to Kano to arrive. As soon as the twin-engined jet came off the taxiway and onto the ramp where the planes parked, we all rushed through the fence and followed it around as it taxied to its parking spot. This involved avoiding several other jets trying to manoeuvre, which was a little unnerving and not the sort of thing they encourage in civilized airports.

As soon as the disembarking passengers were all off, there was a mad rush for the narrow set of steps leading up to the plane. Obviously, nobody trusted they would have a seat. I hung back as my 'procurer of tickets' assured me I would still have a seat. But I quickly realized he either didn't know what he was talking about or had another scam up his sleeve as it was apparent that boarding was a free-for-all, with no order in the way people were getting on that plane, and there were most likely more people trying to board than seats on the plane. I joined the throng of men and women, pushing and shoving with elbows and anything else handy, hoping I hadn't left my move too late. It was more like a rugby maul than boarding a plane, but one couldn't be polite in these circumstances, and I did my fair share of shoving and elbowing with no 'beg your pardons'.

As I was halfway up the steps, the tout gave me my bag, as I couldn't have managed to hold it and shove at the same time. I gave him his US$60, having a sneaking feeling that I was not getting a good deal. On board, a quick survey showed that most of the seats had been occupied and I rushed to get one of the last seats at the rear of the plane. Having seated myself, I was determined to keep the seat no matter whose name was on the ticket I carried. I found I had developed the same mentality as the other passengers in this mad dog-eat-dog atmosphere.

At this point the captain of the plane suddenly appeared, walking through the cabin wanting to know who had let us on, as they still had to refuel the plane. I don't know what he had been doing in the cockpit while the mad mêlée had been boarding. But there was no way I, or anyone else, was leaving the seats they had so vigorously fought to occupy. This was quite simply a matter of squatters' rights. As I sat there, waiting to see if there would be any further developments, I wondered if my luggage would be loaded or if some tout had by now spirited it away and was sampling my taste in clothes. I wondered how they would know who had made it on to the plane and, therefore, which checked bags were to be loaded. Perhaps they were all loaded unless the losers claimed their bags from the tarmac in time. But that was a secondary issue compared to keeping my seat.

So, we sat and sweltered in the rising tropical temperature for nearly an hour, there being no air conditioning and very little, if any, movement of air in the cabin. Someone came around to collect our tickets and I sweated even more for a while over whether there would be a problem. This was a completely alien situation for me, endeavouring to fly to a destination with a ticket that had another person's name on it, and a stranger's name at that. Part of my mind told me that this was unlawful, but that was squashed by the urge to accept this situation if I was to get a flight to Kano. I got away with it or the airline didn't care so long as I had a ticket. And it was Nigeria.

A Nigerian gent across the aisle told the ticket collector how he had paid so much to get a ticket, but didn't get one, and he wasn't going to move. Eventually, after much argument he won and stayed where he was. I postulated as to whether we had both been paying for the same ticket, but I paid just that bit extra and so I had been given the ticket. Eventually, the door was closed, and we took off for Kano, while I figured out how I could claim the US$60 bribe back on my expense account.

Surviving Dictatorships

By 1983 my marriage had been having difficulties for some time, and in May Marion and I separated. To complicate matters further, a few months after my marriage break up, I decided to leave Forestal. It was a difficult time with a recession drastically cutting our payable workload at the company. I thought it would be better to leave before I got a pink slip, though when I put in my resignation, they asked would I reconsider and stay. But the working atmosphere and *esprit de corps* had changed in the previous couple of years, and I felt I could do better working as a private consultant. To help with my income, I had contracted an arrangement with Silviconsult, a Swedish forestry consulting firm, and was on a retainer to do business development for them and to be available for consultancies when they might need me. This came about as I had met with Sten Karlberg, the President and owner of Silviconsult, on several occasions while on assignment and doing business development and marketing for Forestal.

Life as a self-employed forestry consultant was quite successful, and within two years I was earning more than my salary at Forestal. Then in late 1984, Sten asked if I could lead a team to Liberia to evaluate a World Bank plantation project. I had a feeling it was going to be difficult working in Liberia, having heard of the turmoil in the country under its upstart president, former army sergeant, Samuel Doe. He had seized power in a bloody coup a few years earlier. It was a six week assignment, and it didn't take me long to realise my concerns were more than justified.

In fact, it took no longer than the short walk to the immigration desk at Roberts Field, the international airport for the capital Monrovia, after disembarking in the early evening from a British Caledonian flight from London. There, an officious looking individual, sitting at a raised desk, asked if "I had anything for him," after I had handed over my passport. Five dollars was sufficient to get it back again, though with only a twenty-four-hour visa, which meant I had to report to immigration the next day for a further shake down. This was all despite the fact that I had picked up and paid for a three-month visa before I left home in Vancouver. Apparently, such foreign issue visas weren't recognised, or the Liberian scam tram had started in Vancouver.

On the way into town, I experienced what was to be a common problem, around Monrovia, military roadblocks. A group of slovenly, poorly disciplined, but well-armed, soldiers stopped us on some pretext and demanded to see our documents. A forestry chap, who had met me tried to talk with them, but they were quite aggressive and demanded money, hinting that all was not in order with my documents. I wasn't going to argue with a G3 assault rifle pointed at me by a soldier whom I wasn't sure really knew how to handle it or himself. I learnt later that they actually did shoot, if you failed to stop, and a few people were killed in such incidents while I was in the country.

Corruption was all pervasive. Law and order agencies only seemed to exist as a basis for the police and officials to extort money. In fact, after two or three weeks in the country, I concluded that it was almost in a state of anarchy. I had an almost constant feeling of unease, particularly in Monrovia; being wary every time I walked or drove anywhere. Life was far from being carefree and relaxed, as it was necessary to be on my guard and suspicious of most people I came across, including the police and the army. It certainly made me appreciate the freedom and security that we have in many western countries, like Canada and Australia.

The degree to which extortion would be pursued was rather frighteningly demonstrated one afternoon near the project office. Our working discussions were interrupted by a co-worker bursting into the office and breathlessly telling us that George (George Nagel, our economist) was being taken into custody at gun point. I and another colleague rushed out and found George standing with a little man in plain clothes pointing a pistol at his head.

We approached cautiously and asked what was going on. The little man informed us in a brusque, officious way, that George had been caught photographing the State House, home of the President. The whole thing was a trumped-up charge and George denied it. Next, the little man threw in that he had also seen George photographing some other 'sensitive' site, which was also nonsense.

Then the man, who had informed us he was a member of internal security, demanded we move away so he could take George with him to some internal security office for interrogation. We knew that if he got George away from us and into Internal Security clutches it could be difficult and expensive to get him out. Luckily, the local United Nations forester, Eric Hammermaster, whom I had known from my days in Papua New Guinea, had the presence of mind to convince the security man that it was in his interests to talk about the whole matter in our office first.

The security man finally agreed, and we all returned to the office, where Eric and others managed to persuade the little security man, possibly with a little monetary help, that George really was innocent and that taking him into custody would only create problems for him with the United Nations getting involved. There was an audible sigh of relief when the security man left, although, needless to say, George was badly shaken by the incident.

The police had a habit of stopping vehicles to get a bit of cash, usually based on a trumped-up charge of failing to stop at a red light or some such thing. It happened to me more than once. We had set up a working camp in the forests in the west of the country, but every time we drove into Monrovia there was a chance of getting stopped, which added to the unease I felt. This extortion was aggravated by the fact that public servants' salaries were about three months in arrears, and the army two months in arrears.

My counterpart, a forestry research officer, also asked me for "overtime". Normally, I would not have minded paying him something extra if he was at all hard working. But he was just a whinging sloth, who, I don't think, liked field work. He managed to avoid it on most occasions on some pretext or other and I always suspect foresters who don't like getting some mud on their boots in the forest.

As part of trying to determine the state of natural forests and potential for plantations in Liberia, I arranged with a local air charter company for a reconnaissance flight in a small, single-engine, Cessna 185. This hiring of planes in developing countries can be a bit of a gamble because of uncertainties relating to proper maintenance and pilot capabilities but flying can be an efficient way to either get around or get an overview of the forests and trees.

So, we decided to risk it. Two of my forestry consulting colleagues, a Canadian and a New Zealander, and I arranged to fly from Monrovia, using the local airport (Spriggs Payne[10] Field). The plan was to head east, checking the forest, to a point near the border with Cote d'Ivoire, where we planned to land and look at some teak plantations, to evaluate the potential for this species. Little did I know that this venture would see us on the brink of disaster.

I was a bit concerned when our pilot, an African in his thirties, had to ask the mechanic on the ground about the working of some instrument on the aircraft, and it appeared he wasn't totally familiar with this particular model plane. Perhaps I should have cancelled the flight then and there, or at least questioned the pilot about his flying experience and knowledge of

---

10 James Spriggs Payne (1819 - 1882) was the fourth and eighth president of Liberia.

the country. However, I somehow assumed the default position that the pilot was competent overall and knew enough to ask about what might be different with this particular plane.

Spriggs Payne Field, Monrovia, where I had more than one run in with immigration officials seeking money.

Once we had taken off, the pilot seemed to be handling the plane quite well, so we settled down to watch the forest pass beneath us. It was a sunny day with only a few clouds, and no sign of any bad weather - a good day for a flying reconnaissance.

I sat in the right front next to the pilot and used a map to determine roughly where we were while making notes on the forest as we flew over it. Flying below 500 feet, individual tree crowns were visible in the undulating forest canopy that stretched beneath us with varying shades of green as well as the red and yellow flush of new leaves.

This was west African tropical evergreen rainforest, but it was far from a solid mass of trees as logging had opened up the canopy in many places revealing remnant tall trees hung with vines and fresh green regeneration carpeting the open patches.

Approaching the border with Cote d'Ivoire we seemed to be heading too far south from where I estimated the plantation site to be. After a while, I mentioned this to the pilot as well as the fact that our fuel was down to about half. He turned north and we flew, at first seemingly with some direction in mind, but, after a while, in more of a searching mode.

We crossed a large river, which I took to be the Cote d'Ivoire border, but which the pilot, stubbornly, maintained was not. We were definitely lost! And it wasn't a comfortable feeling, particularly with a pilot who seemed inexperienced and refused to recognise his mistakes or shortcomings.

To add to our troubles, I again noted that the fuel was getting rather low. When I raised my concerns about this with the pilot, he said not to worry as we could refuel when we found the plantation strip.

This was not reassuring as it was a Saturday and people were usually off somewhere else rather than waiting round to fill planes, and this would be just a bush strip and unlikely to have any fuel on hand. We also had to find the strip first, and it was obvious that the pilot didn't really have a clue as to its whereabouts or even where we actually were.

At this point I told the pilot to forget our mission and finding our destination and just head back to Monrovia before we went beyond any point of no return as regards fuel. He wouldn't have anything to do with it, stubbornly insisting he could find the strip, although it was obvious, he had very little, if any, knowledge of the area. His incompetence was confirmed, when in desperation, he suggested landing on a road near a village to ask for directions. No way! This was crazy, particularly as there were power or telephone lines near the road. My assessment of the pilot had hit a new low, but we were stuck with this rather stubborn individual.

Tropical evergreen forest over which we flew with the wayward pilot.

Finally, after more fruitless and aimless flying over forest as the fuel gauges dropped towards empty, he was persuaded that he was lost and agreed to turn back. From my dead reckoning, using the map as a guide, I thought if we headed due west we should hit the coast, which ran about west-north-west, or at least come in sight of it. A beach was a preferable landing strip to the jungle. Once we hit the coast, we shouldn't be far from Monrovia.

So, back we flew while I watched the green mass of jungle below and the fuel gauges in front. They were at about a quarter full when we started back, which meant we had used three quarters of our fuel to that point and so would be stretching to make it to the nearest airstrip along the coast or even the beach; let alone back to Monrovia.

As we flew over thick forest interspersed with patches of glistening wet and green swamps and occasional patches of cultivation, the minutes passed, and I watched the needles on the gauges edge closer to empty. I felt quite detached from the reality of the situation. It was as if I was in a car, and we were low on petrol. Though here it wasn't a case of just stopping by the side of the road, but rather one of falling out of the sky or trying to find a half decent clearing to lessen the impact on coming down. Perhaps I felt, subconsciously, that all would be well, although the almost solid mass of trees, interspersed with swamps and small streams, didn't bode well for a safe landing if we did actually empty the tanks. I looked back over my shoulder at my two companions, who sat grim-faced watching the landscape below us.

Eventually, in the distance, I glimpsed the ocean and the beach along the coast and relaxed to some extent. As we hit the beach, the pilot turned north-west towards a nearby airstrip at the small town of Buchanan. One of the gauges was indicating empty when we came in sight of the airstrip. We all audibly blew a long sigh of relief. The pilot flew straight in, landed, and taxied to a shed. But nobody was around and there was no fuel, as I suspected would be the case. The pilot dipped the tanks and announced that we did indeed have a quarter full tank on one side and the other was "on reserve". When I asked what that meant, he admitted it meant "empty". So, the question was, "what to do next?". One option was to try and hitch a ride on the road back to Monrovia, some 50 kilometres along the coast. Given the anarchic law and order situation with the police and army roadblocks, I thought this was perhaps a bit chancy.

The other alternative was that we could try and make it by flying there, trusting that we had enough fuel. We decided on the latter and climbed back on board. Luckily, there was beach most of the way and we flew over this at only about 200 feet in case the fuel gave out. The worst moment was when we had to turn inland to land at the airfield. It was only a few kilometres, but by now we were virtually without fuel with both gauges on empty. There was another audible sigh of incredible relief from us all when the wheels touched the ground, and we were able to taxi to the apron in front of the terminal.

Needless to say, I had words with the charter company and refused to pay them the contract price, though we did agree on some payment. Then, as we emerged from the charter company office, we found ourselves in another confrontation. We were told an immigration officer wanted to see us. I knew the drill from previous passages through Spriggs Payne Field and had that sinking feeling in my stomach, knowing what the confrontation might entail. On both previous occasions I had been accosted by an immigration officer asking official questions about how much money I had and where I was from, as a pretext to getting a handout. On these previous occasions he had failed to extract any money from me as my counterpart proved his worth, by just coming in on the interview. Not being able to have me alone foiled the intentions of the officer.

As it turned out, it was the same immigration man again, probably smelling money when he saw three foreigners arriving. He demanded to know where we had been and asked to see out passports. Hugh Speechly, the New Zealander, didn't have his passport on him, so we would have to do some swift talking. We told the officer we had been on a reconnaissance flight over Liberia. However, according to him there was something else about our flight he needed to ascertain, and we needed to come to his office. Well, despite much threatening and bombast on the part of the officer, we refused to go to his office to "fill in forms", and there were three of us to support each other.

We then demanded to see his identification. This put a different twist on the situation. The bullying wasn't working. We just weren't cooperating. So, after some time, he finally and reluctantly produced an ID card. We duly took down the details. Realizing he wasn't going to get anywhere with us, his officious attitude changed to that of a whining plea, complaining that he was short of money and was asking us to help him out. At first, we all refused, completely put off by his whole attitude. However, as we were all walking out of the terminal, I quietly slipped him a few dollars. I reasoned he may well have been short on funds, given the arrears in salaries to public servants from a bankrupt government. Plus, it is always good not to antagonise such local officials more than necessary, corrupt though they may be. I might have needed his help on a future passage through the airport. But as the seriousness of our narrow escape on our aborted flight sank in over the next few hours, I realized how lucky we had all been, and there was no thought of any more such charter flights in Liberia.

During the mid-eighties, my continuing good relationship with the World Bank, particularly with the Bank foresters, resulted in several short-term assignments for that organization in Africa. I found the Bank were a good bunch to work with, as they maintained a high professional standard. As part of these assignments, there continued to be an increasing emphasis on communities' involvement with the management of natural forests and farm or village forestry. I was also becoming more adept at handling such approaches, adopting a more bottom-up approach, and communicating with the villagers, rather than my earlier top-down way of doing things, which tended to seriously limit the effectiveness of any resulting project activities.

Continuing my involvement with the community management of forests, I had my introduction to Malawi in 1985 on an appraisal mission for a Wood Energy Project. As the British Airways giant 747 taxied to its place on the concrete apron, I looked out from my wide, comfortable Business Class window seat at the low Miombo Woodland stretching away beyond the airport. Closer in, well-trimmed grass surrounded the runways and taxiways. Here was a country that seemed to have some pride in themselves; though, I knew it wasn't just national pride, as I was driven in a small bus to the VIP arrivals lounge. I had been made aware that my hair should not be too long, or I might not be allowed entry to the country, and that women could not wear trousers. I also noted that there was a certain formality here that was not present in other African countries. The forest officer who met me outside the airport and the driver of our Pajero both wore dark suits and ties, despite the temperature being a low 30 degrees Celsius.

These were the dictates of Malawi's autocratic President, Hastings Banda, an ex-Presbyterian pastor. But the neat and formal appearances hid the fact that Banda ran one of the most repressive regimes in Africa. On my early visits to Malawi, I sensed there was a lot of fear among my forestry counterparts and the general populace, as he kept a tight rein on any dissention. People would disappear overnight with thousands being tortured, imprisoned or murdered under his totalitarian regime. On the other hand, there seemed to be a sense of social and community responsibility, which may have had more to do with the innate Malawian character and traditions than any of Dr Banda's dictates.

Unlike most other countries in Africa and elsewhere, the male Forestry Department staff all wore suits and ties, and that included the drivers. I wore a tie in deference to the local protocol, but balked at wearing a coat in the hot, dry climate, except when I had to attend a formal meeting with a high-ranking government officer or minister. In the field, I forgot the tie.

I visited Malawi on several occasions over the succeeding years, supervising the Wood Energy Project, and always staying at the Capitol Hotel when in Lilongwe. Several days would be spent on each occasion, driving the length of the small country through kilometres of low, open Miombo woodland with sun-dried grass as an understory. In contrast was the sparkling waters of Lake Malawi that stretched for over half the length of the country in the east. The appearance of the picturesque lake was deceptive as it had a dark side. To walk along the shore in its shallow waters could well result in an attack of Schistosomiasis, also known as *bilharzia*, with parasitic worms invading the bloodstream, intestines and urinary tract.

Like other countries in eastern and southern Africa, the woodlands were the principal source of firewood and charcoal. This frequently resulted in uncontrolled cutting, particularly for urban markets, with only stumps to remind one of the trees that had once grown there. Over time, these forest wounds would heal with new trees growing from the stumps, although continual large-scale felling would leave the forest somewhat decimated.

As usual, a great deal of time was spent in the field, walking through woodlands or having conversations with villagers. These concerned the management and state of their woodland forests, how they were coping with their own and the urban demand for wood from these woodlands, and the potential or need for growing trees. It was usually an enthusiastic bunch who would gather to talk at the edge of or in the woodland; and women formed a good and vocal proportion of the group. This was not surprising as in Malawi land titles or customary rights were often passed along the matrilineal line.

The men also had their views, and some were very keen to accept help in furthering their tree planting or woodland management activities. This was helped by earlier colonial forestry extension work, though a number of villagers saw woodlots as an investment in the future, not just for the wood, but as a source of funds for perhaps a child's wedding. However, one old codger informed me, when I asked why he had planted his grove of eucalypts, that, "the British made me do it."

During my supervision of the forestry project in Malawi, there was the transition from President Banda's autocratic rule for life to elections for a more democratic government. In 1993, with increasing local resentment and under international pressure, a referendum decided that the one-party rule should end. The following year, Hastings Banda was defeated, in the first elections held, much to his amazement, as he seemed to think he was loved and revered by his people. Prior to this, my Malawian counterparts would rarely mention politics, although, I knew from World Bank colleagues and some local comments that there was a lot of dislike for many of Banda's policies. However, when Banda's end loomed and democracy was on the horizon, the talk flowed freely as we drove around the country. There was a palpable excitement, as if a new-found freedom was about to occur and it was exciting to be part of the party.

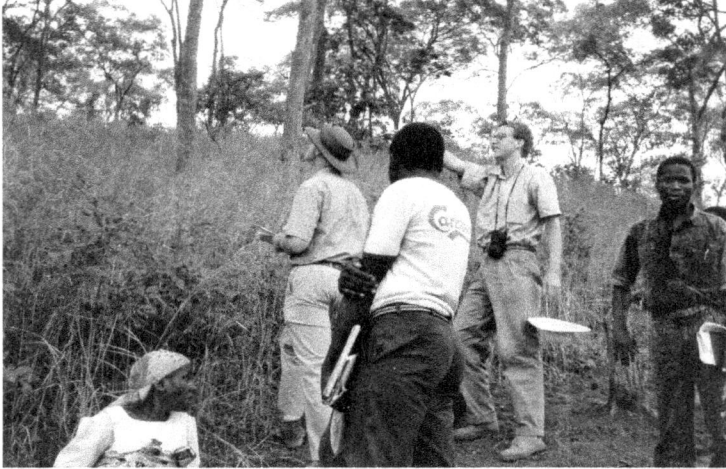

On a site visit in Malawi, 1985.

With quite a bit of work being done for FAO or the FAO Investment Centre[11], I spent several months working in Rome from 1979, when I assisted on a mission to Indonesia to design a forestry project. This followed my first visit to the Eternal City back in 1969, during my tour of Europe from PNG when I was very much a neophyte and somewhat naïve as a traveller. Now, I had quite a bit more experience under my belt and saw and experienced Rome in a different way, particularly as I was spending some time living and working there. I would wander the streets of the old city, inside what remained of the Roman walls, constantly in awe of the fact that ruins of temples and other buildings were actual remnants of the great Roman Empire and early Christianity. It was fascinating to view the interior of so many churches that contained paintings, frescoes, and statues by famous artists, such as Bernini, Raphael, Giotto or Michelangelo. I loved the food and the Roman approach to eating from sidewalk cafés to restaurants or tavernas. The Roman traffic seemed crazy and completely undisciplined, but after a while I realised that it all somehow worked out and I never saw an accident.

---

11 The FAO Investment Centre is part of FAO (Food and Agricultural Organization of the UN) and with funding from the World Bank and other development banks, it helps to prepare projects for funding by these banks.

The main FAO complex, where I found myself ensconced, is in the Aventine area of Rome and is an impressive series of buildings with marble facades, built by Mussolini. The address is Via Terme di Caracalla, with the ruins of the Baths of Caracalla opposite. It is adjacent to the Circus Maximus, and I could often look out the window of the office in which I was working and gaze across to where the ancient Romans raced their chariots, while the Palatine Hill beyond that was the home of emperors and other rich Romans.

On my way home to Vancouver for Christmas, in December 1983, I was seated in a half empty Alitalia DC9 en route to Amsterdam on the first leg of my journey. Life wasn't bad, having survived a mission to Bangladesh and my report writing in Rome would require me to return there in the New Year for another two months. In the immediate future, I was somewhat depressed about spending Christmas on my own, though I would then get to see David and Michael in the days after Christmas. After my separation from Marion in May of that year I was living in a two-bedroom apartment in Vancouver's West End, and I missed the close contact with the two boys.

Although these thoughts and feelings were with me, I couldn't help but relax on the smooth flight with an azure blue sky outside and the snow-covered Alps coming into view through the plane window. As I looked out, I was taken by the woman seated at the window. She had a mass of curly, auburn hair down to her shoulders, an attractive face, brown framed glasses and was wearing a thick knitted pullover. She saw me looking at her and I mouthed some inane comment about how beautiful the scenery was.

We fell into a conversation. She worked for the Fisheries Department at FAO. Well, that was a nice coincidence, and I explained how I was working with the Investment Centre. She was Dutch and was flying to Amsterdam to spend Christmas with her mother. We talked non-stop until the plane was taxiing to the terminal at Schiphol Airport, when I took a chance and asked if she would like to meet when we both returned to Rome in the New Year.

"Yes, it would be nice to get together for a coffee," she replied, smiling.

'Don't push it, Ryan. Coffee is a good start,' I thought to myself. "I'm Paul Ryan," I told her, and she said her name was Ronnie (Veronica) Fontijn.

Back in Rome in early January, I had to wait a week or so until Ronnie came back from Amsterdam. I then rang her number at the Fisheries Department and waited for her to answer with my heart halfway to my throat. We agreed on a coffee date, and over a couple of weeks, we saw each other a few times, enjoying ourselves and each other. I then arranged for a dinner date at a rather nice restaurant, called Il Grotto not far from where I was staying in the Aventine area. They served one of my favourite Italian dishes, spaghetti ala vongole – al dente pasta with only allio, olio and pepperoncino, with clams in just steamed open shells.

Amid getting to know Ronnie, I had been feeling tired and somewhat unwell for a week or so and then, I noticed my stools were black. Checking with the clinic at FAO, I was told to monitor the situation. A couple of days later, at a party to which I had gone, I left early as I was feeling decidedly seedy, and I almost collapsed on the metro coming back to my pension. The next day was a Saturday, but I needed to seek help, so, on the advice of the FAO medical people, I got a taxi to the Salvador Mundi Private Hospital. There, the attending doctor told me I would need to be admitted to hospital immediately as I had a bleeding stomach. But I needed some clothes and toiletries, so, back I went via taxi to my pension.

I picked up some pyjamas and other gear and told a friend and forestry colleague there about my plight. I asked him to inform John Weatherhogg, our stalwart English team leader for the Bangladesh project, on which I was working about my situation. I then set off back to the Salvador Mundi, wondering what was in store for me and feeling rather alone and vulnerable. When John came to see me the next day, all very concerned, I asked if he could contact Ronnie and pass on my regrets at not being able to make our dinner date a couple of days later.

I stayed in hospital for ten days and was quite comfortable in a single room. They gave me some iron or liver extract injections and fed me bread and milk until the bleeding symptoms disappeared, but no cause for the bleeding was found when x-rays were taken. John, meanwhile, had also been quite vocal in trying to get me medevac'd out to England as he was convinced, I would die in a Rome hospital. The public hospitals did not have a good reputation, though the private one I was in seemed okay. The FAO medical officer, a down-to-earth Irishman, refused his request, partly because my situation was not that serious and partly because they didn't agree with John's assessment of the Rome hospital in which I was staying. Still, it was nice to know I had such lobbying being made on my behalf. The interesting part came when they told me I could leave the hospital. The bill came to some 1.5 million lira or roughly US$900. The hospital would not take credit cards and I did not have that sort of cash. So, into the fray jumped John. He had come to pick me up and on hearing of my dilemma, immediately jumped in and paid the bill. Of course, I paid him back as soon as FAO recompensed me.

When Ronnie heard of my plight, she came to the hospital to visit me, which was wonderful, her presence no doubt aiding my recovery. In fact, she came several times to my private room, and we became even more acquainted with each other. What started out with chatting and holding hands ended with Ronnie on the bed with me. I am not sure if the nuns who ran the hospital always approved.

Out of hospital, I soon moved in with Ronnie at her apartment and we developed a wonderful close and loving, intimate relationship with much laughter and sharing of experiences. On that stay in Rome, and on several other stays with Ronnie over the next couple of years, I got to experience Rome more as a resident. There were neighbours yelling at each other across the open central well in the apartment block. There was the frustration of trying to find a parking space on the sidewalk, the luxury of buying fruit and vegies at the local Saturday farmers' market, and the patience needed in dealing with Rome traffic on the way to work. We explored the countryside outside of Rome in Ronnie's old Citroen 2CV and, as both of us loved food, we ate out much of the time and had enormous fun trying out numerous restaurants and their local specialities. Although we developed a very close and loving relationship, it didn't lead to marriage or even moving in together permanently. I had my sons in Canada and Ronnie didn't wish to commit to a marriage and move away from Rome at that time. I was also wary of a marriage commitment after the breakdown of my marriage to Marion.

A Sort of Himalayan Shangrila

My experiences in Africa, particularly in Liberia and Nigeria contrasted with some months subsequently spent in Bhutan in 1985. Early in the year, while at home in my apartment in Vancouver's West End, I received a telegram, which read: *"Could you please reply earliest re your availability for an assignment to prepare a plantation plan for Bhutan over a two-month period. FAO Forestry Department"*. It wasn't much as far as terms of references go, but perhaps the writer had as much concept of forestry in Bhutan as I did. Not having been to the country before or knowing anything about their forestry, I felt it might be a difficult task, particularly given the short time that I had to do the job. Nonetheless, I was prepared to give it a go, particularly as I was keen to see how real my vision was of Bhutan as being a sort of Shangri-La amidst the high mountains and valleys of the Himalayas.

I proceeded to make the arrangements to arrive in the country on 11 February 1985, after a three-day visit to FAO headquarters in Rome, where I would endeavour to find out a bit more about forestry in Bhutan and why a plantation plan was needed.

If this trip had been made prior to 1983 it would have been necessary to have driven into Bhutan from India. It was then that an airport had been opened with an air service commencing in February 1983, with the newly established Bhutanese airline, Druk Air.

Before I could get a seat from Calcutta for the one and half hour flight to the airport at Paro, I experienced something of the isolation of the country and the happenstance way things were organized. Bhutan had only two foreign embassies, and so to get the necessary visa, I had to send a telegram with my personal details to the Bhutan Forestry Department in the capital Thimphu. I then received a telegram back saying that my visa had been granted. Confirmation of this visa then had to be recorded against my name in a large ledger-type book at the Druk Air office in Calcutta Airport, to enable me to get a seat on the plane.

So, after arriving in hot and humid Calcutta from a chilly Rome, via Delhi, on an overnight flight, I made my way down the almost deserted drab corridors of the International Airport to Druk Air's small office. There, a friendly Druk Air agent confirmed that my name was in 'the book' and sold me a ticket for the next morning's flight to Paro. I then checked into the nearby Ashok Hotel to catch up on some sleep before an early start.

In-flight services were rather casual on the small Druk Air Dornier turbo prop, which had most of the twenty or so seats taken. Before starting the engines, the pilot, who was a Sikh, gave us a few details of the flight and told us the cooler in the back had drinks and eats for our refreshment, to which we were welcome to help ourselves.

As we then flew north over the Gangetic Plains of India, I could see the snow-capped peaks of the Himalayas ahead of us and I knew that once we were almost at those peaks we would be in Bhutan. To say Bhutan is a mountainous country is to state the obvious. In fact, there is very little in the way of level ground, except on a few river flats right on the border with India. Some wag in Bhutan told me that the British decided on the border between the two countries by rolling stones down the last hills before the plains and they put the boundary where the rocks stopped. As far-fetched as this may seem, the actual line of the boundary gives the story an element of credibility.

But Bhutan had been in existence as a well-ruled and socially organized country long before the British arrived. It was closely linked with Tibet from the nineth and tenth centuries, when it is considered the first migrations arrived, together with Buddhism, at a time of turmoil and Buddhist suppression in Tibet. Of the several religious schools of Buddhism introduced in Tibet, the Drukpa School was eventually established as the dominant one in Bhutan, and it is from this school that the Bhutanese people derive their name, *Drukpas*, while the country is referred to as *Druk-yul*, which is translated as "Land of the Dragon". The name Bhutan is thought to be a corruption of an Indian term *Bhotanta*, referring to those regions bordering Tibet[12].

The system of dzongs or fortified monasteries that were established across the country and still exist today, helped with the establishment and maintenance of a unified system of government from the seventeenth century, while providing defence against enemies within and without. At that time, Tibet was the foreign enemy, attempting several invasions during the first half of the seventeenth century, all of which were unsuccessful, even when aided in the latter stages by the Mongol army.

Although cordial relations were established with the British in the eighteenth century, conflicting interests saw these relations deteriorate to

12 Source: *Bhutan: A kingdom of the Eastern Himalayas*, with text by Francoise Pommaret-Imaeda, and Yoshiro Imaeda. English translation by Ian Noble. Published by Editions Olizane, 1984.

the point where open hostilities took place in 1864-65, from which Britain eventually emerged as the victor. However, through this period and well on into the mid-twentieth century, very few outsiders spent much time in the country, and it was only through the eyes of occasional travellers that impressions were gained of this largely unknown and mysterious, mountainous land. A monarchy was established in 1907 and the third King, Jigme Dorji Wangchuck was responsible for the gradual opening up of the country to the outside world and for the introduction of economic and social development. Bhutan joined the United Nations in 1971 and the first tourists were permitted in 1974.

It was thus, with a sense of fascination and awe, that I watched as our plane descended over an almost untouched wilderness of forested mountains, deep in shadow on one side and bright with sunlight on the other, while over all this, in the background, rose soaring peaks of ice and snow.

The thought occurred to me, 'Why did they need plantations with all this forest around or was I missing something'. Paro Airport is in the Paro River Valley, situated at an altitude of 2,200 metres (7,000 feet). Like so much of Bhutan, the airport was unpretentious; a single runway, an aircraft parking area and the terminal was a regular house. All this was set amongst a variegated pattern of agricultural fields and dry grasslands with the traditional two-storey wooden Bhutanese houses scattered throughout, usually with poles of white prayer flags snapping in the breeze.

With a limit of only 2,000 tourists a year, and usually only one flight a day, there wasn't a need for large airport facilities. The atmosphere at the airport was one of informality and a lack of officious bureaucracy, which certainly made one feel at ease. This was particularly the case, when, on my second trip to the country later in 1985, they found that I didn't have a visa, even though my name was in 'the book' at Calcutta Airport.

It was no cause for alarm, though, as the immigration officials, graciously, with many apologies, gave me a temporary visa, which I could later convert in Thimphu. How could one get upset about a bureaucracy like this whatever the inefficiencies might have been? This was in stark contrast to my experiences in Liberia and Nigeria, where, passing through an airport was a traumatic experience and likely to cost me plenty in bribes.

Unlike in those countries there was no hint of bribery or corruption from the Bhutanese officials. In fact, my reception in Bhutan was somewhat in line with the attitude of a country whose King[13] had coined the phrase

13 The 4th and current King of Bhutan, King Jigme Singye Wangchuck.

'Gross National Happiness' in 1972 when he declared, "**Gross National Happiness** is more important than **Gross Domestic Product**."

The concept implies that sustainable development should take a holistic approach towards notions of progress and give equal importance to non-economic aspects of wellbeing.

A forestry colleague of mine, David Wright, who worked in Bhutan, related an incident, which again illustrates the easy-going nature of the bureaucracy and administration in the country. About a year earlier, he had completed a supervision of a World Bank Project and a time and date were set for the wrap-up meeting to which senior forest officers would be expected to come. Dave duly turned up at the appointed hour to find that after some time only a few junior officers had appeared. On inquiring where the senior men were, he was told they had another engagement and would not be able to make it. Needless to say, he was furious and went back to the hotel to prepare for his departure the next day.

The Paro Valley where the country's airport is situated.

As he was packing his bags, probably wondering why he had even bothered to come to the country given the apparent lack of interest in the project, there was a knock on the door. There stood a few of the senior forest officers. They weren't really repentant, but they were very sorry that Dave was upset. As they explained it, there was this archery contest at some town about a day's drive away. Now, the Bhutanese are fanatical about archery, and they are always having these contests, which are taken very seriously. At each Olympic Games over the last few decades, Bhutan has always sent a two- or three-man archery team, their only athletes. I don't think they have ever won a medal, but that doesn't take away their enthusiasm. Anyway, these foresters had been to this archery contest, obviously judging that to be far more important than a World Bank Project wrap-up meeting. They then asked Dave if they could have a chat about the project over a few drinks downstairs and all ended amicably, although I think Dave was still shaking his head, wondering about Bhutanese priorities, as he boarded his plane the next morning.

From the airport to the capital, Thimphu, a drive of about forty-five minutes, I got my first taste of the Bhutanese road system. Vehicular roads were a relatively recent phenomenon in the country with the first road, linking the border town of Phuntsholing with Thimphu only being built in 1960. Before that, as one of the older local foresters informed me, people travelled from place to place by walking. For example, he would walk for more than a week from his home in central Bhutan to the border, from where he would get transport to take him to the forestry school in Nepal. It certainly made for a hardy race of people when such walking entailed climbing up and down several thousand metres as they travelled from one valley to the next.

The roads, which were bitumen, but relatively narrow, were constructed with assistance from the Indian Army, using a great deal of labour and not much machinery. Clouds of black smoke would issue from fires under large flat pans, into which bitumen was poured and mixed with gravel as it melted. The gravel was made by groups of workers hammering away at boulders, each, over time, making their own individual pile. Scores of people in a road gang could be seen carrying loads of the hot bitumen and gravel from the fires to the area to be sealed, while others were busy levelling and grading by hand. Labour was scarce in Bhutan, and most of the workers employed on the roads were Nepalese, which by the mid-eighties was adding a degree of ethnic tension between these migrant workers and the Bhutanese. The situation was exacerbated when the goats, which came in with the Nepalese, proceeded to chomp away at the local vegetation, reportedly causing some quite serious degradation.

The many twists and turns on the road to Tashigang, which is typical of how we went from one valley to the next.

Road construction was not easy, given the extremely mountainous nature of the terrain. The narrow bitumen track would wind tortuously up the sides of mountains to connect with the next valley, into which it would descend in an equally circuitous manner, sometimes as much as 2,000 metres. In places, the road was etched out of the steep valley sides with sheer drops of a few hundred metres from the road to a river far below; and there were no safety barriers to protect vehicles from plunging over the edge, making travel both hazardous and a little scary.

Following my arrival, I spent some time in and around Thimphu, staying at a small, country style hotel, named after one of the nearby peaks, Jumilhari. This enabled me to acclimatize to the altitude. My lack of conditioning wasn't that noticeable when just sitting around but walking up a hill for some distance found me very quickly out of breath. I did some jogging around town in the early mornings and climbed a nearby hill, overlooking the town, which helped to make me more acclimatized.

I was also adjusting to the local customs. At the rear of my hotel was a long flat stretch of ground, and it was here that archery contests took place on a regular basis. The Bhutanese men commonly wore their traditional dress of what looked like a short, checked dressing gown hitched up by a belt to about the knees. This covered a white long-sleeved tunic or shirt with the sleeves rolled back over the gown. On their legs were knee-high checked socks. The whole effect was somewhat mediaeval, and this effect was enhanced when they stood around the two-metre high and half-metre wide targets with their bows. They would shoot with amazing accuracy and power over about 200 metres, while some from the opposing team would stand in front of the target until the last second or two. There was also a basketball court near the archery ground, and there the King could be seen occasionally, playing with a couple of other men.

Bhutan is also famous for its brilliantly coloured stamps, and I bought a good collection of them. However, I was rather intrigued by the rather arbitrary postal rates for letters I was sending out to family and friends. While down at the western border town of Phuntsholing, I paid less to post a letter than for a similar letter posted in Thimphu. When I asked the gentleman in the post office in Thimphu why my letter to a girlfriend in Rome cost more than in Phuntsholing, he looked at me and patiently said, "But Phuntsholing is closer to Rome than Thimphu." Who could argue with that?

I had been there a month and was starting to get some thoughts together on a plantation plan, having travelled out on day trips from Thimphu. Then, a visiting FAO Forestry Director and the Bhutan Forestry Department thought I should expand my terms of reference. As well as looking at plantation potential and a plantation strategy, I was now being asked to prepare a community forestry project and make suggestions for improving government forest nurseries. With only a month to go and no extra time available I thought it was a bit of an ask to demand this sort of output in the time available. It showed a lack of comprehension of the logistics and field work required to do a reasonable job; and I said so. Some compromise was made, and it was agreed that my plantation output would be more of a strategy than a plan, but they felt I could still do the rest. I am not sure whether I should have taken this as a compliment on my abilities or just the whim of some technocrat. In any event, I determined that it was just a matter of getting stuck into it and doing the best I could, hoping that people, at a later stage, would forgive any shortcomings in the reports because of the limited time available. This is something few would do as reports usually tend to be taken in an absolute sense and judged without thought as to the time and resources available.

I decided to spend about ten days getting an overview of forestry conditions in the rest of Bhutan, and then identify the components for the community forestry project. This would involve a journey of about 2,500 kilometres, going west from Thimphu, to Tongsa in central Bhutan, and thence on to Tashigang in the far east, with a side trip from Tongsa to the southern border at Gaylegphug. The trip would take me across the middle of Bhutan, through what is referred to as the Inner Himalayas, with much of the terrain at between 2,000 and 4,000 metres altitude. I was prepared for the fact that it would not be an easy journey with several forestry and United Nations officers warning me of difficult road conditions in the east.

Landslides were quite common, and vehicles could be stranded for several days, caught between two such slips. I just had to trust that things would work out and that the senior forest officer who was to be my guide and counterpart would make the necessary logistical arrangements. That trust was to be well tested over the first few days.

We set off early one morning from the hotel in a well-used, Indian-made, Mahindra jeep. As with the Ambassador car, the Indians had been using decades old technology without much in the way of model variations to produce their basic transportation. The Mahindra was a copy of a late 1940s model Willys Jeep. It was relatively inexpensive and did the job.

Our departure was not an auspicious beginning. Having powered the jeep to the hotel, the engine now refused to start. So, we pushed our transport from the front of the hotel so that the driver could clutch start it. I wondered what would happen when we stopped somewhere on the road and wanted to get going again; and these roads only passed scattered hamlets and isolated houses, with no service stations apart from in the very few main towns. Not to be deterred, we drove off down the Thimphu Valley to the small town of Simtokha, where we turned left and proceeded to climb the range separating Thimphu Valley from the Sankosh River valley, and the town of Wandiphodrang to the east.

As with much of Bhutan that is below the tree line and above the cultivated valley bottoms, the slopes were covered with thick forest, as far as the eye could see. It was a motley variation of green, representing different tree species. I noted how the forest changed as we rose higher in altitude with variations also occurring on north versus south facing slopes. Sub-tropical wet hill forests, with broadleaved species, like Oak, Birch, Maple, Walnut and Shisham[14], occupied the lower slopes, particularly on those facing north. On the relatively drier south-facing slopes occurred more open, drier and homogenous sub-tropical pine forests dominated by Chir Pine. Above 2,000 metres more temperate-type forests appeared. The pine forests persisted, although the species changed to Blue Pine, while the other forests started to resemble those in Western Canada, with Hemlock and Spruce, often in very homogeneous stands. Above 3,000 metres and up to 4,000 metres, the vegetation changed again to more alpine forest species with great strands of moss hanging from the limbs, giving the forests a colder and more dismal look.

It was through this kaleidoscope of vegetation types that our jeep laboured, slowly winding its way up one side of a range of mountains

---

14 *Dalbergia sissoo,* sometimes called Indian Rosewood, and a valuable timber tree.

and down the other: sometimes down to a narrow gorge, at other times into a broad valley. In the latter, we would then drive through a mosaic of different coloured crops in the fields that contrasted with the green of the mountains. The scattered houses, which reminded me of farmhouses in parts of Europe, particularly Switzerland, were often quite substantial, being two stories high and built of wood. In fact, the large quantities of wood used to construct these houses, together with the collection of wood for fuel, was causing some degradation of the surrounding forests, particularly the pine forests. The lower floor of the houses was for cattle and storage, the upper floor for the family; and scattered around these houses were the ubiquitous white prayer flags, fluttering from tall poles.

Steep descent from the road to the river and road below, Central Bhutan

As we slowly made our way along the narrow mountain roads, my earlier concerns about the roadworthiness of the jeep didn't diminish and, in addition, I was worried about the exhaust fumes seeping into our cabin that we were keeping sealed because of the cold. There was obviously a leak in the exhaust system and the fumes were coming in through any one of several holes in the floor. I expressed my concern to my counterpart, not that there was much he could have done. He told me it wasn't something to worry about. This registered as another example of the easy-going nature of the Bhutanese or perhaps a certain Buddhist fatalism. Be that as it may, I was not going to be poisoned by the fumes. So, I opened the window a bit to let in some fresh cold air.

As the afternoon progressed, the rain started to come down, which brought to light another of the vehicle's defects. The windscreen wipers didn't work. One of them flailed away ineffectively, while the other just didn't move. Under normal circumstances this would have made driving in the rain difficult. However, we now found ourselves in fog or low cloud so that the combination of this and the rain brought visibility down to just a few metres. In deference to this the driver did slow down. But I was still very concerned about the fact that we were driving along this narrow road, on one side of which was an almost sheer fall of about 200 metres to the river below, and there was very little, if any protective structure, like a wall to keep us from plunging over the edge. I decided I might as well be very Buddhist, and so I resigned myself to whatever my fate might be. The only alternative was to stop and wait for better conditions, which could take some time. If we were going to go over, then so be it and there was no sense in getting all riled up about it, but I did keep a sharp eye on what road I could see.

Passing a yak in the fog as we headed for another mountain pass.

Eventually, the rain stopped, and the fog lifted as night came down, with us still slowly wending our way around the mountains with not another vehicle or person in sight. It had been a long and uncomfortable day and I was glad when the lights of Tongsa finally appeared a short distance ahead as we came around a bend in the road. Then we ran out of petrol! My Bhutanese counterpart was dumbfounded. This had never happened before. Perhaps it was the extra weight of a foreigner on board.

I asked if they just might happen to be carrying a jerry can or two of fuel, something that I thought might be a natural thing to do along such a road with service stations being extremely rare. The answer was, "No, because we haven't had this problem before."

There was no point in arguing about common sense and being prepared. Perhaps that wasn't the Bhutanese way. In fact, it probably was a Buddhist trait. One's fate or karma was set and that was that and practicalities to overcome such a fate were not to be countenanced. So, there we sat on the road, about two kilometres short of our destination while a couple of the forest technicians we had with us went to find enough petrol to enable us to drive into town.

My counterpart and I spent the night in a guesthouse, which the next morning, provided me with a spectacular view overlooking the town at the head of a steep-sided green clothed valley. Just below our guesthouse was the massive, white-walled and red-roofed Tongsa Dzong that originally served as a fortress to guard the valley as well as being a monastery. The original building dated from 1543, but it had subsequently been enlarged in the middle of the seventeenth century. Like so many of the dzongs in the country, its walls were masonry surmounted by an untidy superstructure of wooden buildings, which gave the appearance they were haphazardly constructed afterthoughts.

Our guesthouse was unpretentious, but adequate. However, it was a frigid start to the day when I awoke just after dawn to a heavy frost outside, no heat in the room, and no hot water with which to wash. I had a bath using a dipper to pour the water over me, which was so cold my head ached, but at least I had the satisfaction of feeling clean, as well as somewhat invigorated. The cold nights at these high altitudes meant I was glad of a couple of woollen sweaters I'd bought, though these would usually be discarded as the sun warmed the air.

As we filled up with fuel at the local petrol station, I saw how the Bhutanese dealt with the problem of diesel turning to wax with the cold as it was apt to do in those climes. They lit a fire under the engine. I imagine with practice one could judge how big a fire to construct and how much heat to apply before parts of the engine went up in smoke. As with so many situations in less developed countries, a lack of amenities and necessity meant that more risks are taken to get the job done than in the almost risk phobic atmosphere of developed countries.

Our plan was to drive south to Gaylegphug, on the Indian border, that day, and off we set, wondering what adventures the day would bring. I found it easy to be optimistic with the sun shining through the clear, chilly mountain air.

About an hour down the road, the smell of petrol became overwhelming. It could only mean fuel was leaking over the engine. Not a good situation. So, we stopped to investigate and found the carburettor gasket was worn through. My impatience was becoming obvious, and my beleaguered counterpart felt the need to explain in some detail how the vehicle had only just had a major service and overhaul costing a packet. Well, I suggested some repayment or free service by the servicing station was in order because that gasket was in dreadful shape.

Enjoying some local liquor at a wayside rest house and bar.

But there was no point in being nasty. We had a problem with our only means of transport and, glancing around the landscape it was obvious there was no other help available. We were in the middle of nowhere, surrounded only by mountains and sheep. It was picture postcard scenery, but not the best place to be caught with a faulty engine. I managed to find a soft plastic holder for cutlery from one of my flights to Bhutan, and with my Swiss Army knife I fashioned a makeshift gasket.

That did the trick and saw us once more comfortably motoring along the narrow road. That is, until a few kilometres later, a loud bang announced that we had blown a tire. On inspection I could see why it just popped. It was beyond bald. The spare wasn't much better, and my opinion of Bhutanese preparedness for long road journeys went to a new low. There was nothing for it but to change the tire and press on, though we now had no spare tire to replace any of the rather suspect tires on the vehicle. My only solace was that habitation was sparse and there weren't many nails used for building construction.

By early afternoon I noticed that the engine was running rather rough, and we seemed to have very little power. This time, when we stopped to check under the bonnet, it was the timing. Somewhere along the road someone had switched the distributor leads around and the engine was having a tough time trying to figure out the order in which the cylinders were supposed to fire. I also suspected there were other problems with the engine, which added to its lack of power, given the generally debilitated nature of the vehicle. All this was sending my Bhutanese forester companion into an even deeper depression with more wringing of hands and exclamations about how this just couldn't be happening.

*Our Mahindra Jeep with the bonnet up once again
for repairs.*

We managed to chug along, into the afternoon, up and down a few more well-treed hills and valleys, until, heading up a rather steep hill to a town about halfway to Gaylegphug, the engine just wouldn't cooperate. It was late in the day by this point, and, with the mechanical difficulties along the way from Tongsa, we weren't going to make it to Gaylegphug that day anyway. So, we left the jeep in the care of the driver and set off, up a steep walking track through the trees, to cover the remaining few kilometres to the town, where we checked into a local rest house for the night.

As we were having a meal with a Buddhist monk and a police officer that evening, the driver walked in to inform us that he and the jeep had arrived and that he thought the problem had been fixed. I didn't quite know what that meant, though, I wasn't really assured as, by now, I didn't have much faith in the technical capability of the Forestry Department staff or its drivers. So, we arranged with the police officer, who was also on his way to Gaylegphug, to follow us the next day, just in case.

It was a good thing we'd made this arrangement for after we had coasted down the steep hillside from the town where we spent the night and were labouring up hill on the other side of the river, the engine just stopped and so did the jeep. It seemed as if it was all too much for the old vehicle and the pistons had seized. So, that was that. I find I often get quite philosophical about situations like this. I wasn't worried about deadlines and data and how I was going to put it all together, despite the short amount of time. In fact, standing there in the warm sunshine in such a scenic, forested wilderness, it was difficult to get stirred up about it all, and so it was easy to enjoy the moment, particularly as there wasn't anything more one could do. Perhaps, I was adopting some of the Bhutanese Buddhist philosophy on life.

Some fifteen minutes later the police officer's jeep came up behind us, laden with several, smiling, saffron-suited monks. We managed to squeeze in and there was more room when the monks got out at a dzong along the way. And so, we made it to Gaylegphug a day late and without a vehicle. My counterpart then made an executive decision. He contacted Thimphu and arranged for a much more modern Toyota Landcruiser to take us on to Tashigang in the east.

It arrived late the next day and it was a good thing we had this more reliable vehicle as the road east from Tongsa, was, in places, worse than anything we had been on. I felt as if I was riding a bucking horse as I gripped the hand bar in the front of the cab while we bounced over rough dirt roads for hundreds of kilometres.

It was a fascinating landscape, and I felt very fortunate, as I have often felt in my job, that I had been able to make such a journey and experience such a country, where relatively few other foreigners had been. The forest-covered mountains gave way to drier grass-covered slopes as we drove further east, where the rainfall was much decreased. Some of these grasslands contained lemon grass, a species of the genus *Cymbopogon* and an important source of an essential oil used as a pesticide and preservative, while the grass itself is used in Asian cooking. Iron retorts, for distillation of the oil could be seen scattered along the way.

One night was spent in a dzong. It was a fascinating, almost medieval experience to actually spend some time inside a building that was hundreds of years old and had probably changed little in that time to the present. Although the dzong was an administrative centre and fortress in the past, it was still a spiritual place, which was accentuated by the presence of numerous monks and the pervading scent of incense burning. I had visited Buddhist temples and monasteries before and there was usually this air of mysticism about such places, which was enhanced by the ever present aromas of joss sticks, while benign and ancient Buddhas gazed down on us beings, who were still struggling to make it to Nirvana.

Our replacement Landcruiser being refuelled on the road from Tongsa east to Tashigang.

On this occasion, we confined ourselves to the dormitory and ablutions block, which we shared with several other travellers. The dormitory was a rather dark, high - ceilinged affair, where some half a dozen low beds, covered in blankets of dubious cleanliness, were arranged against each of two opposite walls. With hotels or guest houses few and far between outside of the main towns in the country, the dzongs offered travellers some form of shelter, warmth, and food for the night.

These dzongs were often massive and imposing structures that dominated all other buildings in the landscape, sometimes clinging to the sides of steep mountains to gain solitude and the most advantageous spiritual aspect. Apart from stone foundations and outer walls, they are made entirely of wood and the amount of wood used was prodigious. One fascinating thing about the dzong construction was that no nails were used. The wooden beams were joined using dowels and trunnels, and expertly worked interconnecting joints. Even the heavy wooden doors, like the one to our dormitory, swung on wooden pivots.

A dzong like one in which we spent a night in Eastern Bhutan

That night we had dinner in the house of a woman who worked in some way with the Forestry Department. On arrival, we were shown into a very small living room, into which had been stuffed a low table, a settee and two chairs, while the otherwise bare walls were decorated with pictures cut from magazines depicting cities and rural landscapes from faraway and exotic countries in Europe and North America. I felt quite special to have been invited with my counterpart and wished I had some gift from home to give the lady for the kindness and hospitality she was showing to us.

Our hostess did stay and talk for a while, but after she had served the meal, we were left to eat it on our own, because according to local custom, as a woman, it was not her place to eat with us. I have experienced this same custom in other South Asian houses, though not all, where the wife of my host would arrange and serve the meal, but not stay to eat. I didn't question the custom at the time but found it somewhat awkward in light of our own customs and couldn't help feeling how discriminatory it was, particularly as, in this case, she was our hostess and there was no host.

We made it through to Tashigang District without further mishaps. The semi-arid conditions there contrasted with the green clad mountains I had seen over much of the rest of the country. The mountains were still present, though lower in height, and only scattered trees and scrub covered much of the yellow-brown slopes. After two days in the district, it was time to retrace our steps back to Thimphu and for me to put my observations and ideas together on paper.

142

Having seen what I had, limited though it was, I managed to nominate several sites for a community forestry programme, dream up a plantation strategy and even offer some thoughts on improving nursery production. I then spent the last few days back in Thimphu furiously writing it all up into respectable reports. There was certainly room to spend more time understanding how forestry was operating and the current and potential links with villagers, but not on this visit.

This less-than-optimal approach to development, where bureaucracy and funding restrictions lead to poorly thought out and, sometimes, inappropriate projects and use of project funds I found frustrating. After I had been in the international development forestry business for some years, I felt that somehow or other, I had to make something of a positive impact on each job to make it feel worthwhile from my perspective. This didn't mean submitting a thick report that might not lead to much actual development. No, I felt that I had to make an impact on the ground then and there or give recommendations that would definitely lead to positive outcomes in the future. The impact did not have to be big, just sufficient to give me the satisfaction of actually achieving something for the people and forests in these countries.

Talking to villagers about improving nursery practices.

I don't know to what extent the reports I wrote on this trip had a direct impact on future community forestry or plantation programmes that did eventuate. Perhaps someone did take some pearls of wisdom from this and my other reports. However, I do know I made a positive impact in one small way.

I visited a nursery, near Thimphu, as part of my efforts at improving nursery technology and management. The nursery manager and his assistant, together with six or eight local men sat on the ground, amongst the poly pots with seedlings, with me to hear what I had to say. We examined how they were preparing seedlings, the type of potting mix, how long they kept the seedlings in the nursery and their condition when they were transplanted out. I made several observations about improving the potting mix and ensuring that vigorous seedlings were ready on time for planting.

The men all sat and listened intently with few expressions except the occasional nodding as points were translated. I left with many offers of thanks and largely forgot the experience. However, on my next visit several months later, I happened to visit the same area and learnt that the nursery had adopted my suggestions and that their young, planted seedlings were thriving, compared to indifferent survival and growth previously. It was just a small impact, but a positive and very satisfying one.

The Bhutanese seemed to like my reports while, back in Rome, the FAO Forestry Department thought it was a good effort. I was then asked to go back to Bhutan later in 1985 for a further FAO forestry mission, but this time with a team and covering a more limited area for forest management. There were more road trips, but with more reliable vehicles, as we studied insect attacks on the pines and viewed leach-infested wet sub-tropical hill forests, where the little parasites would wait for you on the rain-soaked leaves. Since then, I have thought fondly of the country, hoping I could return for another visit, though I understand from more recent travellers that some of that serendipitous nature has gone in the move to a more western approach to life, business, tourism, and government. In some ways it is a pity that such is the price of progress and development.

The World Bank and
Washington D.C.

By 1986, the World Bank and I had become well acquainted after quite a few consultancies for the organization, and I was on good terms with several staff. This was helped by the camaraderie induced through the consumption of the odd bottle of single malt whisky or local beer, as we discussed projects and other less serious matters in several African countries' hotel rooms, sometimes late into the night.

In May of 1986, I had a phone call from one of the Bank foresters, Michel Grut. I was in Vietnam at the time, endeavouring to put together a forestry development plan for the country, under the auspices of the United Nations Development Plan. Michel asked me if I was interested in joining the Bank as a wood fuels expert. I was quite taken aback and flattered to be asked. Still, I hesitated and said I would think about it. It seems a bit crazy after I had been offered a lucrative job in such a prestigious institution to say, "I would think about it." However, having worked as a consultant with the Bank for some years, I had got to know it as an institution, and there were an awful lot of procedures and bureaucracy that weren't my cup of tea. So, I spent a couple of months considering it.

In the meantime, I was contracted by the Bank to assist on an appraisal mission for a forestry project in Uganda in mid-1986. It was a difficult assignment in a country that had just emerged from a civil war, with gunfire still being heard at night in Kampala as remnant opposition to the new government of Yoweri Museveni continued to be mopped up. After a couple of weeks in the field and three weeks in the country trying to come to grips with the forestry situation and the issues involved, I was struggling to put together six meaningful components. Eventually, I did manage to design something reasonable, which then went on to form part of a project that I later spent some years supervising as project manager for the Bank.

Meanwhile, the Energy Sector Management Assistance Project (ESMAP) in the Bank, who had asked for my services, got in touch and suggested, as I was procrastinating about joining them, that I come along on a six-month consultancy to help out on a couple of projects, so I could get the feel of working more closely with them. I agreed to that and in September of 1986 found myself in the company of three World Bank staff on a KLM DC10 flying to Sudan, another rather different country and forest situation.

Walking out of the Khartoum Hilton felt like opening an oven door, as the searing hot and dry air hit me. It was over 40 degrees Celsius, and I had been warned that although you don't seem to sweat, as the air is so dry, you need to keep drinking water or suffer from dehydration. And that is the way it was as a small group of us, including a Norwegian Sociologist, Turi Hammer, and Peter Dewees, an American Forest Economist, drove from Khartoum south, through a landscape of alternating low Acacia woodlands, ploughed farmland, and barren desert-like conditions.

We travelled for hundreds of kilometres through such conditions to familiarize ourselves with the forestry situation and the remedial actions the Sudanese were proposing to have the Bank finance. What sort of forestry project this was going to be had me intrigued. The woodlands contained mainly scattered Acacias and Mesquite and then there were a lot of desert-like areas devoid of vegetation.

It was a difficult three weeks in that country, where a recent coup had put an Islamic fundamentalist regime in power, and as a result, life was even more difficult for all concerned. This was exemplified when one of their first acts was to shut down the only local brewery and tip all the beer stocks into the Blue Nile. Did they even consider what that would do to the fish? However, alcohol was not totally absent as we found when we attended a get-together with our Sudanese forestry counterparts. We were served with araqi, a fiery liquor made from dates; and to help with any hangovers there was raw camel's liver; a real treat. On the other hand, the KGB (Khartoum Guild of Brewers) provided us with some home-made cold beer after a late afternoon Hash House Harriers run. It was my one and only hash run, and it felt somewhat weird as a bunch of us foreigners ran through stunted scrub in 40 degree heat, late in the afternoon, following the paper trail and the cries of, "On, on", as local villagers stared at us in bewilderment.

I was back in Sudan in December of 1986 for an appraisal of the forestry project there. At that point I decided that I could indeed join the World Bank and told the project manager of my decision. I felt that if I could stay on an upward learning curve it should be a worthwhile experience and I would cope with the procedures and bureaucracy along the way. Having made the decision, I was quite excited about taking up my position and getting involved with the work that I had already started. So, I moved to the Washington D.C. area in January of 1987. In hindsight it was not the best decision for keeping as close to my sons as they and I would like, although, subsequently, over time, we have maintained a close and growing relationship.

Some of our mission chatting to firewood sellers on our field trip. Firewood was a scarce and valuable commodity

The World Bank was formed in 1944 at the Bretton Woods Conference (United Nations Monetary and Financial Conference), which was held at the Mount Washington Hotel, in Bretton Woods, New Hampshire. The conference and the concepts discussed owed much to the forward thinking of two luminaries of their time: the economist, John Maynard Keynes, and the senior US Treasury official, Harry Dexter White.

Initially, the World Bank was known as the International Bank for Reconstruction and Development (IBRD) and its main aim was the provision of loans to help rebuild countries in Europe devastated by World War II. By the 1950s, the Bank became more involved with reconstruction and development in the more needy nations worldwide, with a heavy emphasis on infrastructure. From there it expanded to its more recent status as the principal lender to numerous developing countries, with its current focus on poverty reduction and promoting prosperity in a sustainable way. It is responsible to some 180 member countries' shareholders via a Board of Governors.

When I joined the Bank in 1986 it had a lending programme for thousands of projects worth some $20 billion. It was also a time when the Bank's policy and focus in relation to forestry was changing. There was an increasing emphasis on people and poverty, as well as the rapidly changing landscape with regard to community involvement in forest management and recognition of the effectiveness of this participatory approach. In addition, there was an increasing concern for the environment, following on from the 1992 Rio Earth Summit[15]. As a result, the Bank's policy moved from forest management for largely exploitative purposes to one that considered people's participation and poverty reduction, as well as the environment to a much greater degree.

It was a sign of the times, as I had been discovering through my work with forests and communities involved with forests. A much broader, multiple use approach to forest management was necessary. This wasn't always easy for traditional foresters who, through their training and experience, had a mindset that considered they were the forest managers and that forests were primarily for wood exploitation, albeit on a sustainable basis. I was fortunate to have gained some experience with the other side of forest management, looking at wood as a fuel and the role of communities in growing this wood in what was initially referred to as social forestry, then subsequently, farm forestry. Some of my colleagues in Forestal/Sandwell had referred to my involvement with this as "Mickey Mouse forestry", reflecting the traditional foresters' thinking.

Given the prestige of the World Bank, it was with a certain amount of awe and apprehension that I arrived at the Bank in Washington D.C. on a chilly January day in 1987 to take up my post. I would be rubbing shoulders with eminent professionals, who were designing and managing multi-million-dollar projects, and I hoped I was going to measure up to the task ahead. My responsibility involved looking at the energy situation in countries, particularly as it applied to households and small industries, with particular reference to wood fuels. It was certainly a learning experience with economics often playing a key role. Luckily, my colleagues were a friendly and helpful bunch.

I had met Chris, who also worked for the Bank, while on the mission to Uganda and our relationship had deepened over the months, with trips to Washington for the World Bank. When I moved to Washington, we agreed to share a condominium in Bethesda, not far outside the District of Columbia (DC) line, and just up from the Potomac River and the canal that ran along the south side of the river.

It was a wonderful experience to be living and working in and around Washington, the capital of the most powerful and influential nation in the world. The World Bank complex was two blocks from the White House, and I would occasionally pass by on the way to the Mall or some

---

15 United Nations Conference on Environment and Development (UNCED), Rio de Janeiro, 3-14 June 1992.

of the shops further east. My lunch time running routes would take me alternatively around the Lincoln and Jefferson memorials, or over the bridge to the Pentagon and down along the banks of the Potomac, which in April were pink with cherry blossoms.

Fascinating though the city was and as comfortable as I felt living in Bethesda, there was something about America that inhibited me from really calling it "home". Perhaps it was the gun violence and nonsensical lack of control on firearms. Almost every day there was a report of gun-related homicides. A lot of this was related to drugs and violence in the eastern part of DC, where virtually ghetto-like conditions and poverty existed, within a mile of the Congress. It was a city with incredible wealth represented by enormous houses, although down the road there was real poverty and hardship with slums.

Tanzania

After my first visit to Sudan in September 1986, I flew down on a KLM DC10 to Tanzania. The relatively modern, though compact, airport terminal on the outskirts of Dar es Salaam seemed at odds with what I had heard of this economic basket case of a country. And so, it was. The reality would be encountered as I emerged, after passing unscathed through immigration and customs, to be accosted by men urging me to take their taxi. Not knowing what the local setup was, I played it safe and made sure that the dilapidated Peugeot into whose boot some fellow was loading my suitcase at least had a taxi sign on it.

I climbed into the back seat and nearly went through the cushions to the floor. After pulling the door shut, I tried to wind down the windows as the air was warm and sticky, then found there were no handles on either door. The driver, meanwhile, was coaching the vehicle's engine, which sounded decidedly sick, to keep going as we motored out through the airport gates. He saw my plight and reaching over, yanked a handle off the front door and handed it over to me with a big grin. From that trip on, over several years, I would use the condition of the Dar taxis as an indicator of economic progress in Tanzania.

The visit to Tanzania was to identify for funding by the World Bank, a forestry project to improve the supply of wood fuels to the urban areas. From what I had heard about Tanzania, the impression was of a country suffering economically and socially. It was just starting to awaken from the economic malaise, which had resulted from President Julius Nyerere's socialist policies that were fostered by the Swedish Government. Amenities were, reportedly, very basic, infrastructure in a state of disrepair and consumables being scarce. I wasn't expecting a comfortable stay, particularly when one of my forestry friends in the Bank told me how he had to take in his own light bulbs, soap, and toilet paper, while staying at the best hotel in Dar es Salaam. So, I was mentally as well as physically prepared for just about anything.

The flight from Khartoum arrived at night and, as my taxi motored through Dar town and the harbour area, the initial sight of the Kilimanjaro Hotel, overlooking the harbour, was quite impressive. At least the power was on, and there were plenty of bulbs to light up the outside of the hotel, so things didn't look too bad.

Conditions apparently had been worse, but my stay in the 'Kili' was not a pleasant experience. After being shown to my room, down a wide but dingy corridor with a tattered and dirty wall to wall carpet that had once been red, I prepared to get some rest. However, the springs on the bed were so bad and the mattress so thin that I put it on the floor to get some firmness. It was then necessary to sprinkle cologne on the carpet adjacent to the mattress. This was to counter the stink from the floor of what appeared to arise from mould and urine and other undefinable decaying substances ingrained in the once red, but now mottled, floor covering.

The beds and other amenities in the room were improved over the succeeding three to four years, like another barometer indicating improved economic conditions in the country as a whole. However, some aspects didn't change a great deal and it was something of a lottery as to what might go wrong on each stay. The water in the bathroom would disappear, and then come back on so muddy that it was almost useless for washing. The air conditioner was uncontrollable and would often pump freezing air into the room, which I endeavoured to control by unscrewing the outlet grate and stuffing paper or cardboard behind. Alternatively, I'd resort to wearing a sweater, to bed. On other occasions it would fail completely, which meant I sweltered in an airless room, because opening the door to the balcony let in squadrons of whining mosquitoes.

Over the next couple of days, I started to get a feel for how the government operated by visiting the Headquarters of the Forests and Beekeeping Division. This consisted of a series of ill-kempt and overcrowded offices on two floors above a branch of the National Bank of Tanzania. It wasn't an environment conducive to deep thought and hard work and, partially as a result of that, and the appallingly low salaries, it appeared that very little of either took place there.

Dar es Salaam, which had an attractive setting by the harbour and the sea, didn't seem to have changed much in the last half century. There were only one or two more modern-looking high-rise structures, and most buildings could have done with some maintenance and a touch of paint. The roads had more potholes than bitumen on many stretches, with some of the holes a serious hazard, containing water up to half a metre deep during the rainy season.

After some preliminary discussions in Dar on what might constitute a future project, my consulting colleague and I, naturally felt we had to get out and see the situation in the field. This colleague was a rather opinionated French Canadian, but despite his strong thoughts on a variety of subjects, we managed to get along well enough over the next few weeks. For the field trip we needed a good four-wheel drive vehicle and a forester who knew what was going on out in the bush. The latter was easier to find than the former. The United Nations Development Programme (UNDP), that was helping with our logistics, had managed to reach an arrangement with the only vehicle hire agency around, apart from the government Tanzanian Tourist Corporation (TCC). I drove out to the agency, located in one of the shanty town areas of Dar, not exactly a prime business location.

The only vehicle available to take us on our 4,000 kilometre safari around remote areas of Tanzania left much to be desired. Parked on the dirt apron of the agency's tin shed of an office, surrounded by an assortment of tin and wood shacks, was an old Land Rover 109 with red curtains in the back windows. Although I knew I was unlikely to get an honest answer, I checked with the owner of the company that the vehicle was in good running condition and that it had at least two good spare tires.

"Yes, yes. No problem," he stated quite emphatically as he assured me the vehicle was in good shape and could handle the trip up to Mwanza, on Lake Victoria, and then back. I had no idea about the road conditions, but I envisaged that they would not be good.

On the day of our departure, it had been arranged that the vehicle would pick us up at the hotel relatively early in the morning so that we could get a good start. So, I started to get a bad feeling when it hadn't turned up by lunchtime. It was useless trying to phone the agency as the phone system rarely connected to anyone. I sent someone off to find out what was going on, while we waited in case the vehicle turned up, and decided to have a bite of lunch in the meantime in the rather grotty restaurant of the hotel. The message came back that they were trying to get petrol. This sounded like either very poor organization or the explanation offered to us while the manager's wife borrowed the vehicle to go shopping. By the time the Land Rover arrived, in mid-afternoon, there were a few more excuses thrown in after I had vented my frustration, but I counted it as a plus that at least we were on our way.

That feeling of satisfaction didn't last for long. We were taking in the woodland scenery about an hour west on the road to Morogoro when the engine spluttered to a stop. Out jumped the driver, up went the hood, and off came the fuel line to the carburettor. This was obviously not a new problem, and I had a gut feeling we had been ripped off and could well experience the equivalent of being up the creek without a paddle. The driver managed to get the motor restarted after he sucked petrol up through the fuel line into his mouth to ensure there was a good flow, then reconnected the line before too much fuel spilled over the hot engine. Luckily no one was smoking.

Given our late departure, we had decided before we left Dar that there was no way we would meet our first day's schedule and travel to Dodoma, a journey of four to five hours on a reasonable bitumen road. I was reluctant to drive after dark because of bandits and the irresponsible and crazy way many of the locals drove. Seat belts were not common, and our vehicle had none, so, there was a high risk of serious mishap. In any event, with the way things were going for us on this trip we would be lucky to make Morogoro by dark.

We did manage that and spent a comfortable night at the Bush Trekker Hotel, which seemed to have been built to imitate a Masai encampment. There was one large rondavel housing the reception, bar, meeting rooms, and dining room, while a series of smaller ones served as rooms. It was a novel idea, but there were few guests with only two other tables being occupied in the large, high-ceilinged dining room that could have been quite stunning, but had a rather forlorn air about it. Although attempts had been made to maintain the place, it was going backwards and suffering from neglect, on the part of both management and patrons.

The next morning, after a quick visit to the regional forestry office, we set out for Dodoma. Morogoro is overshadowed by the 500 metre high rocky mass of the Uluguru Mountains that form part of the Eastern Arc Mountains of Tanzania. The town is spread out at the base of these mountains and is an important administrative and commercial centre, but dusty and uninviting, and we didn't linger.

Miombo Woodlands as seen through much of southern and eastern Africa. Wood being piled for charcoal production.

The road from Dar to Morogoro and on to Dodoma was bitumen and in reasonable shape, running first through villages, fields, and small towns as we moved into the interior. After some time, the woodlands became more dominant. These were the Miombo Woodlands, named after the vernacular name for the tree *Brachystegia,* which, together with *Julbernardia,* were dominant species among the short-stemmed trees, topped by light green foliage. The undergrowth was light, often because of periodic fires that left their charred signatures on the trees' dark grey, rough-barked trunks.

Not long after leaving Morogoro, as the day warmed with a cloudless sky from a cool early morning, we started to climb the escarpment of the east African highlands, through woodlands. Once on the escarpment, although woodlands were still present, scrub, thickets and grasslands were more predominant and their parched and dusty appearance signalled that we were arriving in the driest area of the country.

Approaching Dodoma we passed a gold mining site, set up in scrubby bushland, where individual miners had sunk vertical shafts, some ten metres deep into the red lateritic soil. The numerous deep holes, about a metre in diameter, were closely spaced, but with no notice or protection to prevent someone from taking a nasty tumble down a shaft as they walked unknowingly through the scrub. This local gold mining was a risky business, not only from the danger of falling down shafts and cave-ins, but also from the liberal and uncontrolled use of mercury to extract the gold. Many of the miners had suffered seriously from mercury poisoning; but, this hard, high risk and relatively low return occupation, with no compensation for injury or death was necessary to provide some sort of a livelihood for the miners' families.

Gold mining site near Dodoma with unmarked vertical shafts a danger for the unwary.

Our reception by the forestry people in Dodoma was a bit frosty as we were a day late and they hadn't been informed of our delays. This was something that our counterpart from the Forestry and Beekeeping Division in Dar should have taken care of, but, as I quickly learnt, one could not rely on anyone else to organize logistics. I would often have to make accommodation and travel arrangements for my Tanzanian forestry counterparts in addition to organizing the logistics for myself and my team. This proved to be an interesting experience, particularly as I had no knowledge of accommodation or conditions out of Dar. They were a nice group of friendly people at the Forestry and Beekeeping Division, but there was a serious deficit in the drive and initiative department, as well as in their organizational skills.

Dodoma had the appearance of a frontier town, a collection of low-storied houses, surrounded by low dull green *Acacia-Combretum* scrub and Miombo woodlands. It was intersected by red earth roads whose dust rose with each passing vehicle to drift onto all exposed surfaces and sifted through the windows and cracks into buildings, where it lay as fine, gritty powder on furniture, files, and floors. The town was the proposed national capital and the only half logical reason was because it is roughly in the centre of the country. There was nothing else to recommend it. It was not only in the driest part of the country, but it also lacked adequate water, and, apart from a few decrepit guesthouses, there was only the old Railway Hotel for accommodation.

Over the years since 1986, efforts had been made to improve the infrastructure and accommodation in the town, with parliament having token sittings a few times a year by the mid-nineties. But in 1986, the town was seen for what it was: a road and rail town on the way from the coast to Lake Victoria and a regional administrative centre. It was also where the bitumen road stopped. From here westwards to Lake Victoria and Mwanza, a distance of 700 kilometres, our journey lay over poorly maintained dirt roads, and when I say 'dirt' they were just that and were not gravelled. Of course, I didn't know the state of the roads, but from what I had heard it was going to be a difficult task, particularly given the poor state of our vehicle. We had suffered more fuel starvation problems from Morogoro to Dodoma, and this was compounded by the inability of the engine to generate adequate power for some reason.

There was no choice, though, if we were to get the job done. So, after spending a day and a half in and around Dodoma, including some trips into the bush to get a feeling for the local forestry scene, we started out for Singida, some 230 kilometres to the North West. Having set out mid-morning to have plenty of time for the trip, I had underestimated the problems with our vehicle, and the journey took over 10 hours, with a short break for lunch at a lonely railway siding called Manyoni. This was a depressing place, where we managed to get some tough chicken with rice in a rather dirty and rundown 'restaurant' next to the rail line.

The fuel starvation problem continued to halt our progress every so often, and I was getting worried about the condition of the driver's mouth, respiratory system, and stomach from sucking so much petrol through the fuel lines. After two flat tires we had used up both our spares, and there were no service stations along the way. Then the radiator boiled over. It had developed a leak during our journey, or possibly, even before that. With a lot of stopping and refilling, we managed to make it through to Singida well after the sun set.

The Manyoni Hotel and eating establishment where we had lunch.

In Singida, tired, hungry, and fed up, we drove around until we found a guest house that looked half acceptable. Well, half acceptable was being kind. It consisted of several rooms around a central concrete courtyard, a not uncommon design for guesthouses in Tanzania. The rooms were really nothing more than boxes with a bed, and there was not much space to spare around the bed.

As was usual in such establishments, the sheets seemed to be changed on a weekly, fortnightly or, perhaps, monthly basis, no matter how many guests had occupied the room. However, being so tired, I was content to just have a bed on which I could lie. I did put my shirt from that day over the pillow, reasoning that the smell of my sweat was fresher and better than that of the previous occupants on the pillow.

The bathrooms and toilets were communal, at one end of the concrete courtyard. Using them was not a pleasant experience, particularly the squat toilets, which would have been easy to find on a pitch black, moonless night by just following my nose.

No running water was available for either flushing or washing, but a bucket gave enough for a dip bath and there was a bucket of water and dipper to flush the toilet. It all meant one didn't dawdle over one's toilet.

By ten a.m. the next day we were ready for the road again, with the radiator fixed and the tire tubes patched. It was a bright, clear, sunny day and after a night's rest, we were off to a fresh start and I had a positive attitude, despite our troubles to date.

It was later than we had wanted to leave, but by this time I was resigned to the quirks of our Land Rover and the need to compensate for them.

Attaching one of the balding spare tires on our luckless Land Rover at the town of Igunga in Western Tanzania with our sociologist Idris Kikula

The landscape was now much more open, with large tracts of grassland and then low-lying swampy areas, as we came down onto the flats of the Wambere River system. This river flows from higher country to both the north and the south, and then goes nowhere but into the ground. Before lunch we had two more punctured tires, which again left us without a spare. By this time, I had figured out that the punctures were due to a combination of the rough roads we were bouncing over and the fact that the tubes for the tires had already been patched numerous times.

In fact, when we stopped for lunch in the rather uninspiring town of Igunga and endeavoured to have our punctures repaired, there were so many holes in each tube, that the tire chap ran out of patches. This wasn't the work of the odd nail or sharp stone, but rather balding tires and lousy tubes. So, we headed out on the 90 kilometre stretch from Igunga to Nzega with only one spare.

We had hopes earlier of reaching Shinyanga a further 80 odd kilometres towards Lake Victoria, but this wasn't to be. Another puncture mid-way to Nzega left us without a spare tire and then, about six kilometres short of Nzega, in the middle of scrub and low woodlands, we had another flat. There wasn't much traffic on the road, and, with the sun getting low on the horizon, I decided it might be good to set out walking. I had got my bag down and was preparing to start when someone came up with a brilliant idea. Why not hail a passing truck and use his compressor to blow up the tire that had been partially fixed? Hopefully, the leak would be small enough to allow us to drive to town before the tire became too flat. It worked!

We pulled up outside the Four Corners Guesthouse, with still enough air in the tire for the driver to get the Land Rover over to a service station opposite.

Nzega wasn't discernible from the *Acacia-Combretum* scrub and large granite boulders that covered the undulating landscape until we were approaching the first concrete and mud houses on the outskirts. It was a crossroads town, where four corrugated, potholed, and dusty roads met, connecting Mwanza, Burundi, Tabora, and Dar es Salaam. The town was a motley collection of houses and shops with a central market cum bus terminus and nobody had thought or done much about landscaping or painting.

There were two guesthouses, and in both, the accommodation was far from salubrious, as I found then and on several future occasions in the nineties. The rooms were again located around a central courtyard in which there was a well from where somewhat murky, grey water was drawn.

Even ten years later Nzega still did not have a reticulated water supply, though there was a dam with adequate water located only a few kilometres out of town. The problem was getting funds for pipes and pumping.

Driving through Acacia-Combretum Scrub in Western Tanzania between Igunga and Nzega.

The Four Corners Guesthouse had en suite bathrooms, though. If one could call them bathrooms. There was a squat toilet, which emitted an unpleasant odour, the result of insufficient flushing. The water for this, and for washing, was provided in a bucket from the well, and one could even get a bucket of hot water in the morning. I didn't dwell on how many people had slept on the bed since the linen was last changed. At least we had made it this far and I just put a towel over the pillow and slept reasonably well.

The next morning, after a breakfast of chapattis and greasy fried eggs, I checked with the driver, suggesting he buy a new tube or two, given the state of the tubes I had seen. However, he told me he had almost run out of the money his boss had given him. At this point I was totally fed up with the hire company and its owner. I couldn't blame the driver, who had done a sterling job under trying circumstances, and without decent equipment and the necessary financial or material resources. To hell with it! I decided we needed a couple of new tubes, so I would buy them. This greatly reduced our puncture problem, although the fuel starvation persisted and, on top of that, the rough roads had damaged the right rear shock absorber, while the engine continued to have a problem with achieving sufficient power.

Our drinking water supply was also disappearing at a rapid rate. I had decided, before leaving Dar that we should bring along bottled water, together with some emergency food supplies, in case we got caught out somewhere along the road. The water was hard to find in the one or two shops that looked likely to sell such an item, and I think I bought out the last of the bottled water in Dar, till the next boat. The hot and dusty weather meant that the water was welcome. However, the bumpy roads took their toll on the plastic bottles packed in cardboard boxes and every time we unloaded the gear at the end of the day, a few more bottles were seen to have cracked and leaked their valuable liquid. It meant a certain amount of rationing until we got to Mwanza, as there was no source of decent drinking water in the towns we passed through.

We made it to Shinyanga with only one puncture and spent a couple of days there. It is a regional administrative headquarters town situated on a flat, dry and, for most of the year, dusty plain, covered in scattered acacia trees and thickets. I held talks with local forestry officers, and we drove to several sites in the surrounding scrub and woodlands, with a particular eye to fuelwood resources.

Then it was off on the last leg of our journey to Mwanza, on Lake Victoria. I felt a bit like Burton and Speke who had also come this way and were anxious for a look at the lake that was reported to be the source of the Nile. I imagined them walking through the Acacia scrub and Miombo woodlands with a long line of porters stretched out behind, wondering what might be over the next ridge.

The state of the roads we endured in Western Tanzania. Sometimes it was easier to drive off the road.

Our last 50 kilometres to Mwanza were on what was left of a bitumen road that had been eroded so much from the edges inwards and had so many deep potholes that it was worse than the ungraded dirt and gravel roads. By now, I felt that I would have been in heaven if I had been able to drive on a half decent road and not have to hang on for hours on end as we got bounced around; but heaven would have to wait several years until a World Bank funded road took shape.

I didn't like Mwanza when I first saw it and that impression didn't improve over the following years. Almost symbolic of the run-down nature of the town was the group of railway wagons and engines, lying in a disordered mass and overgrown by weeds, shortly after entering the town from Shinyanga. They were still there ten years later. It was a dry, dusty, dirty, and rather depressing town that became dustier and dirtier over the years, as the bitumen on the roads disintegrated through neglect.

During my last visit there, in 1998, they were hoping for some foreign aid funding to redo the roads, which were, by that point, all reduced to dirt, being bumpy and dusty in the dry season and muddy and bumpy in the wet.

Stretching around Lake Victoria for a couple of kilometres, the town, when viewed from the lake, consisted of low rise and single-story buildings on the strip of land adjacent to the lake. Behind this, all sorts of small houses had been built over the rocky hillsides, with the odd larger building, like the hospital, standing out. The poorer homes were further up the hill amongst giant granite boulders, which dominated the landscape. In the surrounding areas, the same boulder-dominated landscape occurred with only scarce, scattered bushes, giving it a desolate, almost hostile appearance.

According to the older local foresters, the town was not always so arid-looking. As little as fifty years before, it had been surrounded by quite dense woodlands; but these were subsequently obliterated in a conscientious effort to eradicate the tsetse fly and in the quest for wood fuels. The blue waters of the lake were the one redeeming feature. They gave a sense of coolness and tranquillity that softened the nature of the town. However, by the mid-nineties, widespread and massive growth of water hyacinth was clogging the lake shores; in some cases, filling whole bays and virtually stopping boating.

The Mwanza Hotel was better than anything we had stayed in since leaving Dar. It might even have been better than the Kilimanjaro, although both were run by the Tanzania Tourist Corporation (TCC). I felt the word 'tourist' was included in the title without full appreciation for what it meant, as rarely did I find any effort on the part of staff or management to encourage tourism or to make me feel at home, while the hotel accommodation was not designed to encourage visitors to linger any longer than was necessary.

But it was to TCC, in Mwanza, that I now turned for help with transportation. I had had enough of our Land Rover and its problems. Even if we went back to Dar the same way, I was not prepared to put up with the constant breakdowns and punctures. In a report that I wrote to the UNDP about our troubles, I noted that, on average, we only made 50 kilometres between incidents. Now, we were planning to head back to the coast on a more northerly route via Arusha, and that meant crossing the Serengeti.

This vast plain of grass and scattered trees was home to tens of thousands of animals, including a fair share of lions, cape buffalo, elephants, and cheetahs; and there were no service stations or towns across the game park until we reached the Ngorongoro Crater, some eight to ten hours' drive from Mwanza. This was certainly no place to be stopping for repairs every so often. So, I told the driver we were finished with him and would head on without him, thanked him for his hard work, and gave him a little 'something' for all his efforts, though I suspect he may have made a small pile from acting as a taxi on the way back to Dar.

It was a bright, sunny morning as we headed off early in a relatively new Land Rover 110, feeling like we had a new lease on life. Even on the rough roads it felt far more comfortable in this much better vehicle. I have often found it interesting how, when one is in difficult circumstances, small improvements that would otherwise be accepted in quite a blasé way can have an almost exhilarating effect. We had wheels that worked, and we were heading through one of the great natural wonders of the world, the Serengeti National Park, and all as part of the job. This was amazing stuff!

The Western entrance to Serengeti National Park, 1986.

The drive through the Serengeti was unforgettable, although the entrance to the park once again reminded me of the poor state of the country's economy and its unsatisfactory grasp on the management of tourism. The office at the gate, on the western edge of the park, where we went to pay our park fees was run down with the pungent odour of bat dung pervading throughout. The fibreboard ceilings were near collapse and there were no tourist aids or brochures in evidence. Nor were there any tourists to be seen.

On entering the Serengeti, my first impression was one of being completely isolated. Unlike game parks in Kenya that I later visited, there was very little evidence of humans, and we saw no foreigners. During the initial stage, driving from the park entrance, near the shores of Lake Victoria, the road was often in poor shape. I was glad we had a four-wheel-drive that behaved itself, as we drove through low-lying black soil plains, wet and sticky from recent rains; the vegetation varied from open grasslands to woodlands with scattered low trees. There were animals to be seen almost as soon as we entered the park - water buck and baboons.

In the slightly higher and drier plains we encountered vast herds of wildebeest, interspersed with zebras. Then there were the packs of Thompson and Grant's gazelle, grazing with their stubby tails rapidly flicking back and forth, until a disturbance or alarm set them bounding off en masse. We came across elephants ponderously making their way through the bush, tearing down leaves to stuff into their mouths, satisfying their enormous appetites. The lions were resting, lazing under a tree and not bothering about us except for a curious lifting of their heads as we drove within metres of where they were. There was a cheetah on the prowl and cape buffalo quietly grazing, belying the fact that these were regarded as the most dangerous and unpredictable of the animals. We kept our distance.

As we headed east, we wound our way down into the Olduvai Gorge, where the Leakeys had discovered some of man's ancestors, dating back as far as two million years, but also as recent as 22,000 years. What was the countryside like then for these hominoids; and how was it different from today, if at all. I felt extraordinarily privileged to be visiting such sites. From the Gorge, we climbed towards an old volcanic region, now dominated by the Ngorongoro Crater, and as we did so, I looked back in the late afternoon sunshine across the expanse of rolling grasslands through which we had passed. There was an unimaginable vastness about the scene that was awe inspiring. It appeared to be so utterly untouched and primeval. We had only seen one other vehicle on our way through. There was almost something sacred about its nature. It deserved to remain untouched.

Encountering vast herds of wildebeest and zebra on the Serengeti, 1986.

I was to make the same trip on two later occasions during my forestry tours of duty in Tanzania and the wonder at seeing so many animals over such a vast, largely undisturbed, landscape didn't cease. There was some development for tourists in the mid-nineties, but in the eighties, it was only minimal. Tanzania still did not have the tourist panache that its northern neighbour had developed, but that had helped conserve its wildlife resources, preserving them in a more pristine environment. They may have missed the boat economically in the seventies and eighties through Nyerere's misplaced confidence in a socialist system, which included the formation of an ujamaa or villagization scheme. Through it all, they have remained a united and peaceful people, who didn't take themselves too seriously; and they have rich wildlife and mineral resources.

We spent that night in the Crater Lodge on the very edge of the Ngorongoro Crater. From the hotel veranda, I looked down several hundred metres to the crater floor, where elephants and buffalo were barely discernible.

The next morning, early, there was a compulsory drive down into the crater, before heading on to Arusha. This provided another visual feast of wildlife, including the spectacle of a lion and lioness mating, within ten metres of our vehicle. There was another lion on the road to Arusha, just lying in the middle of the road, where it stayed, nonchalantly blocking our path, till it decided to move, after a few minutes. No one got out to shoo it away. From its perspective, we were the intruders.

Back in Dar a few days later, after a relatively easy trip on bitumen roads from Arusha, there were arguments with the hire car owner, who resented our dumping his Land Rover. The fellow had the cheek to claim that there was nothing mechanically wrong with his vehicle and that we should have continued with it. However, I called his bluff and produced a log of all the mishaps and breakdowns for the UNDP to use against any claims the owner may have had, and that seemed to resolve the issue.

As a result of this first trip in 1986 and a subsequent visit in late 1987, I reasoned that the most sensible option to provide wood for fuel to the urban centres was to manage the Miombo woodlands and *Acacia-Combretum* scrub. The knee-jerk solution to wood fuel shortages at that time was to plant trees, and that was appropriate in many situations. But, as my travels in the country had shown, Tanzania had some 32 million hectares of woodlands and scrub, with species that were preferred by the local people for both firewood and charcoal, compared to plantation trees like eucalypts or exotic acacias.

It then occurred to me that it would be great if we could get the local villagers involved in undertaking the sustainable management of these woodlands and scrub. After all, they had once had tenure over these woodlands before the Germans expropriated them and made them public forests. This would mean redefining the village boundaries in line with those that existed before ujamaa.

A lion and lioness after mating in the Ngorongoro Crater

The concept of communities participating in the management of forests was not new. Of course, people dwelling within or on the fringes of forests had been doing something like that for millennia; sustaining the forest to satisfy their needs for food, fuel, and shelter. This had been the case in Tanzania before the German colonists took control and alienated the communities from their traditional forests. Elsewhere, many forest-based communities were continuing with this practice, such as I experienced early in my career in Papua New Guinea. However, a new approach had been undertaken in the West Bengal State in India in the mid-seventies, initiated by a forester with whom I later worked with in the World Bank, Ajit Banerjee. Here a system of joint management of state forests between the state forestry agency and the local communities had been undertaken with success.

I didn't know much about the Indian participatory forest management in 1986 and 1987. I just thought it made sense to have the people manage the forests as the Tanzanian Forest and Beekeeping Division hadn't been doing a very good job of it and lacked the manpower and financial resources to do the job in the future. To me, it was an exciting concept that seemed appropriate to the circumstances.

During my first year at the World Bank, I continued to be involved with the preparation and appraisal of the Sudan Wood Energy and Forestry Project, spending more time in Sudan. However, in 1987, my main task was to follow up on the work I had done the previous October and prepare what was to be called the Tanzanian Woodfuels and Forestry Project, costing some US$20 million. This wasn't going to be a big project by Bank standards, although it was big enough, and would have a number of innovative ideas, so I was nervous about doing a good job and preparing a worthwhile project; particularly as this was my first such project preparation as a Bank staff member.

After my years working as a project manager for Forestal and dealing with the private sector approach to forestry investment, I was determined to apply some of the same rigorous criteria to the financial and technical feasibility of the Tanzanian project. It was also important that the sociological aspects be adequately covered. So, both an expat and local sociologist were included in the team, to get the communities' input and to try and understand what their priority needs were, from both men's and women's perspective.

Turi Hammer was a sociologist from Norway, and we had worked together in Sudan, while Dr Idris Kikula provided essential local knowledge, being the Director of the Institute of Resource Assessment (IRA) at the University of Dar es Salaam. There were three other specialists on the project preparation team: an Indian forest economist, an English charcoal expert and a Canadian forester. I had scheduled for the mission to take four weeks in-country, an unusually long time for such preparation missions. But we had a lot of territory to cover and needed to thoroughly understand the issues and the best way of achieving our objective of providing an improved source of acceptable woodfuels to the urban centres.

I travelled to Tanzania in May to meet with the Forests and Beekeeping Division and prepare the ground, prior to our upcoming mission to design the project. The Bank allowed us the luxury of travelling first class when flying over more than eight hours. I did, however, try to remember that it was a privilege and not a right, which attitude stood me in good stead when the Bank, a few years later, relegated us to travel business class. Of course, several airlines, like British Airways, were quite prepared to upgrade us back to first class to get the business, knowing that the Bank was worth several thousand international person trips per year.

I even made a couple of trips across the Atlantic from Washington on the Concord with this arrangement, which was an exciting and novel experience. On the first occasion, there was the anticipation while waiting in the British Airways first class lounge at Washington Dulles, then boarding to find that the interior was quite narrow with only two seats on either side of the aisle, though these were rather luxurious leather recliners. I felt and heard the power from the engines and then the afterburners, as we roared down the runway and lifted off, but reaching twice the speed of sound at some 1300 miles per hour was achieved gradually after we had cleared the coast, with no sensation of increasing speed. Then flying at more than

60,000 feet, the sky was a deep blue, much darker than at lower altitudes. Four hours later we landed at Heathrow, in about half the time, compared with the regular jet Atlantic transits.

For the preparation mission in September 1987, the Kilimanjaro Hotel in Dar es Salaam was our base, though we spent over two weeks in the field. This time, with a certain degree of economic liberalization in the country, we had decent four-wheel drive vehicles, Pajeros from a newly formed company - Gogo Safaris. I felt grateful to the support consultants I had chosen, as they were an experienced bunch and we got along well together. When in Dar, we would routinely meet in my room in the late afternoon to have a few drinks and discuss our project preparation progress in a convivial atmosphere.

Sociologist Turi Hammer with Masai women during project preparation mission, 1987.

We came up with a plan to involve communities in a programme of joint management of their redefined woodlands. In addition, planting of trees by households and communities to augment their supply of wood for fuel and construction wood was needed in areas devoid of adequate forest resources. To support this and to earn additional revenue, villages would be encouraged to raise tree seedlings in communal nurseries, while an improved forestry extension service would provide technical support and guidance for all these activities.

The only incident to mar our experience was Turi Hammer being injured in a vehicle accident when her Pajero, driving at some speed, in the dark, hit an unmarked pile of gravel on the road outside Dodoma. Turi was thrown over the front seat from the back seat and injured her back. She, and the other occupants of the car, who were uninjured, were lucky, as had the vehicle hit the side of the gravel pile it could have rolled. The following night, four people were killed when their car overturned on the same pile of dirt. This ended Turi's efforts in the field, though her back improved and she stayed until the end of the mission.

Back in Washington, I faced some criticism from a few of my World Bank colleagues who felt that giving the local villagers control of the forests was asking for trouble and that they would proceed to cut them down in an unmanaged way. I argued that the villagers had *de facto* control over the woodlands as the Forest and Beekeeping Division was so weak. I felt that reinstating their customary rights that had been taken away by the German colonial administration early in the twentieth century, would give them de jure control over the woodlands with some form of tenure. This would provide an incentive for the villagers to manage the woodlands sustainably and protect them from outsiders' keen to cut and supply the urban markets. In fact, for much of Western Tanzania there was already a community management system in place for sustainable management of pastures, the *ngitiri* system, which could possibly be adapted to our purpose.

Others at the Bank argued that there was insufficient knowledge about managing these woodlands to warrant investing several million dollars via a Bank loan. Well, after a bit of wandering around the woodlands and talking to local foresters and farmers I was convinced that one would be hard put to severely degrade the forest with any management efforts. In fact, the Miombo Woodlands are incredibly resilient. Where trees had been cut down for farming, there was a lot of regeneration from root suckers, and areas that had been cut down many years earlier were now fully fledged woodlands again. I confirmed my beliefs by visiting a couple of retired English foresters who had served in East Africa and were now working at Oxford University.

After much debate, senior Bank management agreed that the project had merit but needed some additional components. The management of forests by communities would require a revision of the existing land policies and demarcation, titling and registration of forest land. It was also considered beneficial to map vegetation and forests throughout Tanzania, to understand the exact nature and extent of the resource. A second preparation mission was undertaken in 1990, and, after appraisal of the project and negotiations with the Government of Tanzania, it was finally approved by the Bank's board and became effective in July of 1992 as the 'Tanzanian Forest Resources Management Project'.

By this point, in the early 1990s the concept of participatory forest management using local communities was being more widely accepted and applied. I took up the reins as the Bank's project manager for this Tanzanian project, though I still wasn't quite sure about how we would get such community forest management to work satisfactorily, particularly the sociological aspects. Having learned from my earlier work with communities managing forests or tree planting that the traditional forester's top-down approach was ineffective and failed to understand the issues, I was now set on a villager-up approach with a lot of sociological input.

A lot of time was spent over the succeeding six years, visiting communities and talking with both the men and women, who were now taking over control and management of their woodlands. The first thing they did was to protect the woodlands from outsiders who might wish to cut down trees for timber, charcoal production or firewood. Even this simple exercise had some very heartening results, with degraded but now protected woodland regenerating and growing. Often, as we sat with the villagers in the village or walked with them through their now reclaimed forest, I sensed their enthusiasm for rehabilitating their forest resource.

Fortunately, in early 1993, I moved with Chris, to Nairobi. We had married in 1989 at a small ceremony at an Anglican Church in Pittsburgh, where Chris's mother lived. However, by 1992, I was getting fed up with some of the office politics within the Bank in Washington and was considering getting out and heading to Australia. Since, moving to the US, I found I was being increasingly drawn back to Oz. Each time I visited my mum and sisters, I found it hard to leave. There was something familiar about the bush, the birds, the lifestyle and the attitudes of people that was drawing me back. I hadn't felt this way while living in Canada. Perhaps it was the different atmosphere and conditions in the States or just a dormant urge that was resurfacing to return 'home'.

Then, I was offered a position in the Bank's regional office in Nairobi. This would get me out into the field and away from office politics and meetings in Washington. But I only agreed to go if Chris was transferred to Nairobi as well, to work there with the Bank. It took a while for this conundrum to be resolved as usually spouses or partners were not allowed to work in the same offices of the Bank. And so, Chris and I packed up our belongings in the Bethesda condo to be shipped to Nairobi. After a month's stay at the Norfolk Hotel, a relic of the colonial era with rooms scattered around enclosed gardens and lawns, we moved into a rented house at Lakeview, in the north of the city.

Security was a concern in Nairobi and the World Bank directives insisted that our house be in a secure location, have a secure, lockable, internal room in case of home invasion, have several silent alarm buttons located around the house to summon the security firm's baseball bat carrying guards, and have a secure gate with a 24-hour guard. Car hijacking was of particular concern with an average of over 2,000 such incidents occurring annually. So, our new Land Rover Discovery had a shift lock, and I was always wary of any vehicle following at night.

Over the five years I was in Nairobi, David and Michael came out several times and, as part of our bonding, we visited most of the national game parks. This included a night at Treetops Lodge in Aberdare National Park, where we watched all manner of animals, including elephants, come to drink at the waterhole. We glamped in Masai Mara National Park and saw lions feasting and part of the annual wildebeest migration across the Mara River. We petted a tame rhino and were nudged by a snotty warthog at Sweetwater Lodge in central Kenya. I then took them on a camel safari in northern Kenya, sleeping out under an amazing starry sky, with lions roaring not too far away. Time was also spent on the coast in luxury hotels by the beach.

Being based in Nairobi enabled me to be much more closely involved with forestry projects, for which I was task manager, in Malawi, Tanzania, Uganda, Ethiopia and Kenya. I also provided occasional assistance to a forestry project in Zimbabwe. All of these were within two hours flying time, while I could drive to sites in Kenya and Tanzania, using one of several Bank four-wheel drive vehicles.

I particularly enjoyed motoring down to Tanzania with one of the Bank's drivers, in either a Pajero or a Nissan Patrol. Starting early in the morning we might head through western Kenya towards the Tanzania border, stopping on the way for lunch at some eatery in one of the towns like Kisii. The menu choice was ugali[16] with some sort of stew or fried chicken with chips or rice. I found the ugali tasteless and would opt for chicken and chips. Alternatively, we would drive from Nairobi south to the border near the town of Arusha, in the shadow of Mount Kilimanjaro, a much shorter trip.

Crossing the border into Tanzania was usually a bit of a process when bringing in our vehicle and it could take half an hour or more going through the bureaucracy on the Tanzania side. From there on, in the west, the road deteriorated until we got close to Lake Victoria where we would usually spend the night, sometimes at Musoma. The accommodation was

16 A white mass of stiff maize flour porridge that was a staple in East Africa.

very basic, though later there were one or two half decent hotels to be found. The next day we would proceed to Mwanza and get on with touring the project sites with local officers.

On several occasions, it was easier to fly down to Dar es Salaam, particularly if I had meetings there. I would then usually head up country in a new project Pajero with the Project Coordinator, Mr Musocqua, a portly, smiling, religious and honest Tanzanian, with whom I became quite good friends.

It seems that every country has to have its own airline. Something to do with national pride and independence, although it's debatable whether some can afford the expense; and I often wondered about maintenance. Tanzania was no exception, though goodness knows they needed an airline. It is a large country, and the trains are bloody awful, while many of the roads don't deserve to be called by that name. I have seen smoother creek beds.

I had flown Air Tanzania several times, both within Tanzania and regionally, without any significant problems. Stories abounded of cancelled flights and long delays, but I seemed to have led a charmed life with ATC (Air Tanzania Corporation). At least that was the case until I took a flight from Mwanza to Dar es Salaam. This was in March 1996, and I had been touring around Mwanza and the Tabora Regions doing field work for the mid-term review of the project.

On several previous flights from the airport at Mwanza to Dar, all had gone without a hitch, with the plane usually being roughly on time. On this occasion, they had a substitute plane doing the job, a Boeing 737 from Air Toulouse, as one of the two Air Tanzania 737s was in Ireland for an overhaul. It was comforting to know that they were serious enough about maintenance to send their planes all the way to Ireland for such major services.

We boarded the plane from the small, usually overcrowded terminal on the northern outskirts of Mwanza, and headed to Kilimanjaro Airport, between Moshi and Arusha, in the shadow of Mount Kilimanjaro, arriving at about three p.m. Then, while sitting on the plane waiting for refuelling to be completed and passengers to embark, an announcement was made asking us to disembark as there was a fuel or oil leak. So, we wandered across the hot tarmac to the terminal, wondering what was going on and resigned to the usual delays and lack of information as to what the problem was or when it would be fixed.

I have always found the most frustrating part of flight delays is the lack of information. It isn't the delay itself that is so much of a bother but being kept guessing as to what is going on and how long one might have to continue to wait. Some airlines or airline personnel do seem to try and keep the passengers informed. Others seem to have forgotten they have passengers or feed them half-truths, which seemed like an insult to our intelligence. Delays 'due to technical problems' is the usual catchall phrase that can mean anything from the incoming flight having just crashed on landing, to the captain's loss of his contact lenses or a flat tire.

Now, it should be pointed out that a lot of people flying from Mwanza to Dar buy fish caught in Lake Victoria before going to the airport. The Tilapia were regarded particularly highly and were even exported to Europe. The fish were usually packed in unsealed cardboard boxes without the benefit of any insulation, ice, or refrigeration. But it was only a two-hour flight, and the cargo hold would get quite cold at 30,000 plus feet, so there was no cause to worry that the fish would spoil.

We had the same loosely tied boxes of fish on our flight, but with the addition, as I learnt, of some four tonnes of fish for transhipment to the UK that night on British Airways. Sitting in the late afternoon sun and the warm tropical evening air at Kilimanjaro was not going to help the fish one little bit.

I spent my time wandering around the airport, which was deserted except for the passengers from our flight and the attendant ground staff. In contrast with Mwanza, the terminal here was relatively large and modern, though quite stark in its features, having been built with the idea that overseas airlines could land and disgorge hundreds of tourists for the nearby game parks and Mount Kilimanjaro. For a while, some airlines, such as KLM, Ethiopian and perhaps British Airways had obliged. However, problems with the runway and landing guidance systems, coupled perhaps with a lack of passenger interest, meant that the airport was now mainly used for domestic traffic. It may have received about half a dozen flights a day, so it wasn't exactly throbbing with life. And it was stuck out in the middle of nowhere with only acacia scrub and grasslands visible for some distance. On a good day, though, one could see the majestic might of Mount Kilimanjaro a few kilometres to the north, with its perennial snow-capped west peak.

After some time, we learnt, partly through an official announcement and partly through scuttlebutt, that our plane wasn't going anywhere for a while, but that a replacement jet was coming from Dar to take us through to that city. It turned out this was the plane that was due to fly from Dar to

Nairobi but was now being sent to pick us up. Goodness knows what the Nairobi-bound passengers, who had checked in down in Dar were being told.

With some relief, we then watched as our replacement plane finally landed and taxied to the tarmac in front of the terminal at around six-thirty p.m. We were anxious to be away and streamed out to board the plane as a disorganized rabble, while the ground staff were still transferring our baggage and several tonnes of fish. Finally, all were seated and waiting for the door to be shut and the plane to start rolling. At that point, the captain came on the intercom to inform us that we would not be going anywhere as there was a blackout in Dar and no lights at the airport.

Tanzania in general, and Dar in particular had been having serious problems with power shortages for some time – due to low capacity, poor maintenance of equipment, and, more recently, a low water level in the hydro dams because of drought. Nevertheless, the airport was supposed to have had a backup generator to offset such outages. It was unclear whether the persons responsible had forgotten to provide diesel for the generator, that there was no money for diesel or that it had broken down and had not been repaired for some reason. All were possibilities. I understand a Zambian Airlines plane was taking off when the blackout occurred and it continued hurtling down the runway, and into the air, using only its own lights.

Nobody had any idea when the lights would come on in Dar - another case of keeping the customers in the dark about what was going on. So, we sat on the plane or wandered over to the terminal building. It was all a bit lackadaisical on the part of the airline staff, but that seemed to be on par with what I had come to expect. No refreshments were provided, but I had a bit of chocolate and some trail mix, which I shared with a few passengers.

Finally, at about eleven p.m. we were told to board as the lights were back on. Great! We settled into our seats, forgetting the dreary hours we had waited as we anticipated arriving at our destination. The engines were started, and we taxied out. Then, before we got to the runway, we turned around and came back to park in front of the terminal. I thought perhaps they had forgotten something, but after a minute or so, the captain announced that the lights had again gone out in Dar.

Needless to say, there was much moaning and gnashing of teeth, together with a sense of frustration. I tried to stay on the plane and sleep, as it seemed the most comfortable place, but, with no air conditioning, the air was so thick and smelling of stale sweat you could have cut it with a knife. After a while, I went into the terminal building, where I found a row of plastic seats and tried to stretch out and get some shut eye. It was not very comfortable, and I wasn't too successful, but it was the best I could do under the circumstances. Then, at around three a.m. in the morning, we again got the word to board.

Naturally, I felt a certain amount of scepticism about our chances, but it wasn't long till dawn when we wouldn't need lights anyway so 'what the hell'. This time we did take off and actually made it to Dar, landing at about four a.m. As we waited, tired and a bit fed up, for our luggage to arrive at the carousel, we could smell the fish while the baggage cart was still some distance away on the tarmac. My suitcase, when I retrieved it, was covered in fish slime and stank to high heaven. Luckily, there was hardly a soul around as I walked into the posh Sheraton Hotel lobby at about four-thirty a.m., having gone halfway around Dar in one of the few taxis we could find at that hour of the morning, but sharing it with several people going to different parts of the town.

The power outage had played havoc with the hotel computers, and they were still not working, but the hotel in its efficiency had a plastic card-key ready for me and I gratefully made my way to my room, with a porter gingerly towing my stinking suitcase. However, on opening the door, I found a man asleep in the bed. He wasn't pleased, but then, neither was I. Back at the front desk, in an otherwise deserted foyer, the porter was sent off to try several other rooms that should have been vacant. He came back to report one that was, so I was finally able to settle in, wash off most of the fish slime from the bag, have a shower and fall into bed for a few hours' sleep before meetings with my Tanzanian forestry counterparts at about nine a.m. that morning.

When I left the World Bank and Nairobi in July of 1997, the Tanzanian Forest Resources Management Project was well on its way to being successful, and I was able to spend more time there, assisting in a supervision mission in late 1998. A new land policy had been passed by the Tanzanian Parliament, which would give villagers back customary rights over their forest land and protect such land from exploitation by outsiders. Some 3,600 village boundaries with woodlands had been demarcated.

The use of the *Ngitiri* communal resource management concept to initiate joint forest management of over approximately 90,000 hectares of woodlands was deemed as a good start, with the potential to be replicated over a much wider area in a subsequent project. Forest resource and land use mapping was completed for the entire country, so that the forest managers and shareholders could now assess the nature and extent of their resource.

These maps were kept and were able to be updated in the Tanzanian Natural Resource Information Centre established under the project.

While I was off managing projects in Tanzania and elsewhere in Eastern and Southern Africa, Chris was not being idle back in Nairobi. She had broken through the glass ceiling regarding her position with the bank and had been assigned as task manager for a couple of serious projects in Kenya. This meant spending time away in northern Kenya, which didn't always coincide with my absences.

Chris was keen to have a child and she did become pregnant in 1990. Unfortunately, that had ended, sadly, in a miscarriage. Subsequently, we had not been successful. After Chris visited a fertility clinic in London on her way back from a trip to Washington D.C., she told me that first it had to be determined whether my sperm count and activity was up to scratch. I was somewhat put out by this, having already been responsible for three pregnancies. After some months of reluctance, I relented and got a script from my local GP for the test, which would be undertaken at Nairobi Hospital.

I didn't want to make a big issue about it, and I waited till Chris was away on a mission. I then drove up to the hospital and went into the outpatients' department. There, I nervously approached a counter where people seemed to be submitting specimens or applying for tests. I told them that I wished to have a sperm test. The white coated technician told me in rich African tones that I needed first to pay at the cashier and pointed to a cubicle with a wire mesh front.

I joined the queue for the cashier and when my turn came, the large Kenyan lady behind the desk wearing a colourful flower-patterned dress barely looked at me as she said, "Yes, what you want?"

I replied in a semi sotto voce voice, being conscious of those close behind me in the queue, "I need to get a sperm test."

She looked at me quizzically and said quite loudly, "What you want?" Somewhat louder this time, I repeated my request. "That will be 150 shillings," came the unemotional reply as the lady proceeded to write out a receipt for me.

Back at the specimen/test counter I presented my receipt to the technician, who then reached under the counter and produced a small plastic container.

"You can use the bathroom down the hall there on the right." So, I proceeded to the bathroom, which had a large bathtub and toilet and was reasonably clean. The atmosphere was all somewhat clinical, and I was unsuccessful in producing a sperm sample. Back I went to the specimen counter and, rather embarrassingly, told the technician I had been unsuccessful. I asked if I could bring in a sample from home where the ambience would be more conducive to producing the required specimen. Yes, that would be possible, but I would need to get the sample to the hospital within thirty to forty minutes of it being taken, to get a valid result.

Now, from where we lived in Lakeview it would take fifteen to twenty minutes to drive to the hospital with no traffic. However, on a weekday morning the traffic congestion could double that time. So, I decided that a weekend run was my best option and confirmed with the technician that his department was open on a Saturday.

"Yes, of course we are," came the abrupt reply.

Early the following Saturday, with Chris still out of town, I set myself up, both mentally and logistically to deliver the sample. With everything ready to make a dash in the Land Rover Discovery, I produced a sample, carefully packaged it to insulate it, and headed down to the hospital, glad that I had achieved my objective. I was at the specimen counter within twenty-five minutes and proudly presented my specimen container to the technician on duty telling him it was for a sperm test.

He looked at the specimen then at me and said, "This is no good. The technician who tests such samples does not work on Saturdays."

"But I was told you would be open on Saturdays by the man here last Wednesday," I exclaimed with more than a little disappointment and frustration. The end of this saga was not yet in sight it seemed.

"Sure, we are open," the technician blithely replied, "but the man who tests such samples doesn't work on Saturdays."

Well, it was going to have to be a weekday run. The technician confirmed that if I got it to his counter within forty minutes of it being taken it would be okay; but I had to wait at least three days before taking another sample. I also confirmed that if I got it in by about seven-thirty a.m. it would be okay. Three days later, I went through the procedure again. Judging my timing to get it in as early as possible to beat the morning rush traffic, I managed to deliver my specimen and have it accepted.

In the end, my sperm test was of no consequence as in mid-1996 Chris announced that she wanted out of our marriage. I was stunned. I asked what had brought this about, but she refused to tell me or couldn't tell me, except that it wasn't about me or another man. Of course, I felt that I must have played some part in her decision. For some months, I continued to feel devastated by the breakup of our marriage, which wasn't helped by having to work in the same office as Chris, even though she had moved out of the house. She also wasted no time in getting a separation agreement set up and a year later a divorce was finalized in the state of Maryland.

One Saturday morning in early 1997, while driving to the Bank's office in Nairobi to put in some extra work, a thought suddenly came into my head that I hadn't been laughing so much in recent months. And, with further thought over the next few days, I realised that I was not happy working with the Bank. In fact, I was rather stressed with the workload. I had also felt for some time that I was losing touch with my forestry profession and becoming more and more immersed in Bank procedures and non-forestry project matters, even while based in Nairobi.

However, I felt I was in a position to do something about the situation. I didn't have a wife, David was starting on his public relations career, and Michael was doing well at university. So, I decided I would quit the Bank and move back to Australia later in the year. When I discussed my situation and decision with my wonderful manager, Sushma Ganguli, in Washington, she suggested I could try for a more technical position or move back to Washington. However, the Bank had moved away from having select technical expertise units some years earlier and moving back to Washington with more meetings and bureaucracy didn't appeal to me. So, with some regrets, I left the Bank and Nairobi in early July 1997 and headed back to Australia, via Washington and Vancouver, to try my luck at consulting once again. As it turned out, much of the consulting ended up being with the Bank, but now I could concentrate on the technical aspects of projects and leave the rest to the Bank persons involved.

An Introduction to South Asia

Bangladesh is one of those countries that doesn't hit the world's headlines except when there is a natural disaster or a *coup d'état*. I'm not talking about your regular disaster with perhaps a few score people killed and substantial damage to property. In fact, that probably wouldn't even make the news in Bangladesh. This is a country where some forty percent of the land is flooded annually, and it's just considered part of the normal agricultural nutrient replenishment cycle. It happens when the Meghna, Jamuna and Padma Rivers (the main distributaries of the Ganges), swollen by monsoon rains upstream, spill into the low-lying fields, leaving a rich deposit of silt from India and Nepal, to foster good harvests in the succeeding year.

The people have learnt to accommodate these annual floods by building houses and roads on higher ground. Such flooding is only significant, and a disaster declared, when sections of roads and villages become inundated. This is a country where a significant disaster means the loss of tens, if not hundreds of thousands of lives, with property loss affecting millions more; and it doesn't just happen once every fifty years or so. The cyclones that sweep up the Bay of Bengal from May to October could result in this sort of catastrophe happening every three or four years. With winds in excess of 120 kilometres per hour, and often over 200 kilometres per hour, accompanied by tidal surges, the flat low-lying coastal areas, including any villages, stand little chance. In the early nineties, during one cyclone, approximately 400,000 people lost their lives, while death tolls of over 100,000 were not uncommon. I heard stories of men, who had stayed behind to protect their properties and possessions, tying themselves to trees to survive - and some actually did, but what a terrifying experience and what guts it must have taken to stay behind.

In November 1983, I flew into Bangladesh to be part of a team to prepare a World Bank forestry project. My terms of reference for this mission and later visits to supervise a subsequent project, would be directly linked to these cyclonic disasters. This was because one of the principal components was further expansion of a mangrove planting programme in the Ganges River Delta - the largest delta in the world - and along the Chittagong Coast, with the aim of reducing the destructive effects of the cyclones, particularly the tidal surges.

This concept of planting mangroves in the silt deposits from the rivers had been originally tried several years before by the Bangladeshi.

Such plantings had resulted, after several years, in additional land being formed by accreting and stabilizing the vast quantities of silt brought down by the rivers. Mangroves planted on almost completely submerged mud flats enabled these flats to grow steadily in height as the mangrove trees themselves grew. After several years, the silt accumulated to the point where there was little, if any, inundation with the tide. Some fifteen to twenty years further on, this newly accreted land could be used for grazing or agriculture in a country desperately short of arable land, while the trees could be cut for fuel and poles.

When I subsequently visited the area again in 2000, I found that the 150,000 hectares or so of mangrove plantings had, indeed, been successful in alleviating the effects of the cyclones, so much so that any thought of cutting them for land and fuel was being delayed until sufficient depth of plantings had been achieved.

My arrival in 1983 was a particularly uneasy time for Bangladesh, although, I'm not sure when one could say they had a comfortable and stable situation, with strikes (hartals) and mob violence being an ongoing occurrence during subsequent visits. It is the sort of thing that added a degree of apprehension and tension during my time in the country. I wasn't aware, though, of any civil unrest as I made my way through the protracted process of clearing customs at Dhaka Airport, together with several returning Bangladeshi, many of whom had at least a couple of enormous suitcases. These would spring open on the customs inspections counter to reveal masses of assorted goods and clothes obtained overseas, for which the poor blighters probably had to either cough up a handsome bribe or pay duties.

I heard some word about recent riots and disturbances during the first couple of days of my stay in Dhaka, but the civil unrest problems really only came into focus during a visit to the Principal Secretary for Forests and the Environment. This gentleman was nicknamed 'Actually' by my colleagues because every second sentence actually contained the word 'actually'. There we were listening to him sprout on with all his 'actually's', while I sat actually pinching myself to stop from actually laughing, when the sound of a large mob shouting drifted up from the compound below.

A glance out the window revealed a rather agitated crowd intent on their grievances being heard. So, it was suggested that we should leave immediately by the back way in case things got brutal. I am not sure I ever understood the reason for the riots on this occasion, apart from being related to serious grievances by students and some of the less well to do among the population.

Newly established plantation of Keora mangroves in Ganges Delta on accumulated silt.

A 15-year-old Keora plantation on accreted silt flats in Ganges Delta.

We returned to our hotel, the Sonargaon, to have lunch and to prepare for our departure at five p.m. that afternoon by boat for the delta area. It was not entirely unexpected then, that at about one p.m. we learnt that the government had declared a curfew from three p.m.

This put a bit of a spanner into the works as we were not prepared to depart at such short notice. Nevertheless, it was agreed that we would try and make it out to the docks on the river before the curfew time.

While we hastily packed, our fearless leader, one John Weatherhogg from the FAO Investment Centre, managed to persuade a taxi driver to make the trip with us, for considerably more than the standard fare. I had tried a few minutes earlier and had reported that I couldn't convince several taxi drivers to take the risk of being out when the curfew came into effect, but I obviously did not have John's touch.

The shortest route to the docks was through the most troublesome part of Dhaka - the area around the university; but we were committed and so off we sped, with only about thirty minutes to do a trip that usually would take forty minutes or more. I didn't know what to expect, never having flaunted a curfew when the orders were to shoot on sight, but there wasn't anything to do but hope for the best.

Luckily, the streets were largely deserted at that point, with only a few police evident, and so we were able to arrive at the docks with minutes to spare for us and the driver. We made our way to the ferry, which was already boarding passengers.

After stowing our bags in our somewhat old fashioned, though comfortable, cabins, we made our way to the upper foredeck, where we were able to sit and have a cup of tea, while watching for any indications that the riots had started. The river was calm with a few small boats making their way by sail or with oars. On land, the usual din of traffic and the babble of people was noticeable by its absence, with hardly a soul in sight.

The Rocket ferry that we took from Dhaka to Barisal

By the time of our five p.m. departure, there was no sign or sound of any trouble, as we moved out into mid-stream on the Buriganga River and proceeded to head down stream at a fair clip on our way to join the Meghna River. Given the amount of other traffic on the river, I thought we may have been going a bit too fast, although, a boat nicknamed 'the rocket' had a reputation to live up to. A few years later, I heard that the same ferry had sunk in an accident, with many lives being lost, with, I understand, excessive speed being a contributing cause.

Meanwhile, back in Dhaka, as we heard a day or two later, riots had, indeed, taken place, and the next day, the situation was even worse, with a curfew all day and thirty-four people killed. Similar riots occurred in Chittagong, where a colleague of mine, John Davidson, found himself being stoned by a mad mob as he tried to make his way to the Forest Research Institute. Luckily, his driver kept his head, and with John lying terrified on the floor of the Landcruiser, they surged on through the mob to safety. He was still pale from the incident when I saw him several days later.

The next morning saw us in the thick of the delta with mangroves very much in evidence. The ferry dropped us at about breakfast time at the town of Barisal, approximately 120 kilometres south of Dhaka. There, the district forest officer and his colleagues together, with a Forest Department launch, were waiting for us, and we headed south to the mouth of the delta, where the mangrove plantings were taking place. It was a relaxing trip, on smooth water with sunny skies, as we headed along the delta. There were at least a couple of hours between stops, and I watched the dhows, with their often brightly coloured triangular sails gliding in on the wind from the Bay of Bengal, the smaller fishing boats anchored with their nets across the current, and the passing seascape of islands, as we chatted about mangroves and forests and past experiences.

Sails on cargo ships in the early morning as we explored the Ganges Delta

The newly planted mangrove seedlings were almost under water at or near high tide with only their tops showing above the waves. I got into the spirit of things and jumped overboard to wade knee deep in glutinous, sucking mud and waist-deep in water, to view the seedlings up close and personal. It was a weird experience doing this a few kilometres from the nearest land. The only way to move one leg forward was to gain purchase by leaning on a small boat that accompanied us or on someone else. It was hard work as the mangroves, in this case Keora (*Sonneratia apetala*), prefer nice sticky mud, rather than sand.

After our inspection of the planted mangroves in the delta we headed west from Barisal to Khulna, through mile after mile of naturally occurring mangrove stands lining the many waterways associated with the delta. We passed mangrove-clothed islands with whimsical sounding names such as Char Kukrimukri, often seeing deer on the shoreline.

We were now aboard the Khulna District Forester's launch. This was a marvellous old boat, with teak decks, polished brass fittings and wood furnishings that dated from the early part of the twentieth century when such vessels were more the norm. Originally, it had been powered by steam, but now had a diesel engine. Seeing the beautiful furnishings and the old, varnished wood gun racks that held the necessary firearms against tigers and other wildlife, I began to imagine what it must have been like in those bygone days, when life was probably less complicated and moved at a slower pace. We didn't see tigers this time around, but they still have quite a presence. Taking a walk to view mangrove forests further to the west, in the Sundarbans, we came across pug marks suggesting that one was not too far away.

The mangroves, in which we had been walking, wading, and working, are a fascinating eco-system. There are several different genera and species and their position on a shoreline and their rate of growth are linked very closely with their varying abilities to adapt to the different degrees of salinity present. The salinity, itself, is influenced by tides and the amount of fresh river water present. As roots need air to survive, the mangroves have adapted by having stilt roots that rise above the water or pneumatophores – spikes that stick up out of the mud like snorkels to provide oxygen to the roots.

Mangroves have, traditionally, been much sought after as a good source of fuel, either as firewood or for conversion to charcoal. This has led to large areas being decimated in Asia, on the east coast of Africa and in South America; and this destruction of mangroves has also adversely affected fish and prawn stocks as they obtain food and shelter from predators in the murky mangrove waters.

In 2000, I was back in Bangladesh to help with the implementation of another World Bank funded forestry project that included further mangrove establishment. On that occasion we didn't get to the main mangrove areas in the delta. It was the start of the monsoon, and it was no time to be mucking about in boats on the exposed Bay of Bengal coastline, for, as one divisional forest officer told me, "The seas can be very furious at that time."

On a subsequent mission in January and February, the following year, the seas were almost glassy calm in the stillness of the winter haze, with temperatures dropping as low as 10 degrees Celsius at night, and poor exposed citizens were dying from the cold. This time we were going to have good look, not only at the mangroves that had been planted, but also at the vast area of natural mangroves that make up the Sundarbans, home of the Bengal Tiger.

I joined Rob Epworth, an Australian from the World Bank Dhaka office, his wife, Barbara, and Tajul Islam, the Bangladeshi, from the World

Bank, who was in charge of the project, together with his wife and teenage son. After flying from Dhaka to Jessore in the west of Bangladesh, we were met by forestry officials, who accompanied us as we drove south to Khulna, through flat, irrigated farmland and small towns, on the usual narrow Bangladesh country roads, raised above adjacent paddy fields. In Khulna, after a bit of a chat about mangroves and some lunch at a local restaurant, we boarded two launches for our mangrove exploratory cruise. The married couples got the only cabin on each boat while I joined three Bangladeshi foresters in the low-ceilinged forecastle of one launch. This was a rather roomy affair with several bunks arranged along the sides and in the centre, so we weren't exactly overcrowded.

Our meals were prepared in a kitchen that consisted of a couple of tiny rooms no more than a meter and a half wide, into which had been squeezed two gas single burner stoves, together with assorted pans and pots, plus containers of food. The cook did a fantastic job, squatting and sweating before his stoves, creating three or four different curries plus rice for lunch and dinner, as well as two curries with fried eggs and chapattis for breakfast. Our fresh meat came from a batch of hens in two coops located in the lifeboat over the stern.

After steaming for much of that first night on the boat, we dropped anchor in the early hours of the morning with a crashing rattle of the chain as it made its way overboard from the chain locker just forward of my berth. In the early morning light, just after six p.m., I thought I had better get into the head to shave and wash before the others. The steel deck was wet with dew in the chilly air, but after a few exercises to stir the blood and loosen the muscles, I had a cold bath, using a cup to pour water from the tap over myself, not stopping to think too much about how cold the water or the air was.

Having dressed in the few warm clothes I possessed, including a woollen sweater, I stood and watched the sun rise through the mist over the waterway. In the near distance, a score of fishing boats gently floated out from the shore with the tide, while extending their nets. The scene was so peaceful in that stillness and soft light of the early morning, and it was repeated over the next several days as we made our way through the mangrove channels. Under such circumstances it was hard to conceptualize the frantic hustle of peak hour commutation in the world's cities or the ravages of war occurring in a dozen separate locations. Here, isolated in the waterways and among the trees of the world's largest area of mangroves, all was as it should be, and breakfast was just about ready.

The Sundarbans, which comprise the western portion of mangrove forest in Bangladesh, is spread over 602,000 hectares. It stands adjacent to the Indian border, and there is a smaller area of mangroves on the West Bengal State side. It was declared a forest reserve in 1875, but there has been heavy pressure in the last few decades on the tree and land resources as population pressures to the north pushed people into illegal harvesting of wood and conversion of forest into agricultural and grazing land. Such pressure was understandable given a population density in Bangladesh of 970 per square kilometre. By contrast, India, which one considers is grossly overpopulated, has a population density of 290 per square kilometre, China has 130 and Canada 4 per square kilometre. By 2001, the number of such fringe dwellers dependent on the Sundarbans had risen to an estimated 500,000. With all these threats to the ecology, the government decided to set aside 140,000 hectares in the southeast of the Sundarbans to preserve the unique flora and fauna of the area. This was declared a wildlife sanctuary and a World Heritage site in December 1997. The rest of the mangrove forests were supposed to be managed on a sustainable basis.

After breakfast each morning, we headed off to see something of what the project was assisting and to observe how both the natural and planted mangroves were faring. This involved cruising along the waterways in the launch or, when the channels became too shallow and narrow, transferring to one of several speedboats. On either side of the waterways and on the islands, the leafy mangrove trees grew down to the water's edge, sometimes with branches partially immersed at high tide. As the tide receded, it left the trees high and dry, usually with the tree canopy cut off on a distinct line above the ground - the height to which the many large herds of deer grazing along the banks could reach to browse. The shoreline was a mass of brown glutinous mud across which the occasional rather large crocodile would be basking.

Sliding onto the edge of the shoreline, we jumped off into the mud and trudged up into the trees. There were always two or three forest guards accompanying us, armed with ancient Lee Enfield 303 rifles, to protect against tigers. I did wonder just how much protection they would actually provide, and I asked one guard how often he practiced shooting.

"Not very often and not for a long time," was the reply. "We don't have enough money to buy extra ammunition."

So, I realised, if we did actually confront a tiger who was interested in having a piece of us, we could have been faced with either no protection from fleeing guards or a wounded tiger, due to poor marksmanship, not a comforting thought.

I was pleased to see that within the Sundarbans sanctuary, which is home to 373 species of fauna, including tiger, spotted deer, monkey and wild boar, there now appeared to be a minimum amount of disturbance. We came across the odd fishing boat taking an illegal catch, which the forest officers confiscated on the spot. In one instance we acquired several sacks of illegally caught mud crabs. There may have been illegal cutting of wood inside the forest which couldn't be seen from the fringes, but we saw no evidence of this during our walks, nor did we come across any boats carrying wood, the most obvious giveaway of such illegal activity.

During our tramping through natural and planted mangroves on recently formed islands (chars), we noted that the Keora trees, the main species planted in the mangrove afforestation programmes tended to be somewhat self-limiting in its habitat. As the silt and mud accumulated and the 'char' became higher and less subject to inundation causing the salinity of the soil to change, the Keora trees ceased to grow and suffered increasing attacks from nasty little borers, which chewed away at the inside of the tree trunks. As a result, a large percentage of the Keora trees were recorded as being dead or dying after reaching twenty to twenty-five years of age. In the natural stands there is usually some sort of mangrove species secession with other species, more adapted to the conditions taking over. We did view some very successful trials the Bangladesh Forest Research Institute had been undertaking, whereby they were planting the successional species in the plantation.

But we weren't just looking at the trees. Some time was also spent trying to see at least one of about 400 tigers supposedly resident in the Sundarbans. We did come close, picking up several recent pug marks and, in one spot, near Katka, coming across the remains of several deer, one of which appeared to have been devoured only the night before. Perhaps, though, it was fortuitous we didn't come face to face with one of these magnificent, but dangerous, animals as I didn't have faith in our trusty guards' abilities to prevent a tiger having one of us for a snack.

Fishing was a major pastime, an industry and means of livelihood in the mangrove areas, as they are ideal fish and shrimp or pawn breeding grounds. On this occasion we were in the middle of the fishing season, after the monsoons and cyclones had departed, leaving more favourable seas and winds. Outside the sanctuary we came across numerous small to medium sized wooden fishing boats tending their nets, which were strung out across the waterways to trap fish as they moved with the tides. There seemed to be little in the way of regulation of the fishing with what appeared to be many undersized fish being caught, and our Bangladeshi counterparts mentioned that overfishing was a problem.

Fishing boats strung out across the waterways.

On the outer or more southerly parts of the mangroves, we came across larger fishing boats as they set out for or returned from the fishing grounds in the Bay of Bengal. These wooden boats, with their high prows and sterns and a wheelhouse built towards the stern, had similarities to sixteenth century European ships, except that, instead of sails these had diesel power. Otherwise, the design for these fishing vessels seemed to have changed little in the last six hundred years since Vasco de Gama sailed this same region on his incredible voyages of 'discovery' that opened up South Asia to Europe.

Part of the fishing business involved the sale of dried fish and we stopped at two villages where fish drying was a major occupation, one on the island of Dublar Char and another some twenty kilometres to the north. After tying up at Dublar Char we walked along the foreshore of reclaimed mangrove swamp. An incredibly strong fishy stench wafted out to greet us and a further two hundred metres brought us to its source, a hectare or so of land devoted to fish drying. At this point, the sickly smell of rotting fish was almost unbearable. The atmosphere was more that of a charnel house than a food processing area, and I wondered how much of the fish was actually drying in a way that made them edible and how much was just decaying. I don't know how the locals managed to live in houses that were close by. However, this was their livelihood and quite a lucrative one at that, so I guess one can put up with and get used to some noxious odours if there is worthwhile money involved.

Fish drying on Dublar Char.

Small fish and shrimp were spread over dozens of woven palm mats on the ground or on raised benches. Strung up between and around these were medium sized fish, such as a sort of garfish, hanging on thin poles supported above the ground. Then there were larger fish, like groupers, which had been sliced open several times longitudinally, then hung in such a way that the strips of flesh were expanded to form a sort of basket or grotesque Chinese lantern. With the heads still on, complete with staring eyes, each of these fish looked like some sort of alien creature.

I like fish: raw, salted, pickled, dried, fried, poached, and grilled, but none of the fish lying out there being withered by the sun and checked out by innumerable flies appealed to me in the least. The presence of a very shallow, fly-blown open-air latrine in the next field only added to the rich stench. I took advantage of this but had to climb some rickety stairs and balance on an equally rickety platform, made from sticks, over a suppurating aboveground cesspool. Back on board our launch, the cook, taking advantage of the local fish supply, then proceeded to prepare a dish of dried fish for lunch. I declined after a token taste that brought back the rotten odour on the recently departed char.

An interesting aspect of this deltaic area was the degree to which we encountered shallow newly-formed silt or mud banks, usually some distance from existing land. There was a remarkable amount of silt being deposited as we can attest to, being stuck on several occasions during low tide, even in the speed boat, in open water. In places these sites were easier to detect, where a dense growth of a sea grass broke the surface of the waves. As we approached the island of Nijhumdwip on the southern fringe of the mangroves during our last day, it was fascinating to see fishermen walking knee deep in the sea on mud banks a couple of kilometres from land. The local foresters estimated that a further 200,000 to 300,000 hectares of such silt banks would be formed to a high enough level over the next ten years to plant mangroves, a valuable addition to the land area of the country and a buffer from cyclonic storms.

All in all, it was a fascinating journey, during which we covered over 1,000 kilometres through the waterways that crisscrossed the mangroves and across more open stretches of water between the relatively recently formed islands that were often covered in mangroves planted in the last 35 years. It was a wonderful and relaxed way to explore and view the many facets of the mangrove ecology, as well as understand and experience how people lived and worked in this environment. After the placid waterways, I now had to spend several days on the narrow rural roads, on our way to viewing several dry land forests, dodging buses and trucks, whose drivers had scant regard for any rules or anyone's safety.

Communities and Forests in The Hills of Nepal

At about six a.m. I was running through the almost deserted, narrow streets of Thamel, that tightly packed section of Kathmandu that has a myriad of small shops selling pashminas, yak wool sweaters and local artefacts, travel and trekking agents, restaurants and bars. Only the occasional shop front was open; but as I moved into the older, less-touristy section, cupboard-sized shops selling fried dough in various forms already had their kerosene or gas stoves hissing away under bubbling vats of oil, the white dough bobbing in the bubbles. Garbage trucks were scooping up piles of fetid rubbish from the road, skinny dogs cruised looking for trouble, and finding it occasionally with an unwanted interloper, and the odd motorbike or scooter emerging from an even narrower lane with someone on their way to work. By evening, the streets would be jammed with cars, people, rickshaws and hawkers; but for now, I could move without too much hindrance, being careful to watch my step on the uneven paved road and through the scattered garbage and occasional dog droppings.

This was 2005 and I was in Nepal as Director of an AusAID-funded community forestry project, which had been running, in one form or another for some 30 years. It was not my first visit to the country, having spent some weeks there 22 years earlier in 1983 as part of an FAO team investigating the feasibility of building a pulp mill near the town of Nepalgange in the western Terai, the flat plain bordering India before the start of the hills, then leading to the mountains that form the Himalayas. The narrow, winding road down from Kathmandu to the Terai, passed by magnificent stands of flowering red Rhododendrons and white Magnolias as we descended a couple of thousand metres. In contrast, I found the Terai was a rather depressing place with bad roads, dirty towns and nasty cheap hotels. For the equivalent of $2 one got a concrete bench with a mattress and pillow, both smelling of several previous occupants, and I didn't linger at the common, stinking toilet and washing facilities.

This time in Kathmandu, thirty to forty minutes of running and walking around the streets saw me back in the relative luxury of the Yak and Yeti Hotel and then by eight a.m. I was on the road in the project's[17] maroon Toyota Landcruiser with its large, yellow kangaroo stencil on the bonnet. The two forest officers from the project districts were my companions as we headed out of town, having picked up Mike, the Project Team Leader,

17   The Project was the Nepal Australia Community Resource Management Project.

and Anthony, the Community Development Advisor at the project office on the way.

The Nepalese hill communities had been undertaking a form of community management of their forests since the mid-1970s, when they had got fed up with the forests in their areas being mismanaged by the government forestry agency. They were being overcut by entrepreneurs, particularly cutting Sal, a valuable hardwood. With the help of aid agencies like AusAID, there had been a lot of success, and the slopes were once again turning green with tree cover, either natural regeneration or plantations. In addition, there had been increased benefits to the villagers, though not always on an equitable basis, with caste distinctions playing a part and the lower castes, particularly the Dalits or Untouchables, often missing out on their fair share of benefits.

We moved out of the crowded and expanding urban sprawl of Kathmandu with its multi-story square-shaped concrete and brick buildings, whose main variation was the size, but not the shape. The narrow, almost two-lane road was the start of the highway to the Chinese (Tibet) border and rose above the rice paddies of Bhaktapur District, interspersed with the occasional massive brick works.

A left turn off the main highway saw us on one of many narrow winding roads, climbing into the hills surrounding the Kathmandu Valley. Passing through the occasional security force roadblock was a reminder of the ongoing conflict with the Maoists. The next day's papers carried word of four security force men killed in a fire fight with the rebels in the Kabhre Palanchok District, our destination for the day. On an earlier trip that year three or four of us had driven ourselves into the hills for a reconnaissance. I was nervous about doing such a trip unescorted and was glad when we descended back down to Kathmandu, having seen some evidence of Maoists activities, such as stuffed dummies swinging by the neck from trees. It was far from a secure environment, but we felt the calculated risk to our doing our work was acceptable. The understanding was that we would not be as important targets as government people in government vehicles. At the same time, the project was endeavouring to help the rural people, which was partially what the Maoist were also supposedly trying to do.

The lower hills with their multiple stepped terraces gave way to rice paddies in the valley bottoms, but higher up, we drove through degraded broad-leafed forest and pine as we passed the small tourist resort town of Nagagot. There was more of the same terrace cultivation and forests, until we finally topped the ridge under the gaze of soldiers manning a sandbagged machine gun emplacement near a military base.

The eastern side of the ridge was the Kavre Palanchok District and the road deteriorated to a rutted track, softened by pine needles as we descended through dense pine stands. It should not have been so dense, as we were into forest managed by local communities and the local Community Forest User Group (CFUG) should have been thinning the pines and generally managing them to better effect. At least that would have been the ideal situation but getting the ideas and techniques across takes time; in this case it would seem it was taking years.

As we wandered through the pines in the cool mountain air blended with the aroma of pine resin, we discussed how the plantation's full potential could be used to benefit the community. Eventually, members of the CFUG joined us and we all sat on the dry pine needle duff in filtered sunshine.

Discussions ensued, and it was good to actually get in touch with reality in the field, after planning for this final year of the project, based on reports, hearsay and one previous quick trip to the districts. The locals told us how the CFUG had come to be some 11 years earlier, at which point they said these hills were barren or covered in low scrub, after being almost totally deforested through indiscriminate cutting. Now they had a valuable asset in the pine plantation, from which they were already getting income through the sale of logs.

CFUG in Janagal Range Post discussing the management and use of their pine plantations while sitting in a stand badly in need of thinning

But they also had some problems in managing these forest assets. In several smaller pines, we had seen quite a bit of die-back or the browning and dying off of needles in the upper branches, the position on the tree where active growth is normally most vigorous. The villagers mentioned there was also a root fungus, with both ailments a concern as they reduce tree growth.

The die-back could have been at least partly due to nutrient and/or water stress brought on because the trees had not been managed properly. It was a shame to see a valuable resource not achieving its production potential because technical inputs and support were missing or inadequate. The result was that the villagers who were managing the forest were not obtaining optimal benefits to improve their livelihoods.

After some two hours, our combined group meandered down a dirt road to the local village, about 100 metres below, and perched on the side of a spur, with terraced maize fields all around. There was more talking in and around the user group's dark dry-stone office that had been built with their earnings from log sales. We then set off down the road, if it could be called that, to the district headquarters at Dulakel, for a spot of lunch at a local hotel. We were running late, as is usually the case on these field visits, given all the talking that goes on.

I felt such discussions were important to get an understanding of the local situation from the community's perspective. But, from experience, I had found that even when I thought I understood the community situation and how they managed their resources, on a subsequent visit I would find I hadn't got the full picture and thus a complete understanding of why outcomes were not as planned. To me, sitting down with a group of villagers and talking about all sorts of issues over a cup or two of tea, rice wine, or country liquor was as worthwhile or even more rewarding than asking direct questions in a more formal way. Village people aren't in as much of a hurry and time isn't usually of such great importance as it is to us foreign interlopers, for whom time often seems in short supply.

The next stop was down a very steep walking track, where a group of some twenty women, all dressed in red, were gathered under a pipal tree (a Bengal Fig). They were all Dalits (untouchable caste) and had not got a fair go until the project came along about a year ago, with a Women's Empowerment programme. As they explained, they had already realised the need to improve themselves before the project provided inputs.

Literacy training had been a starting point as all had been illiterate, but they knew empowerment meant more than that, and they were keen to improve their situation with regard to such things as health, nutrition, and income. Women were second-class citizens in Nepal, even those in higher castes, but these Dalit women were doubly disadvantaged as Dalits just don't usually count as part of the community. It was, therefore, heartening to hear how these women had improved their lot, and were now voicing their opinions in public meetings, and already getting concessions.

At first, they sat on an embankment under the Pipal tree while a few self-consciously gave answers to our questions and a young boy lolled in a fork of the tree above them, watching the scene. We sat below them on a small flat area, but as the discussions progressed, first three women then a few more moved onto a mat much closer to us.

The discussion became increasingly animated with several women answering questions or just voicing their ideas. All the while, in contrast, I noticed a young woman sitting somewhat apart on the bank with a small girl. The sadness in the woman's demeanour was palpable and seemed highlighted by the attention-seeking of her daughter whom the woman held with great tenderness. I wondered about her situation and what was making her appear so sad, in contrast to the animated enthusiasm of the other women present.

Meanwhile, the rest of the women were explaining how the CFUG committee had been providing loans to them, but the women had negotiated a reduced interest rate of 10 percent instead of the established 12 percent.

Thuliban CFUG, Women's Empowerment Group

Dalet women enthusiastically explaining their achievements as a group

Although the women had asked for 8 percent, they still felt they had got a good deal. They had also started a savings group to provide funds for themselves and had managed to obtain a hectare of forest land from the community for their own use and were growing improved pasture grasses for their household cattle. These weren't large concessions or achievements, though they were a start.

Undaunted, they had a plan to start a cardamom plantation the following year for which they needed another 1 to 1.5 hectares. They were talking with the CFUG committee, trying to work out a benefit sharing deal. This was women's empowerment at work and wonderful to behold.

A lone Dalit mother and child, who did not seem to be so enthusiastic about developments.

196

However, the CFUG committee were apparently reluctant to allocate more land. Indeed, it seemed that the community, although having undertaken a wealth ranking survey and providing benefits to all members equally, were still reluctant to fully adopt measures that would raise the livelihoods of the most disadvantaged in the community – the women and the poorest villagers. We listened as the women explained how several poor families could not afford the fees to join the CFUG, particularly when back fees to the establishment of the CFUG were being demanded, albeit with a ten percent concession. There was still much to do, but there was some movement towards a more equitable distribution of benefits being developed.

The afternoon was moving on and we had too as well. I wondered how much further we would continue down into the valley, and thought of the long hike back up, regretting I had not brought my water bottle, as the afternoon sun was hot and the air dry.

We headed further down the steep slope to look at the women's group forest, which still needed a lot of work, and then on to another forest area where I could see further unused potential in the dense Sal regeneration. Little thought had been given to thinning here. In fact, remembering other Sal regeneration in the districts, there seemed to be either a reluctance to thin and improve the stand for production or a lack of knowledge about how to manage such forest.

It seemed a shame, as there was much potential to both provide income or subsistence benefits from cutting the small timber for fuel or poles, as well as to enhance the opportunity for more valuable benefits from larger trees in the future. These Sal trees may not have had the potential to reach the heights and volumes of their cousins down on the more fertile lands of the Terai, but they could still prove to be a valuable resource.

After we had descended several hundred metres along a few kilometres of this steep uneven track, we passed through a cleared area of forest where another group had been experimenting with a variety of tree species. This group was more innovative and were trying different approaches to managing their forests as they later showed us further down the slope. They had actually done some thinning and were cutting the Sal to be used as firewood by CFUG members. The group were also keen to do away with the pine forests or plantations and replace them with broadleaved species, some of which were part of trials we had seen. They felt the pines dried out the soil and did not allow anything to grow under them, whereas the broadleaved species provided leave litter for fodder and compost, a multiple-use benefit. This was local community knowledge coming to the fore to enhance benefits from their forests. They were also considering leasing land to outsiders, to plant commercial tree crops, a rather innovative approach to the use of their 62 hectares of forest land.

Anthony Willett, the Community Development Advisor standing in Sal regeneration on a steep slope in Keraghari Range Post, showing potential for stand improvement.

We sat and chatted in a picnic shed they had built among scattered pines, using their own funds. It was being used by the local towns people for a charge of NR350 (AUD$7) a time; an achievement of which they were duly proud. The committee treasurer did most of the talking and seemed to be the main leader, while the chairman sat nonchalantly, with his arms draped over the back of the pipe bench, nodding in agreement at times. The community were quite active in social mobilization. They were sharing benefits amongst their members, including the distribution of firewood for a price and on the condition that each hamlet that received the firewood provided volunteer labour. Small development grants were also available for poorer groups from the CFUG committee.

The sun was getting low on the horizon as we walked down through more Sal and pine forests to the highway below. On the way, I remarked, not for the first time, how some soil moisture conservation works, such as contour trenches, might improve growth of the Sal regeneration. Further down the hill, one of the parties pointed out how my idea might work. There was an irrigation trench dug across the slope and below it the trees and vegetation were decidedly more vigorous than above the trench, having received more ground water because of the trench.

I really had thought it would be a good challenge to climb back up the way we had come, and had psyched myself for the effort, but that was not in the plan. We needed to be out of this valley before dark for security reasons, although we were persuaded to have a cup of tea at the small wayside tea shop owned by the group's treasurer. There we sat under an overhang of the shop, which was part of a two-story mud-faced house. The sweet milk tea, in glasses, was scalding hot, but helped to allay our thirsts to some extent, while we continued our discussions with the treasurer, though by this stage my brain was moving into neutral.

Driving back out of the valley into which we had descended, we stopped at a local restaurant cum bar near to the top of the watershed and hanging precariously over the valley. The view from the terrace was of the valley below in the gathering dusk, and, in the distance to the north, the white peaks of the Himalayas were visible through the haze. We deserved a few beers and sat with the district forest officers for the usual debriefing and general chit chat that occurs on such occasions, when inhibitions are down and opinions are high, particularly as the level of beer is lowered in the bottles. It was well and truly dark by the time we left, with a clear starlit night above and the twinkling of scattered lights below in the valley indicating that the communities were at home for dinner. We made it back to Kathmandu by nine p.m. knowing that this last stretch of road down into the Kathmandu Valley was quite secure.

An Introduction to India

As our plane flew low on our approach to landing at Mumbai Airport, I wondered what lay ahead on this trip to such a populous country who's fascinating, and at times, turbulent, history I had read so much about. The city seemed to be a jumble of grey, concrete, unpainted multi-storied buildings with narrow streets full of vehicles and people. Closer to the airport, we passed over a mass of tattered shacks, crowded together, then over an open dirt field where dozens of the poor shack dwellers were squatting. I wondered, at first, what they were doing, and then I realised that this was their toilet facility, and they were defecating.

On the way from the rather run-down airport into the city centre, we passed more of these shanty towns, and I could see how the shacks were often constructed with cardboard and tin; the latter being metal drums that had been hammered flat and then somehow fastened to form patchwork walls and roofs. And drifting in through the open window of the Ambassador taxi came the putrid smell of clogged and polluted drains filled with a grey liquid and numerous pieces of debris.

So, this was India. I wasn't impressed. The poverty and poor sanitation were all pervasive, especially in and around the urban areas. Then there were the people - so many and everywhere.

This was an assignment to a country where I was to spend a great deal of time over the succeeding thirty years and, in the process, got to understand and appreciate so much more about India, its people and its customs. This trip, in 1982, was also a further step along the social and participatory forestry lane. Forestal had been asked by the Canadian International Development Agency (CIDA) to design and appraise a social forestry project in the state of Andhra Pradesh, towards the south of the country.

Our aim was to assess the demand for wood in communities as well as the potential and interest for such communities to grow trees. We then needed to reach a consensus with our counterparts in the Andhra Pradesh Department of Forests about how a social forestry project should be developed. This included the planting of trees by communities or farmers on their lands, but also for trees to be planted along roads, railway lines and canals, as spare land for planting trees was scarce. I feel we did something right because when I began spending more time in AP from 2000, I found that a major source of trees and local income along the coastal area was from farm plantings initiated through our project, mainly using Casuarinas or Coastal She Oaks (*Casuarina equisetifolia*).

The next day, at Hyderabad Airport, as we emerged from the airport terminal, numerous beggars assaulted us begging for alms. Many were in a pitiful, bedraggled state or maimed, some kneeling on wheeled boards and pushing themselves along with bandaged hands or on pads made from old tires. On the streets of Hyderabad, the capital of Andhra Pradesh, the piteous plight of the poor was much in evidence. Numerous small cardboard or tin shelters acted as homes, although some had no such shelter and lay on the footpaths. I sometimes wondered if the bodies I avoided as I walked along were actually alive. Perhaps, some weren't.

Hyderabad in 1982 was like one enormous village with few high-rise buildings and it teemed with people. We spent several days in the field: most of them in the coastal regions. This involved many hours driving along narrow, bitumen, rural roads. Our Mahindra Jeeps dodged horse or oxen-drawn carts, a variety of other vehicles, including high-sided, brightly painted trucks, people, and even elephants, as well as a few other cars and trucks. Luckily, there weren't too many other vehicles, as drivers, ours included, tended to overtake on blind corners and seat belts weren't an option. Occasionally, our driver would overtake with another vehicle approaching in the opposite direction, forcing the other vehicle off to the side of the road. There were no repercussions, with this sort of driving being accepted as normal. Admittedly, the roads did not allow for high speeds, which was a saving grace.

Our field trips around Eastern Andhra Pradesh took us through a range of rural vistas. Much of the time, our route passed through cultivated fields and villages, with little open space or bush between the communities. The forests tended to be in the hillier areas and varied in condition from stands of tall trees with thick undergrowth to more open and degraded forests. The latter were usually teak-dominated in the north of the state, while the other, more mixed forests, often with bamboo prevalent, occurred towards the coast. Low scrub forest was dominant in the drier south and offered little in the way of either wood or non-wood produce for local communities.

The team would usually stay overnight in Forest Department or other government rest houses that had been established throughout the state and were a common feature in India. These, usually well maintained, though often ageing, bungalows were a hangover from the time of the British Raj. They were generally comfortable, and the Indian food was very good, with lots of it. I also experienced for the first time the culture of command and control that existed within the Andhra Pradesh Forest Department. The terminology was apt, even down to nomenclature, with low-ranking staff being referred to as subordinates and the lowest office workers were called peons.

There was much saluting by subordinate staff of more senior officers, and replies of "Yes, Saar," with no questions asked. When we would arrive at a guest house several uniformed subordinate staff would, invariably be lined up and saluting as we drove in, giving me the impression that we were serious dignitaries arriving, rather than a bunch of foreign foresters. Even junior professional officers would kowtow to their superiors with very little, if any, questioning or opinions given, unless they were asked, and opinions seemed to be rarely sought.

I got my first dose of 'Delhi Belly' about halfway through our three-week stay. Unfortunately, it struck rather suddenly in Bangalore Airport as we were waiting for our flight back to Hyderabad after a field trip through Andhra Pradesh and Tamil Nadu. Having to seek relief in a rather smelly, dirty, squat toilet was not very comfortable, but the phrase 'any port in a storm' came to mind. Despite taking a couple of remedies, my malady persisted until I left the country and headed to Greece for a business development visit on the way back to Vancouver. After that first nasty bout, I rarely suffered other tummy problems in many subsequent visits to the Sub-continent, despite the many months spent in the rural areas of India and Bangladesh.

There were a couple of visits to India in the early 1990s, looking at woodfuels supply and demand issues and the effect of urban demand for woodfuels on surrounding forests, which wasn't good. Until the Government of India introduced a programme of subsidized liquid petroleum gas (LPG) for use by urban dwellers, a considerable area of forests had been destroyed adjacent to towns and cities. On the other hand, the lack of wood for fuel in rural areas meant that households only had half of the energy needed to cook adequately, with dried cow dung playing an increasing role in cooking, to the detriment of agricultural land fertility. I had an interesting time discussing woodfuels with several learned gentlemen in various institutes and government in Delhi, Dehra Dun and Hyderabad, as well as spending some days roaming around the countryside, seeing how degraded lands could be used to grow wood for fuel.

On a morning in November 2000, I found myself at Hyderabad Airport, being met by a representative of the Andhra Pradesh Forestry Department, before being driven to the Banjara Hotel, where I waited to hear from someone at the Forest Department. I had been asked by the FAO

Investment Centre to lead a mission to evaluate the World Bank Andhra Pradesh Forestry Project and do an implementation completion report.

This was to be an eye-opening experience. The project's components included participatory management and rehabilitation of forests by forest fringe dwellers, improving plant propagation and productivity through applied research, and biodiversity conservation. Eventually, a phone call from the Additional Chief Conservator (the Indians certainly have a way with words) of the Forestry Department, Mr. K. Subba Rao, informed me that a vehicle would be sent to pick me up after lunch and he hoped I had had a good rest following my flight. Having spent some time being briefed on the project, I found myself, two days later, sitting next to the Principle Chief Conservator of Forests, Mr. S.J. Mukherji on the well stuffed back seat of an Ambassador sedan: a squat solid looking copy of a 1950s Morris Oxford.

This short, lean, but lively man, wearing black trousers and a white shirt with rolled up sleeves, was something of an expert on the joint management of forests with communities and I was somewhat nervous accompanying such a leading figure in AP forestry. However, we settled down to a comfortable relationship as our driver expertly dodged other vehicles, pedestrians, bullock and horse carts and the inevitable wandering cow. The drive was somewhat nerve-wracking at first until I gained some trust in the driver's abilities, although, I reserved my trust in his judgement, particularly when it came to overtaking other vehicles on blind corners.

As we drove along the narrow bitumen rural roads, I learned from Sri Mukherji the origins of the project and some of its achievements of which he was rather proud. Stopping at villages that were involved in the project, we would invariably be met by a greeting committee of villagers who proceeded to anoint us with the red dash to the forehead and lay a lei around our shoulders. In my case, I often ended up with several leis placed there by villagers' keen to welcome this foreign 'dignitary'.

Through discussions with the APFD officers and talking with villagers, I was discovering what an innovative and successful project this was. It was evident that there was an enthusiasm among many of the APFD staff, though not all. Messrs Subba Rao and Mukherji explained that it had taken perhaps two years to change the mindset of the APFD officers and subordinate field staff. For decades, such staff had communicated in a very top-down and patronizing way with forest-related communities and farmers growing trees. They were used to the role of regulating and policing, not communicating and cooperating with villagers. There had also been much graft and corruption with field staff; sometimes forcing the poor villagers to pay bribes to prevent prosecution for even minor forestry related infringements. In fact, I learned from more than one officer that such field staff were some of the most hated government officers. And with good reason, as these officials were quite literally robbing already impoverished people, who were probably illegally taking wood or non-wood products from the forest, just to survive.

Arriving at one of the communities to inspect progress. Is this what is referred to as being overlaid?

Now, there was a major shift in the approach to sustainable management of the forests. It must have been incomprehensible to the villagers and hard to understand for the forestry field staff. This joint forest management project was actually endeavouring to co-opt communities to protect and manage areas of government forests allocated to them, and in return, to receive benefits from the same forests for themselves.

I can imagine the first response by many villagers when such an approach was suggested. "Go on. Pull the other leg. Do you think I came down in the last shower," or the Indian equivalent to such words? After all, there was an intrinsic mistrust of government and government schemes by village communities, based on decades of abuse of power and maltreatment of villagers; and the insurgent Naxalite[18] movement was feeding on such discontent.

But over time, communities had come to accept what was being proposed through the project as genuine, or at least, something which it

---

18 Between 1980 and 2010, the Naxal (Maoist) movement was firmly entrenched in Andhra Pradesh. The causes for the Naxal insurgency were economic exploitation, poverty and social marginalization of the Dalit and Adivasi population in rural and remote forest areas of Andhra Pradesh.

was worth becoming involved in. Of course, what also helped change the attitudes of the villagers was the prospect of earning money for labour, using funds provided through the project for forest improvement works. I heard stories of how previously shunned APFD field staff were now being welcomed by the villagers and offered cups of tea.

To the north of the state, near the town of Warangal, on the second day of our field excursion, we stopped at the village of Macherla. Here was a village forestry group (*Vana Samarakshan Samithi* (VSS) in Telegu, the local language) established through the project with some 200 hectares of forest assigned to them in 1997 for protection and management. Previously, they had seen the forest being degraded and disappearing, with thieves taking good teak. Now, they considered the forest as their own, even though legally it was still a government forest reserve. They had chased off wood thieves, and the poorer element in the village were earning wages through the project to rehabilitate the forest and establish soil and moisture conservation works like staggered trenches or gully plugs and check dams. The forest was yielding sustainable benefits in non-wood forest products, fuelwood and grass, with increased benefits expected in the next few years.

In another village forestry group, Nizampeta; apart from forest benefits, a women's thrift group had been formed with 20 members. They were each contributing up to a total of Rs600 (US$12) a month, which the project would then match. This would enable a fund to be established for lending among the members. In this case they were charging three percent interest. Other groups charged two percent.

This meant that women had access to affordable credit to purchase necessary items for their homes or for their children's education, rather than having to borrow from loan sharks who charged up to 60 percent interest. These women's thrift groups were also empowering women to undertake joint ventures, such as making smokeless chulas or cooking stoves, purchasing a sewing machine to make clothes, and making candles from animal lard. Some groups were federating, further empowering the women to stick up for their rights or obtain concessions within the community or from government officials.

One objective of the project was to ensure the advancement of women. At one village, we were met by a relatively young female VSS chairperson. She proudly showed us the community's achievements, including two hectares of planted clonal eucalypts that would be harvested for pulpwood in a few more years, as well as planted bamboo that would shortly yield culms for sale. There was no doubting the overall community enthusiasm, as men and women smiled and nodded, while I discussed future plans and prospects with this dynamic woman. It was difficult not to be buoyed by her enthusiasm and the achievements of her community.

We would usually arrange to have lunch and would then spend the night at one of the many APFD or another government agency's rest house. Often, as we approached the rest house, FD office complex or even a forest site, we would be met by several khaki uniform clad subordinate forestry staff, who would come smartly to attention and salute as we drove up. This was a vivid reminder of the command-and-control operational management system applied within the APFD. I sometimes found this quasi-military performance amusing, particularly when it came to issuing and obeying directives. Although, as I later spent more time working with the APFD, I found it a definite constraint to initiative and progress in field operations.

This first association with the joint management of forests between communities and the APFD created a very positive and favourable impression, and I gave the first phase of the project a glowing evaluation, which, of course, the AP foresters were very happy about. I was particularly struck by the enthusiasm and competence of a number of the APFD forest officers, as well as subordinate staff in the field, and this despite the fact the concept was a new one and so different to their regular approach to managing forests and the forest fringe communities. Their initiatives were already showing impressive results. This included a tree improvement programme that was producing eucalypt and various fruit trees' planting stock with much improved yield potential.

After this successful first JFM project in AP, it was almost a foregone conclusion that there would be a follow-on project, and there was – the Andhra Pradesh Community Forest Management Project (APCFMP). This was to be a bigger and better version of the earlier project and I was asked by Irshad Khan, the World Bank Project Manager, to take part in the design and implementation management of the new project. As a result, over the next ten years, I would spend about three months a year working with this project, as well as contributing to several other World Bank community-based forest management projects in the states of Kerala, Uttar Pradesh, Uttaranchal, and Assam.

This all meant that I spent a lot of time transiting through airports in India, which could on occasion be a lengthy and irritatingly bureaucratic procedure. In Hyderabad, the capital of AP, there was rarely any problem. Initially, it was a smaller airport with few international connections, but even with the new Rajiv Gandhi International Airport, outside of town at Shamshabad, which opened in 2008, there was not much of a problem, even less, in fact. It also helped that I was always met on arrival by a range officer from APFD, together with a car and a driver to conduct me to my hotel. The security people at Hyderabad Airport were far from officious. On one occasion, they found a Swiss Army knife I had inadvertently left in my carry-on bag. Rather than confiscating the offending 'weapon', the officer kindly arranged for me to collect the knife on my return in a few days' time.

It was a different scenario at the very busy Delhi Airport, particularly when it came to international flights. On my flight to Rome via Zurich at the end of the AP Forest Project evaluation, I enjoyed the pleasant and efficient service of Swissair in their spacious business class cabin. This contrasted with the chaos at the Delhi Airport international terminal. Experience had shown me that a double degree of patience was so often needed at this terminal, particularly when departing at one a.m. with most flights to Europe leaving sometime after midnight.

First, there was a scrum to get into the terminal where a police officer checked each person's ticket. I had the help of a tout cum porter, who imposed himself on me and then wanted Rs150 at the door. I was prepared for this scam, and I knew that Rs50 would have been more than adequate, but I gave him Rs100 as he really did sound desperate, and I had it to spare.

I was then faced with a lengthy queue to get my bags scanned before check-in. The Swissair check-in was swift, efficient, and painless as one would expect from flying business class with such an airline. Then, there was the immigration queue, where passports were checked with departure cards and boarding passes. It was similar to when I entered the country; the officers moving with almost exaggerated slowness, thoroughly checking all documents with the pedanticism inculcated in Indian government bureaucrats. Occasionally, one of the officers would find fault with a person's documents, which, of course, meant conferring with his senior officer.

All this queueing and checks would take about 45 minutes, but I had time to sit down and get a drink in the Taj Lounge before joining the security check prior to entering the departure lounge. At the head of the security check queue, my boarding card was again checked by a police officer to see that it had been stamped by another official at a desk just after the immigration check. The purpose of this check escaped me as the immigration officer had already stamped my passport, and boarding card.

After I put my bag on the belt for the x-ray surveillance scanner at the security check, I joined all other passengers to be subjected to a full body pat down while standing on a low box, having removed all items from my pockets, which were placed on a table with the boarding pass. There they were subjected to close scrutiny by the security officer. The box was probably a health and safety addition to prevent back strain among security officers while they checked one's lower limbs.

This was all in lieu of going through the electronic surveillance scanner, which may not have worked. But it wasn't done in an overly officious manner. In fact, once they saw I was an Australian, the subject of cricket and various cricketers would then be discussed while the patting down took place. At the end of the body check, my boarding pass was again stamped, and I picked up my carry-on baggage which had been duly stamped on a specially provided I.D. tag.

The final queuing occurred at boarding. It wasn't just a matter of airline staff checking boarding passes and passports. Before this there was another security officer who checked that our boarding passes had the requisite number of stamps from officials who were supposed to stamp them, and that our hand baggage tags had been stamped at the security check point.

Having reached the airport from my Delhi hotel in a small rickety taxi nearly two hours before the scheduled departure of my flight, I had spent over an hour of that time in queues. The rubber stamp industry in India was thriving.

Community Management of Forests, a Win-Win Situation

It was February 2004, and not a bad month to be in south-east India, weatherwise. The days are hot, but nothing like the furnace temperatures of April and May when the thermometer stays in the 40 degrees Celsius during the day, or the more sauna-like conditions of June as the South West monsoon hits. I was in the coastal region of Andhra Pradesh State doing one of my periodic field visits to check on a community forestry project being funded by the World Bank; something I had been doing about twice a year for the last three years.

We had left the small hotel with its makeshift plumbing at around six a.m. just as the local citizens were stirring and a few health-conscious souls were out for their morning walk in that cool freshness, before what promised to be another hot day. After a quick South Indian breakfast with sweet milk tea at the nearby Forest Department rest house on the edge of the town of Srikakulam, my Indian colleagues and I set out for a morning in the field. Now, after travelling the smooth surfaces of the bitumen roads for an hour or so, our Indian SUV was jolted about as we made our way over rough dirt tracks to the community awaiting us among the forested hills and farmed narrow valleys that formed the border between the states of Andhra Pradesh and Orissa.

This was one of over five thousand such communities that were participating in the Community Forest Management Project that I had been involved in for the past three years. The community we were to visit that clear, hot February morning was typical of those involved in the project, if anything could be called typical in the socially and ecologically diverse landscape that makes up the state of Andhra Pradesh, or India in general.

This community was made up of tribal people, as were over half the communities involved in the project, meaning that they consisted of ethnic groups that predated the Moguls and other migrants who had arrived in the last two thousand years. Perhaps they were somehow related to the people, who supposedly made their way across India to as far away as Australia some 50,000 to 60,000 years ago.

The tribals or 'scheduled tribes', as the Indian government refers to them, tend to be more homogenous and lack the caste system that is still prevalent in much of India. In many cases, through an ironic twist of fate, their ancestors might have been forest dwellers, living for centuries in a symbiotic subsistence existence within the forest before the British expelled them. This was done, first, to convert forests to agricultural land to gain taxes, and second, because they were considered a threat to scientific forest management and conservation.

Eventually, legislation and forest reservation broke the traditional organic link between tribals and the forest restricting or denying usufruct rights to forest products. In some areas, such tribals still recognise a form of customary tenure over the forest lands. This, and the fact that they seem to have more of a community spirit, has tended to make the tribal communities more suited to community or participatory management of forests.

Prior to the introduction of the project, these forest fringe communities had been largely without a sustainable means of livelihood, often lacking sufficient land to grow even subsistence crops. Any legal income had usually come from male family members who had found work by migrating to provincial towns and cities or working as farm labourers. The result was that many wives were without their husbands and children without their fathers. So being on the fringe of both society and the forest they had opted, through necessity, to make use of the latter as the nearest available source of land and goods, notwithstanding the fact that to do so was illegal.

They cut down trees to plant crops in a type of shifting cultivation called "podu", as well as illegally taking wood and non-wood products for both personal use and to sell. But they remained desperately poor and were usually without basic amenities. As a result of this uncontrolled exploitation, the forest, which often contained valuable teak and other hardwoods as well as many non-timber products, had become heavily degraded.

In some areas, this degradation was so bad that the trees had largely disappeared; being replaced by areas of grass and scrub with most of the remnants of remaining trees reduced to high stumps with coppice shoots only two or three metres high. At the same time, ground water had been so adversely affected that wells and streams had dried up. In fact, what was happening was that the forest fringe and adjacent communities were destroying the last major source of their livelihood, having no framework or means of controlling or managing the exploitation in a forest over which they had no legal tenure. It was a classic case of the tragedy of the commons.

Similar scenes of impoverished communities linked with degraded or destroyed forest resources and the associated landscape can be seen throughout many third world countries. However, a few enlightened souls had recognised several years earlier that the concept of endeavouring to conserve and manage forest resources by locking them up within a reserve under the control of ill-equipped, under-paid and, often, corrupt government forestry agencies didn't work when there were desperately poor communities on the fringes or even within the forests who relied on such forests for their very existence. So, in a similar example of what I had proposed in Tanzania, the enlightened souls decided to use these communities to protect, manage and enhance such forests, in return for an equitable and sustainable share of the forest resources. After all, as I found in Tanzania, the forest-based communities had *de facto* control of the forests, despite the best efforts of the forestry agencies; and as mentioned earlier, the forebears of many of these communities had sustainably managed these same forests for centuries prior to the imposition of colonial administrative and control systems.

Under the project in Andhra Pradesh, each selected community was being given the opportunity, as honest citizens, to take over the protection, rehabilitation, and management of 200 to 300 hectares of forest, with project support. In return, they would be entitled to harvest for their own use and for sale both wood and non-wood forest products on a managed basis. The communities would thus have a vested interest in protecting and sustainably managing the forest resource.

For the first few years, there was also financial support to pay for initial community involvement in the rehabilitation and protection of the forests and to generally get things going. Overall, the interest and involvement had been very positive. Villagers were improving their livelihoods and becoming better off, and the migration from the villages had been reversed, while at the same time there was a noticeable improvement in the forests, and ground water levels were much higher, not only in the forests, but also in nearby fields and villages.

For the latter part of our journey that morning we had been passing through uncultivated fields, many of which would be used for paddy rice. But this was the dry season, and with the monsoon rains in October not coming, the farmers were looking forward to the next rains that were due to start soon, otherwise food would be in short supply. The dry, dusty, brown plain fields became less frequent as the valleys became narrower and the hills closed in. It was here that we finally arrived at our destination. Beside the track stood representatives of the expectant community, together with several uniformed forest range officers and their subordinates. There were also a couple NGO (non-government organization) officers who had been helping to organize and train the community.

I would often feel rather self-conscious turning up at these communities, where, sometimes, drums and horns would greet us. From their small pond, expectations were that some bigwig representing the World Bank was coming with several Forest Department officials. From my big pond, perspective I was not a bigwig, but rather a consultant who was trying to help the project to succeed. Nevertheless, I understood the situation and was grateful for the welcome, complete with at least two leis of marigolds thrust over my head by eager women. The forestry staff in their khaki uniforms came to attention and saluted smartly, and I gave a namaste, the traditional Indian greeting of joined hands[19], to many, and shook hands with the leaders as well.

There was much smiling among the general throng of people, while the leaders tried to look suitably important, but, at the same time, appeared eager to please. As with many such welcomes throughout the project area, the people seemed quite happy that we had come to see what they had been doing with their allotted forest area. We were visiting this community because, rather than be shown some of the better managed forest areas, I had asked to be taken to a poorly performing community. According to the local APFD officers, this community had been having trouble maintaining trees they had planted to enrich some of the degraded sites, and they weren't making much headway in collecting non-timber forest products or making money. Well, now we would see what the situation really was like.

This community forestry management group, or VSS as per the Telegu acronym, was called Kummearivaleasa. Some 25 villagers, of which more than half were women, some with young children or babies, gathered under a canopy that had been put up for the occasion. We, the visitors, sat on chairs at a table and were served with some biscuits and water. The villagers sat on the ground, which had been covered with several mats. There was a quick introduction in the local language and then the VSS chairperson gave us a history of the VSS and what they had been doing since its inception in 1996.

All this was interesting, but as is often the case with such get-togethers and in line with a certain Indian formality, it was largely scripted stuff. I was keen to get into the forest and see what was actually happening on the ground and have an on-site dialogue with the villagers. So, we trooped out from under the canopy and walked down, through a grove of mango trees, across a dry creek bed and up a slope into a rather dry forest. There were gaps in the forest growth, which had been planted with various non-timber forest product seedlings, though many of these looked decidedly sick. Big trees

---

19 "Namaste" is a very beautiful and spiritual greeting; roughly translated as "may the God in me greet the God in you".

were few and far between, and the whole area looked to be badly degraded, with little sign of much successful rehabilitation over the six years of the community's involvement.

However, as we discussed the situation, under a brilliant blue sky that was becoming steely with the heat, it became clear that the villagers didn't see their efforts as a failure. They had been very actively endeavouring to rehabilitate and manage their forest legacy, as soon became clear. This included efforts to establish seedlings in the open areas, but the last two rains had failed to arrive and, despite hand carrying water to each seedling, many had succumbed to the dry, hot conditions[20]. Nevertheless, some seedlings were surviving and would be expected to bear fruit and provide incomes in another two to four years.

Meanwhile, they had been tending the existing trees that bore several non-timber forest products (NTFPs), like the small, round, green soap nut fruits that are used for washing; the flatter green *Pongamia* nuts, which yielded a useful engine oil and substitute for diesel; the round, green bitter amla fruit, high in vitamin C and is used in pickles; and, finally, the dried fruit of the Bixa plant that produces a brilliant red food colouring. They were also getting dried firewood and eventually their efforts would produce some important timbers. Production had increased, for example they were now getting 150 bags a year of soap nuts compared with only 50 prior to the formation of the VSS. The problem, as they pointed out, though, was that they could not access the markets, being isolated and somewhat at the end the road. Without such access, their productive efforts earned little money, and the situation was leading to despondency.

I could sense that these people, who, with very little other means of livelihood from the surrounding lands, and, who, therefore, relied heavily on the forest, were keen as mustard to make things work and had put in a great deal of effort.

They kept urging me into different areas of the forest to view their regeneration achievements and produced baskets and bags of the various products for my Indian colleagues and I to inspect. But the ultimate in innovation came to light when they told me they were planning to set up an internet kiosk or website at the nearest town to better market their NTFPs. This particularly applied to the Bixa colouring that was mainly sought overseas. It turned out that the state government, which had a rather far-sighted chief minister, was providing funding to bring IT to just such rural communities and, these villagers were determined to take full advantage of it.

---

20 Temperatures in April and May, prior to the monsoons can be consistently above 45 degrees C, with very low humidity, and little or no rain from September to May.

The VSS committee chairman with an Andhra Pradesh Forest Department section officer in a degraded community forest with a soap nut tree in the background and a regenerated Pongamia sapling centre right.

A collection of non-timber forest products being produced from the rehabilitated community forest: clockwise from top left, bixa, Pongamia nuts, and soap nuts.

I was definitely impressed. In fact, standing there in this degenerated forest miles from the nearest decent road, water tap or light switch and other services, the concept seemed almost surreal; but they meant to do it.

They were certainly one step ahead of the Forest Department officers, who didn't even recognise the problems related to the slow development in the VSS. Like so many such rural communities I had seen associated with this project and others in India, they were far from being a downtrodden group feeling sorry for themselves and looking only for the next government or donor handouts.

With a few monetary lifelines, some technical inputs and a lot of hard work, they were significantly improving their incomes and their lives; and, although this particular forest area was still languishing in a somewhat degraded state, other communities that had different products, better fortune and more accessible market links, were showing a marked improvement in livelihoods and overall forest cover, with excellent potential for future production of timber and other wood and non-wood products, on a sustainably managed basis.

I wasn't sure of the practicality or feasibility of their web marketing, but we discussed their plans and aspirations, and it was agreed with the local Forest Department staff that they would help. The APFD was now also aware of the general marketing problem, something they should have caught up with if their communication with the villagers had been more effective. However, the implementation of community forest management was still a learning experience on both sides, and most were willing to learn so that improvements could be made.

Part of the problem was that the majority of the FD staff were not commercially orientated, but they were definitely on a sharp learning curve. Incidentally, so was I, particularly if we were going to ensure that there was some solid degree of sustainability established among a major share of the five thousand plus forest communities that fell under the project before it ended in another five years.

After an hour or more of rambling around the community's forest, while holding animated discussions under an increasingly hot sun, we found our way back to the shelter of the mango trees and, there, shared a cold drink before saying our farewells and heading back down the rough track to the coast and the city of Visakhapatnam.

I was travelling with Ramesh Kalaghatgi, a senior officer of the Andhra Pradesh Forestry Department and a friend after working on the project together and undertaking numerous field trips together over several years. I had met Ramesh on my mission to evaluate the earlier forestry project in AP. He was a very likeable man, of medium height and slightly stouter build, which his wife, was constantly trying to contain, while I would thwart her efforts by bringing Ramesh bags of macadamia nuts every time I visited. We became firm friends as we then spent countless hours travelling by road and rail, visiting communities, as well as sharing quite a few glasses of beer or whiskey while discussing forestry and other matters. He was well respected by the AP and Indian forestry fraternity for his knowledge and solid work ethic. It was to a large degree thanks to Ramesh that the AP Community Forest management Project was so successful.

It was now mid-afternoon, and after a hasty lunch at the forest rest house in Vishakhapatnam, we were jostling our way through the crowds on the overpass to platform number five to claim our two second class, air conditioned, two-tier sleeper berths on the express to Tirupati. Express is used fairly loosely by Indian Railways, as this train would take sixteen hours to cover the 750 kilometres from Visag (the short name for Vishakhapatnam). There were slower trains and then there were the super expresses that might take an hour less to do the journey.

It was a hot afternoon, with the temperature in the mid-thirties, and the stench from the human faeces that lay scattered on the railway sleepers next to the platform rose up from under the waiting carriages. This was a feature of many India train stations, particularly where trains terminated. The toilets on board just have holes in the floor and everything passes straight through to the tracks. Nobody seemed to consider regulating that passengers should not go while the train was at the station and, consequently, there was often quite a mess on the tracks.

There wasn't time to dawdle, admiring the ambience, as our train was due to leave and we had to find our carriage along the line of some twenty carriages of various classes, all painted in the dull Indian Railways blue. These ranged from non-air-conditioned seat or sleeper class, which already seemed to have excess passengers hanging out the windows, through our second-class sleepers to first class.

We eventually found our berths and, with the help of the accompanying forest officers, stuffed our luggage under the seats and settled in for a long, slow journey down the coast of Andhra Pradesh.

The train wasn't crowded, or at least our section wasn't and, so Ramesh and I were able to stretch out on the two bench seats opposite each other that would later form the lower berths and our beds for the night.

These were preferable to the upper births, which were narrower and harder, more difficult to climb into and had nowhere handy to put one's shoes and small bag with valuables. On top of that, the air conditioning vents opened almost directly onto one from the roof and they refused to be closed off. So, it was a case of pulling the blanket right over one's head or stuffing some cloth into the vent, as I did on my subsequent trips, or freezing.

Our train headed north out of Visag and then turned inland to the west to join the main line from Calcutta to Chennai (Madras). At first, we passed the back side of urban Visag. One doesn't usually take the train to get a scenic view of towns and cities and it is no different in India.

We passed several level crossings with cars or trucks waiting behind the barrier. There weren't many pedestrians in sight, but I knew these had probably sneaked under the barrier and scuttled across the track at the last minute as the train was approaching. Then we were out in the countryside passing the well-treed coastal hills, which gave way to parched grasslands and vacant fields. The rains hadn't come last year, and the usually dry countryside had an even more parched and desperate look about it.

We continued our journey through the late afternoon, passing barren fields, grassy hillocks, and small towns and villages, stopping at the occasional station. As the red sun was setting across low hills and scrub land, we pulled into the large commercial town of Rajahmundry on the banks of the Godavari River. There, a senior officer from the local Forest Research Institute had been instructed to meet us with some dinner, which he brought on board in two hemp bags. Ramesh then pressed him to stay with us for the ten-minute journey to the next station, across the 2.7 kilometre long bridge spanning the Godavari. This gave me an opportunity to find out how his forestry research and training programme was going. We chatted as the train made those hollow metal sounds that it sometimes does when crossing over a bridge, with echoes seeming to reverberate off the wide flowing stream far below. After our research colleague had left us at the next station, we tucked into the food he had brought on board. Fried rice, vegetable Manchurian, and chicken curry, all presented in plastic Tupperware-type containers. There was more than sufficient, though I daresay, not terribly fattening, which is probably the reason that, unlike many other assignments, I often lost weight on Indian trips.

The porter had provided each of us with a brown paper bag containing two clean, ironed sheets, a blanket, and a pillow. The sheets were tucked into flaps down each side of the bunks with the result that one ends up with a somewhat decent looking bed. I got myself into a comfortable position and read for a while, by the light of a convenient bed lamp. I turned out the lights and tried to get some sleep as the train rocked its way south along the track to Tirupati. Ramesh was already sawing it away over on his bunk and we had been joined by the Indian version of the travelling salesman who now occupied one of the upper bunks.

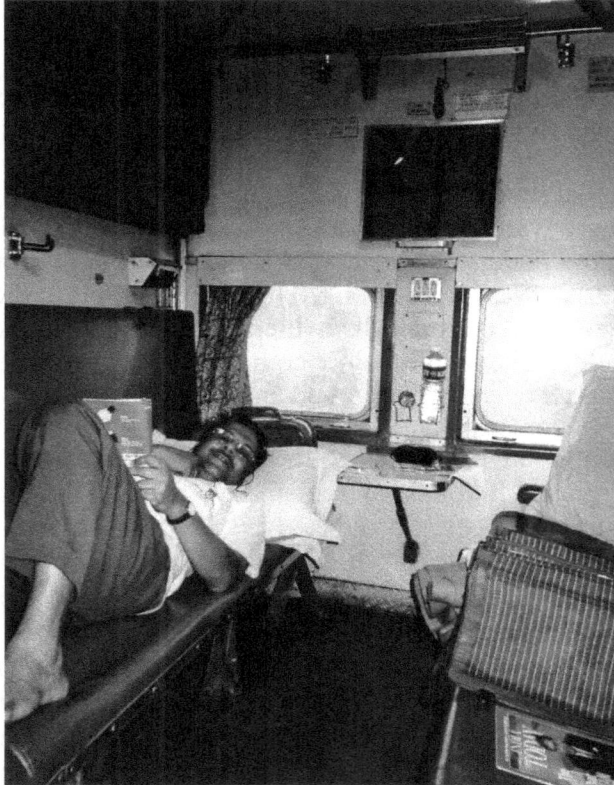

Ramesh relaxing shortly after we left Vishakhapatnam

I must have dropped off for two or three hours, broken intermittently by an increase in the rocking or our stopping at some station. It was dark in the carriage, except for the light from each end that filtered in through the curtains that had been drawn across our cubicle and I fumbled under the bunk for my shoes, then made my way down to the loo at the end. This comprised a stainless-steel western style sit-down toilet on one side or a squat eastern style toilet on the other side. In either case, there was a bit of an art to keeping one's balance while peeing, as the train swayed from side to side. There was a hand valve that released some water for flushing and generally the toilets were reasonably clean in second class AC, although somewhat wet on the floor.

A few more hours of disturbed sleep and the porter came around quietly telling us that we would reach Tirupati in ten minutes. It was four-thirty a.m., and I was quite awake and alert. Though knowing the amount of good sleep, I had actually had, I wondered how long this feeling would last, with a long day in the bush planned, during which I was supposed to ask intelligent questions and pick up on the salient points on how the project was doing. As the train pulled into Tirupati station, it slowed to a crawl, almost as if it was reluctant to arrive, although I daresay, that this also had something to do with the fact that our carriage was one of the last. The others up front had already arrived and passengers were leaping onto the platform.

Finally, we alighted onto the dimly lit platform and were greeted, after a few metres, by the local divisional forest officer and a couple of uniformed subordinates, who grabbed my leather bag. It was always so good to be met by these efficient and friendly Forest Department staff, who eased my arrival, particularly at such early hours. At the station entrance, as scores of people milled around, we piled into the standard government issue Ambassador car. The driver made his way through the usual ill-kempt streets of an Indian district headquarters town, which were still largely empty of the people and vehicles that would fill the streets in a couple of hours.

The hotel was about one and a half stars and didn't look too bad as we approached. With the customary Forest Department efficiency, our rooms had already been signed for and the keys were in hand as we were shown directly to the rooms, passing through a large foyer in which the smell of incense hung heavily. The source of the aroma was not hard to miss as there was a heavily decorated altar at one end of the foyer. Perhaps I should have mentioned earlier that Tirupati is one of the major pilgrim sites in India. The actual pilgrimage shrine is at Tirumala, about ten kilometres from Tirupati on a high flat-topped mountain, where there is a golden temple to Lord *Venkateshwara.* Ramesh told me in the train that the temple was second only to the Vatican in terms of pilgrim visitors, and that is quite possibly true, given that it would take only a small proportion of the 600 million Indian Hindus within India, to make up the pilgrimage numbers. On an average day some 50,000 pilgrims drive up to the temple, and on holy days it may reach 100,000. If you wished to visit the bathing of the deity by the priests, which is done once a week, there is a seven-year waiting list.

My room at the hotel was comfortable and clean, but there was only enough time for a bit of a rest, a shower and change of clothes before meeting other forest officers from the division, then a standard south Indian breakfast of idli (dumplings made from pulses), samba (a watery veg. curry) and chutney, before heading out to see how some forest communities were managing their forests.

Although I may often be fighting tiredness after such overnight train journeys, I would rarely fail to be uplifted by the day's activities, visiting forests and the communities who manage them. I have often thought how fortunate I was to be able to undertake such travel and work experiences, meeting people of such different and diverse cultures within their own environment. At the same time, I was hopefully having at least a small positive impact on these people's livelihoods and on the forest environment.

August is a reasonable time to be travelling up country in Andhra Pradesh. If fortune has smiled then the rains have come and should almost be finished, which means the fields are green with new crops and the forest and scrub is full of fresh green leaves. It is still hot, but nothing compared to the oven dry heat of April and May in the pre-monsoon season.

In August of 2005, the rains had come and so the green had returned, at least with a sufficiency to change the landscape and provide the farmers with hope, unlike the previous year when the parched and hungry look of the land had continued after the rains should have come. As I journeyed by road from the town of Kakinada, on the coast, the tanks were full and the Godavari, where we crossed it near Rajahmundry was a mass of rushing water across the whole 2.7 kilometre width between its banks under the bridge.

One of the stops on this field visit in AP was the community of Banjaragudem in the Paloncha Forest Division, West Godavari Circle. Many of the 96 families in this community were at their wits' end, and to survive they were resorting to desperate and illegal activities in the nearby forest.

The agricultural land, as doled out by the government in small parcels to the poor and landless, had been insufficient to maintain a family. If they were lucky, they had one to one and half acres on which they were growing pulses, a dietary staple, whereas two to three acres was required to support a family with dry land agriculture. However, many families had no land at all. With insufficient or no land on which to grow subsistence crops, one of the few ways open for parents to support their families lay in obtaining work as farm labourers. This might give some INR4,000, the equivalent of USD100, over a four-month period. If the rains didn't come or were insufficient, the yields from subsistence crops of those able to grow them suffered. At the same time, the opportunities for income from farm labour would greatly diminish.

To provide food for their families, many members of the community had resorted to illegal shifting cultivation or what they called 'podu' in the remaining nearby government forest reserves. This uncontrolled and unmanaged activity was inevitably degrading what was once lush high forest, increasingly each year, to the point where the forest was little more than scrub, with remnants of teak trees only two to three metres high.

The nearby forest also provided another means of livelihood in the form of non-timber forest products, such as Tamarind, broom grass, medicinal plants, Usiri (small, sour, vitamin rich fruits from a small tree, widely used in food), beedi leaves (the shiny green leaves of *Diospyros melanoxylon,* or tendu tree, which was used to roll beedis or cigarettes), bamboo culms and Vada leaves (the large leaves from the *Bohenia* tree, used to make disposable plates). By collecting these NTFPs a family might add a further INR1,000 a year to their income. But the collection of these products was also uncontrolled and unmanaged, which was further degrading the forest and the future sustainability of such products.

The community probably recognised the intrinsic value of the forest as a means of livelihood and as an environmental asset; but their desperate straits and the absence of any sustainable management of this government reserve forest meant that they were destroying their last remaining source of livelihood.

The community at Banjaragudem VSS was tribal. I later learnt from some of the community's more vocal members, that the forebears of the current villagers had lived in thick forests in the same area where today there were sorry, much degraded remnants of such forests as islands amidst the agricultural fields that have supplanted much of the forests. Their ancestors subsisted, at least in part from roots, tubers, leaves and other products from the forest in a symbiotic and sustainable relationship that existed for centuries, as it did in large areas of forests all over India.

In 1998, the community heard of a joint forest management scheme being introduced by the Andhra Pradesh Forest Department with funding from the World Bank. Whatever, their prior relationship with the Forest Department, the Banjaragudem community became convinced that joint forest management would provide worthwhile benefits. Undoubtedly, an initial attraction was the money that would be paid as wages to villagers to protect and rehabilitate the forest that had been allocated to them. But there was more to it than labour wages, as the enthusiasm and subsequent physical results attested.

Perhaps they also recognised, as recent research had shown, that the diet obtained largely from the forest was healthier and contained more nutrients than that obtained by consuming planted cereal crops. Whatever their motives, they were now enthusiastically following the advice of the

Forest Department in protecting and rehabilitating the natural forest, as well as planting short-rotation forest crops on degraded forest sites.

Their first action, in 1998, had been to protect the remaining natural forest from their own and outside encroachment and illegal harvesting. Stand improvement treatments were then undertaken. After seven years of such management this forest, which contained quite a lot of valuable teak coppice from roots and stumps, was showing potential for future teak production. From a rather ragged collection of scattered coppice and low bushes, no higher than two metres, the current forest was a dense growth of regenerated teak and other trees over eight metres high.

It would be another 30 years or so before decent sized teak trees could be harvested, but some returns would come from thinning the stands that would be necessary to promote maximum growth on the better stems.

In the meantime, income had already increased for the families, from the improved production of NTFPs that resulted from the protection and management of the forest applied earlier.

However, it was going to take some time for a reasonable income to accrue to the community through the sale of teak wood products from the rehabilitated natural forest. To help provide an intervening and shorter-term income, small plantations of eucalypts, bamboo or non-timber forest products were established, with the help of the project on heavily degraded forest land. The bamboo would start yielding an annual saleable harvest of culms after as little as three to four years.

Villagers from Banjaragudem community, together with AP Forest Department officers in front of a seven-year-old Eucalypt woodlot.

The first of their earlier planted eucalypt plantations were due to be felled the following year with the wood being sold to a pulp mill. The community leaders estimated they would harvest about 100 tonnes and receive 1.8 lakhs (180,000) rupees or the equivalent of US$4,000. This was a vast sum of money to them, given their current family incomes averaged 12,000 to 15,000 rupees per year. And there was more to come.

When the bamboo and Usiri they had planted started producing in the next few years that income would be increased by another 1 lakh rupees or US$2,200 per year. If this level of income could be maintained on an annual basis, the average community household income, including the enhanced subsistence and cash benefits obtained through improved productivity of NTFPs in the now managed forest, would rise by approximately 60 percent.

In agreement with the Forest Department, at least 50 percent of the revenue obtained from the sale of forest products would have to be reinvested in either establishing new forest assets, such as plantations, or managing the existing ones. The rest could be distributed amongst the VSS members, as they decided or used it for community projects such as the building of a hall or a school. However, the reinvestment also meant income for those willing to work as labourers on such forest development and management.

It wasn't just a matter of re-investing in the management of existing community forest resources or new forest asset establishment, as decided by the Forest Department. It was now time for the members of the community to take matters into their own hands and decide on the future of their forests and the management of those forests or the establishment of new plantations.

The harvesting of eucalypt plantations here and elsewhere would be something of a watershed in the communities, as they realised that they were actually getting revenue from these plantations, and it was not just some self-serving government scheme. Moreover, this realisation, and the continued support from the Forest Department was helping to build trust between members of the community and the Department.

As part of that decision-making process, a business or livelihood plan was being drawn up, with guidance from Forest Department officers, but with the community making decisions on what to plant or manage and how to manage the costs involved with such actions.

In some communities, the decision had been made to re-invest 100 percent of the revenues in new plantations of mainly eucalypt and bamboo, to build their community forest-based assets and improve their medium-term revenue situation.

The overall project aim was to ensure that as many communities as possible reached a point of sustainable self-sufficiency with regard to community forest management, although it was recognised that for as many as half of the communities, achieving that objective would be difficult. This meant ensuring that the communities had the necessary management skills to plan, budget for and manage future forest management operations effectively and transparently. It also meant ensuring that those benefits obtained from their forest operations were distributed equitably amongst the community members.

It was also important that there be sufficient income, both in the short and longer term, to give the families concerned a sustainable livelihood, and thus enable them to continue to protect, develop and sustainably manage their allotted forest areas without overexploiting them.

Where the forest was reasonable or sufficient plantations of wood crops, bamboo or NTFPs had been established, this could be possible through the sale of such forest products. In all cases, strong and intelligent leadership would be important.

However, to improve the income situation for community families, particularly in those areas with poorer forest-based resources, alternative means of income generation had been adopted. These included value addition to forest products such as the production of incense sticks from bamboo, but also apiculture, sericulture, fish farming, and the production of vermi-compost. To assist in this, community enterprise groups had been established in relation to a particular product, with such groups federating to give better marketing leverage and mutual support.

On a later visit to AP, we were on the road out of Hyderabad just after six am, as the sky was beginning to lighten for another day. Leaving the barely stirring city and heading out on a good bitumen road for Khammam in the north of the state, we stopped for some breakfast of idli, sambar, vadha and dosa on the way. The roadside restaurant or daba was a low garishly painted building with dirty wooden floors and rickety wooden tables and chairs; but the food, served in tin bowls and plates, was hot and tasty. It was March 2007 and the start of eight long days on the road visiting several forest divisions to see how the community forest management project had been progressing.

At the well-forested district of Khammam, we were met by the Conservator for Khammam Circle, Kamwait Singh, a tall good-looking

Sikh, who was reputed to be an excellent cricket player. He was also a good storyteller, with a dry sense of humour and little respect for certain bureaucratic procedures that got in the way of efficient operations. Kamwait Singh proceeded to conduct us around his forest area, stopping at communities involved in the project to view and discuss progress, much of which was very impressive.

A community enterprise group involved in making incense (agarbathi) sticks from bamboo

March in AP is what is referred to as the start of 'summer', which is the period of warming after the cooler winter months, before the rains come in June. Splashed across the fields and visible in the forests were the bright red flowers on the Flame of the Forest tree (*Butea monosperma*), whose leaves were used for making leaf plates.

I was told this flowering is the signal to prune back the leaves on the beedi trees, from which, in 40 days' time they would pluck the large fresh leaves used for rolling beedis or cigarettes, providing a valuable source of family income. There is an irony here in that the species of tree providing the beedi or tendu leaves (*Diospyros melanoxylon*) is actually the same genus as the very valuable ebony tree.

Another source of local income and sustenance was the Mohar tree. These, sometimes quite large trees, with masses of purple flowers in season, can be seen retained in agricultural fields, as well as throughout the local forest. The flowers are used to make a local liquor, while the nuts give an edible oil.

From Khammam Circle, we meandered through mixed high forest interspersed with villages, down to the coast at Kakinada, near the mouth of the Godavari River. Coming down from the hills onto the coastal plains, we stopped at Rampet and walked up a dirt track to inspect a new project-funded community-based eco-tourism site, set up to provide better livelihoods to the local people. An ancient temple in the area played host to some 14,000 people in one day during the temple's festival, shortly after the site was opened that January.

It must have been one hell of a crush, although, apart from the temple, the eco-tourist attraction is a rather unimpressive stream with a couple of waterfalls. Ladies and gents bathing areas had been set up where a few deeper pools existed, and these might comfortably accommodate a couple of dozen people at each site. One can only imagine the sea of humanity as they tramped up the narrow dirt road to the temple and these bathing holes. What was also of interest was that the whole operation was run by women.

We stopped for lunch at another site, Maredumille, which was a combination of a jungle camp with tents and village style accommodation. There, balancing a tin plate on my lap, I was served the camp specialty, spiced chicken cooked in a bamboo culm, with rice and a veg curry.

Having reached the coast, we boarded a Forest Department launch to check out sites where local fishing communities were rehabilitating over 2,000 hectares of mangroves. This was a massive community operation to manually dig out channels enabling mangroves that once populated the area to once again naturally regenerate.

Meanwhile, further down the coast, communities were establishing shelterbelts on the sand dunes. This was all part of a 200-kilometre-long bio shield being established to provide future protection from cyclone storm surges and tsunamis.

On a beach, under a blazing sun, we watched Casuarina seedlings being watered by hand, as the villagers explained how high the tsunami in 2004 had come up over the shoreline. In the same area, 25,000 people had lost their lives because of a storm surge caused by an earlier cyclone. The Casuarinas were planted directly into the sand dunes, one meter apart, and in belts 100 metres wide with each plant being hand watered at least once a week from wells dug nearby. The whole operation was mainly undertaken by women. Not only did the communities benefit from being paid to establish the shelterbelts. They would subsequently, be able to harvest wood for firewood and poles from thinning the Casuarinas, once they were about three years old.

Digging channels to allow sea water in as part of the mangrove rehabilitation process in Guntur District.

In the south-east of the state, we were into the dry zone, where the forest was no more than scrub, though at one time there had been much taller trees. By now, many of the main 'highways' in India had been upgraded from two-lane roads to divided four-lane highways. However, there were several deficiencies in the road construction as it often was not possible for vehicles to turn into or out of side roads if they needed to cross over to the opposite side, because of concrete median divides. The solution, of course, was typically Indian. Vehicles would just drive down the wrong way until they could cross over. This made life in the fast lane rather scary as one could meet an ox cart or lorry coming from the opposite direction.

Our base in these drier areas was the bustling town of Nellore. In this region, there was not much point in trying to improve the local forest through natural regeneration. It was better to plant trees. So, the project provided future livelihoods for the forest fringe communities by establishing plantations of eucalypts and local fruit or oil nut trees. They had done rather well, both the plantations and the communities, with a number already harvesting older and poorer plantations, receiving as much as Rs1 million (US$20.000), though Rs400,000 to 500,000 was more common. This was just the start with more communities due to harvest increasing quantities of pulpwood from their new, clonal, higher yielding plantations in coming years as the plantations matured. Using funds received, re-investment plans were being drawn up by the communities with the help of the Forest Department, to enable further expansion of their plantation assets.

There was a very positive atmosphere associated with the project in these communities. Usually, we would be greeted enthusiastically by the villagers, sometimes with drums beating, but, as always, with leis placed around pur necks by village women. We would then be pelted with marigold flower petals as we walked down a track to the village, where the community would be gathered, often under a large tent. My Indian counterparts would usually take off their leis almost immediately, but I felt I should keep mine on for a bit, considering the effort they had gone to make or to buy them and because it seemed to be a special occasion for all concerned.

Establishing Casuarina shelterbelt on coast.

Bio shield shelterbelt after three years.

Ramesh and I caught the overnight train from Nellore back to Hyderabad, arriving at six-thirty a.m., which gave me enough time to have a shower and prepare for meetings at the Forest Department before heading off the next morning to the northwest of the state for a look at some teak forest areas. Having breakfast on the way at a forest rest house, we arrived at Nirmal to be met by the Divisional Forest Officer. After another quick cup of milky tea and a chat about activities in the division, we drove off along bumpy and dusty roads to be met by more villagers.

It was nearing noon, on this hot, dry day with only a few scattered clouds to give an occasional break from the sun's heat. Three men stood waiting for us in the partial shade of some dusty roadside trees. Being March, many of the trees were leafless, while the adjacent fields and low scrubs were bare of most ground cover and showed the parched effects of several dry months since the last rains. The men's dark skin showed the results of years of almost constant exposure to such harsh conditions and contrasted with the white shirts and longyis that two of them wore, although the latter also showed the result of exposure to the dust and grime. The third and youngest looking of the three, though he was middle-aged, was neatly dressed in dark grey trousers and a shirt that hung over the trousers. In his breast pocket was a pen and his attitude, though friendly was quite businesslike. His name was Ram Reddy, Chairman of the management committee for Pyaramoor VSS.

Chairman Sri Ram Reddy of Pyaramoor VSS (centre) as he proudly showed us the community's rehabilitated teak forest in Nirmal Division.

This VSS had been formed in 1997 under the previous JFM programme. They had 400 hectares of degraded teak forest that, in 1997, had been nothing more than one-metre-high scrub on rather rocky, hilly land. The chairman was bursting with pride at having a World Bank consultant to whom he could show the community's achievements. He had a good reason to be proud, as the teak forest that was only one-meter-high scrub some eight years ago had now grown to around ten metres.

As we roamed through the dry, leafless forest landscape it seemed that Ram Reddy was intent on showing us all his 400 hectares of forest. It was easy going over much of the area and I would have loved to have spent more time admiring the rejuvenated forest, but I needed to see more examples of community forest management in the short time available. So, we pulled up Mr Reddy, who was striding ahead, and I explained my situation, asking if we could have an abbreviated version of his forest tour, to which he graciously acceded.

Back at the forest guesthouse, where we were to spend the night, we undertook our usual ritual of sitting around with a beer or whiskey, to chat with the local foresters before dinner at about nine-thirty or ten p.m. Apart from forestry, the other main topic was cricket, with the Cricket World Cup being played in the Caribbean. The Indians are mad about the game and their key players are treated like Bollywood film stars. I awoke the next morning to the stunning news that India had been beaten by Bangladesh, a team ranked low down in the list. There was much analysis of the game and grumbling by my counterparts throughout that day, with forestry taking second place.

By 2010, as the AP Project was ending, and as I formed part of the Project Completion Report team, I could reflect on a wonderfully satisfying, rewarding as well as a great learning experience. After some ten days again in the field visiting communities and assessing the achievements of the project, the evaluation team spent some days putting together our findings in the relative comfort of the Green Park Hotel in Hyderabad.

I would have preferred to stay out in the bush with the rural communities, mingling with the village men and women and the APFD field officers. There, a meal could cost the equivalent of one dollar or less at a local daba and I could spend the days wandering through plantations or forests, even in the heat, drinking coconut water from young coconuts cut open by the local forest guards or dancing to the beat of the drums as the villagers greeted us. As we drove between sites, there were often lively and interesting discussions with Ramesh and other senior forest officers not only about forestry matters, but also about religion, politics and social mores.

It was a much-varied communal and forest landscape that I had been privileged to travel through many times in the previous eleven years, visiting some 600 of the 5,000 different village communities participating in the project, some more than once. I had witnessed the positive changes that had occurred to both the forests and the people. In the process, I had got to know many of the forestry officers and field staff and even some of the villagers through repeat visits and had always felt warmly welcomed and a certain comradery.

I had seen badly degraded forests slowly grow and reform into the forests they should be, clothing the hills and countryside in a denser forest green. I had witnessed how impoverished communities had adopted the forest allocated to them, held it dear and protected it, even though they may have received only meagre financial benefits initially, and had sometimes been physically abused by poachers. There was a sense of ownership, that saw them beating off thieves with sticks and stones. As they so said often to me, "this is our forest." A trusting working relationship had developed between hitherto distrustful community members and AP Forest Department field staff, particularly when benefits from the forests began to flow and were retained by the communities. For some communities, the rewards had been substantial, enabling them to improve their livelihoods and invest further in, what they saw, as their forest assets.

I had seen how with good leadership from within, communities had protected their valuable teak forest assets from outside poachers, sometimes sustaining injuries in their defense. This same leadership, supported by the APFD field staff, had done wonderful work in rehabilitating the forests to greatly improve the productivity; thus, benefiting both the forest and the communities. At the same time, the APFD had shown great initiative in setting up value addition enterprises for some of the forest products being harvested. Such schemes will help ensure the community's financial sustainability and the sustainable management of the forests in their care. In addition, increasing numbers of women were finding their voice and leading communities; over 500 by project closure. Similarly, I observed how so many women had gained a degree of financial independence and even a greater sense of empowerment through thrift groups and other women's business groups, fostered by the project.

By the close of the project, approximately 50 percent of the communities involved – 2,600 communities - had achieved the status of being able to sustainably manage their allocated forest area themselves with only technical help from APFD. A further 25 percent – 1,300 communities - were almost at that point, only needing some further input or awaiting the benefits that would shortly accrue from their rehabilitated forest. This was a wonderful achievement, signifying a win for both the forests, which hitherto had been progressively badly degraded, and the people, who had been impoverished with nearly 60 percent living below the poverty line.

Epilogue

By the close of the Andhra Pradesh Community Forest Management Project in 2010, my life as a forestry consultant was waning. I was still interested in doing further consultancies, and I did receive a couple of requests from FAO. But over time, these requests petered out, as my contacts in the World Bank and in the United Nations moved, and I didn't actively seek further work as I had done earlier. My life was becoming more involved with spending time with my sons, David and Michael, in Canada and Australia. Both were now married with children, and it was important for me to maintain close links with my sons and grandchildren. For about three years, Michael, who had a post-doctoral fellowship with Griffith University, resided just down the road on the Gold Coast, with his wife and daughter. That enabled much close contact between us, and I was down there shortly after their second daughter was born in 2014. Then, they moved back to Vancouver in Canada, and I would spend time there either before or after I spent several weeks in Toronto with David and his family.

However, the lure of the forests continues to involve me, though now as a volunteer, working with Noosa and District Landcare and Noosa Council to restore and manage the local coastal bushland or hinterland forest on the Sunshine Coast in Queensland. At the same time, my forest-related learning continues as I also prepare and present talks on forests, trees, and wood subjects to local organizations.

Writing has also occupied some of my time and, in the process, I can reflect on a rewarding and satisfying forestry journey. This applies particularly to the work done in Tanzania and then in Andhra Pradesh, with the latter being a fitting climax to my forestry career that had started with forest villagers and their forests in PNG and then progressed through numerous countries. Although I had experienced and learned much from a technical point of view, the linking of forests and people's wellbeing was the most rewarding aspect. It added a certain transformation from being just a forester who dealt with and managed forests and trees, to one who understood and appreciated the special bond between so many communities and the forests they relied on and managed for their livelihoods.

According to FAO[21], over one billion people in tropical countries live in or near forests and depend on forests for food, energy, and shelter, as

---

21 Food and Agricultural Organization of the UN, State of the World's Forest, 2018.

an economic safety net or as a direct source of income. Of these, about 250 million of the world's poorest people rely almost solely on forests for their subsistence and survival, many of these in Africa.

I feel that community participation in the sustainable management or conservation of forests is something that needs to be further considered, particularly for tropical forests. So many communities have had a history connected to forests from which they have derived most or part of their livelihoods. Currently between 25 and 30 percent of forests in developing countries are being managed by communities with varying degrees of success.

However, it has not all been good news. My first assignment as a consultant after leaving the World Bank in 1997 was to design and prepare a Forestry and Conservation Project for Papua New Guinea, with funding to come mainly from the World Bank. The country and forests that I left in 1972 had changed after independence in 1976. Over time, law and order had degenerated in the urban centres while the forests were under increasing threats of mass degradation, particularly from the mid-1980s onwards. Foreign logging companies, particularly from South-East Asia, were taking advantage of government corruption, as well as local villagers' ignorance and hopes for a brighter future and undertaking unsustainable logging operations to satisfy a growing export market. At first, most of the village communities were duped into thinking they would get improved infrastructure, roads, schools and other benefits, as well as cash payments. These developments did occur to varying degrees; but most were of a temporary nature. At the same time, the villagers' forests were being heavily degraded by often brutal selective logging operations for only a few trees per hectare that left perhaps fifty percent or more of the forests decimated, including precious fruit and canoe trees.

A major focus of the project was the return of sustainable forest management control to the villagers and the improvement in the villagers' potential for obtaining benefits from their forests. At the same time areas of environmental risk were to be conserved and sufficient forest to maintain ecological and biodiversity integrity was to be set aside.

There was a lot of discussions with the PNG Government and particularly with the PNG Forest Authority about undertaking the project, but subject to several conditionalities. These were agreed to by the government and the project started implementation in 2001. However, within a year, it was obvious that the government and the loggers were not prepared to change their ways and meet the conditionalities. So, the World Bank closed the project.

However, that is not the end of the story, because people power came to the fore. Many village communities were fed up with their forests being wrecked and a non-government organization entitled the Eco-Forestry Forum has done a sterling job in keeping the government honest to a greater extent, in relation to the forests, their logging and sustainable management. At the same time, the villagers are now wiser with regard to managing their forests and allowing logging to take place.

In 2011, determined to see how the communities in Andhra Pradesh were managing their forests and benefitting from such, I made a private visit to AP. I was warmly welcomed and escorted around several communities, observing, that despite the closure of the project, the Government of AP was continuing to support communities' forest management. It was heartening to see there was even further progress in the rehabilitation of the forests and continuing benefits to both the people and the forests under their care and protection.

www.ingramcontent.com/pod-product-compliance
Lightning Source LLC
Chambersburg PA
CBHW072103020426
42334CB00017B/1610